REVOLUTIONARY WRITING

Revolutionary Writing

Common Sense Essays in Post-Political Politics

Edited by
Werner Bonefeld

Autonomedia

Autonomedia
POB 568 Williamsburgh Station
Brooklyn, New York 11211-0568 USA

Website: http://www.autonomedia.org
Email: info@autonomedia.org

Printed in the United States of America

Contents

FOREWORD

The present volume draws on contributions to the now-defunct journal *Common Sense*. The journal was published between 1987 and 1999. With its 24 issues, it operated "against the current." It was devised as a means of critical inquiry into the class struggle. The aim was to reflect on "the relationship between revolutionary theory and practice" and keep each "on the boil."

This volume provides a snapshot of twelve years of *Common Sense*. However, neither does this volume do justice to the scope and variety of what we published, nor does it represent the best of *Common Sense*. There is no best of something as if it were a top-forty activity— there is only critique. *Common Sense* was founded against the backdrop of the anti-poll tax campaign in Edinburgh, Scotland, by comrades from the University and the Unemployed Workers' Centre. After the defeat of the poll tax, the journal transformed from a more-or-less local discussion forum into a "proper" journal. We kept its heterodox Marxist perspective but "internationalised." In fact, and not only in Britain, it was a rare journal; it published the articles that the academic industry does not approve of and which, in the late 1980s and early 1990s, were most difficult to obtain.

Common Sense was a platform for heterodox Marxist publishing — for a Marxism that takes itself seriously and does not entertain the academic industry as a means to an end. The journal collapsed in 1999. The reasons for its demise are many. This is a fact and nothing more than the fact will be reported here.

This volume keeps alive and available some of the stuff we published for the struggles of today and tomorrow. The book is neither a resumé nor an anthology. There is no resumé. One hears in the media, from the academic industry, and learned commentators, that the utopia of the society of the free and equal, has run its course. There is nothing odd about this view: such declarations are the business of the bourgeoisie and express their class interest. This volume is dedicated to a different task. It doubts that the misery of our time amounts to the best of all worlds and agrees with Marx that all relations in which Man [*Mensch*] is a debased, enslaved, forsaken, despicable being have to be overthrown. Besides, who would object to the insight that theoretical mysteries find their rational explanation in human practice and in the comprehension of this practice?

Some, of course, will object: their respectability, profitability and purposeful rationality rests and feeds on, and subsists through, this denial. Contentment with existing conditions amounts to the espousal of democracy as a democracy that is consumed in death. The present volume is devoted to the utopia of the democracy of the living, the society of the free and equal, where humanity is purpose and not a means.

WERNER BONEFELD, DEREK KERR AND BRIAN MCGRAIL

Editor's Preface

The present volume differs considerably from the originally planned format for a *Common Sense* anthology. This format would have had the advantage of including many different articles dealing with a variety of topics from the Zapatistas to the working class under Nazism. Although this would have provided a more accurate reflection of the material published in *Common Sense,* its disadvantage seems clear: a volume that contains a diverse mixture of arguments and concerns. Besides, some contributions which should have been included could not be used because of copyright restrictions. This volume, then, is designed as a focused, rather than representative, account of one of the central themes of *Common Sense.* For this reason, some contributions that had originally been selected had to be left out and some have been included which had in fact not appeared in *Common Sense.*

The volume is in three parts. Part I includes chapters on the significance and character of "critique" ("Open Marxism: Subversion and Critique"); Part II examines contemporary developments ("The Insurrection of Labour and Global Capital") and Part III contains contributions on the emancipatory dimension of Marx's work and its contemporary significance ("The Critique of the Political"). Although all contributions argue from a heterodox Marxist perspective, the volume does not speak with one voice. Instead it offers an intersecting of distinct accounts. The shared basis of all contributions is their general critique of the entire system of bourgeois categories. This critique is not a critique for critique's sake. It is a determinate critique, a critique which determines the forms of capital as perverted form of human relations. In short, the contributions are agreed that Marx's critique of political economy is realised in its negation: the society of the free and equal.

Hopefully this volume will be only the first of many, to allow the circulation of those additional contributions which have not been included here.

Werner Bonefeld

ACKNOWLEDGEMENTS

With the exception of Chapter 11, all contributions have previously been published in English as follows:

"A Critique of the Fordism of the Regulation School" and "The Crisis of Public Space" were first published in *Common Sense,* no. 19, 1996.

"Capital Moves" was first published in *Capital & Class,* no. 57, 1995.

"Constituent Republic" was first published in *Common Sense,* no. 16, 1995.

"Destruction as the Determination of the Scholar in Miserable Times" was first published in *Common Sense,* no. 12, 1992.

"Development and Reproduction" was first published in *Common Sense,* no. 17, 1995.

"From the Revolution Against Philosophy to the Revolution Against Capital," "The End of Work or the Renaissance of Slavery," and "The Politics of Change" were first published in *Common Sense,* no. 24, 1999.

"Human Practice and Perversion" was first published in *Common Sense,* no. 15, 1994.

"In the Beginning was the Scream" was first published in *Common Sense,* no. 11, 1991.

"Marxian Categories, the Crisis of Capital and the Constitution of Social Subjectivity Today" was first published in *Common Sense,* no. 14, 1993.

"Reappropriations of Public Space" was first published in *Common Sense,* no. 21, 1997.

Revolutionary Writing

Common Sense Essays in Post-Political Politics

Part One

Open Marxism: Subversion and Critique

1
IN THE BEGINNING WAS THE SCREAM
John Holloway

In the beginning was the scream. When we talk or write, it is all too easy to forget that the beginning was not the word, but the scream. Faced with the destruction of human lives by capitalism, a scream of sadness, a scream of horror, above all a scream of anger, of refusal: NO. The starting point of theoretical reflection is opposition, negativity, struggle.

The role of theory is to elaborate that scream, to express its strength and to contribute to its power, to show how the scream resonates through society and to contribute to that resonance.

That is the origin of Marxism, not just of Marx's Marxism, but presumably of our own interest in Marxism. The appeal of Marxism lies in its claim to be a theory of struggle, of opposition, of negation. But that is not what Marxism has become.

Today Marxism is probably more discredited than ever, not just in the bourgeois press or in the universities, but also as a theory of struggle. The experience of the Soviet Union and Eastern Europe has been crucial in this respect; the identification of Marxism as the official ideology of the state has meant that the struggles against the state have taken the form not of struggles inspired by a "truer Marxism," as was hoped by many in the west for so long, but of struggles against Marxism as such. But it is not only in the East that the statification of Marxism has led to its rejection. In the West too, the surge of Marxism into the universities in the late 1960s and early 1970s has led in some degree to its desiccation. Borne into the universities on a wave of working-class struggle, Marxist theory has tended to be sucked into the general separation of theory from practice which characterises the university as an institution. As the wave of struggle, which provided the basis of Marxism, has ebbed, many Marxist academics have completely abandoned Marxism; even worse, perhaps, many have not, but have carried their Marxism with them as they adapt to the institutional structures and professional pressures of the university. Often this is not the result of conscious choice, but rather the result of the dynamics of non-choice; work in the university has its own dynamic which constantly tends to separate theoretical work from any political base. The result is often a Marxism which is far more sophisticated, but no less determinist, than the old "orthodoxy" of the communist parties.

In both cases, with the state ideology of the East or the sophisticated academics of the West, Marxism has lost its scream. Class struggle remains a category, but the simple statement at the start of the *Communist Manifesto,* that "the history of all hitherto existing societies is the history of class struggle," is in fact abandoned. Class struggle in these theories is still seen as being influential, but only within a broader framework, variously interpreted as the conflict between the forces and relations of production or simply as the "laws of capitalist development." Class struggle is important — of course (so "of course" that it can simply be taken for granted) — but it must submit to the "inescapable lines of tendency and direction established by the real world" (Hall, 1985, 15). Struggle is subject to structure, and since structure is the structure of capitalist society ("the real world"), Marxism in this version becomes quite simply a theory of capitalist reproduction. The "inescapable lines of tendency and direction established by the real world" are quite simply the functional requirements of capitalist reproduction, so that these theories are not only structuralist, but also functionalist. And then, with all thought of rupture or revolution long forgotten, these theorists move from analysing what is necessary for capitalist reproduction to prescribing what is necessary, to making policy suggestions and advising the state, still, of course, using the language of Marxist theory and making obeisance to the importance of class struggle. It is little wonder that many who are actively involved in anti-capitalist struggle feel little attraction to such Marxism.

And yet a theory of the scream is more urgent than ever. It is more urgent than ever because capitalism is both increasingly fragile and increasingly terroristic. The scream will continue as long as capitalism does, but there is a real danger that Marxism as the language of the scream, as the theory of protest, could get lost. Marxism as a theory of determinism and as an ideology of the state is discredited, but it is more urgent than ever to develop Marxism clearly as a theory of struggle. There is of course a long tradition of emphasising struggle as the central element of Marxism, a long tradition of what one might call "left Marxism," but it is a diverse and often subterranean tradition, without very clear continuities. Many of those who politically have insisted on the self-organisation of the working class have retained theoretical concepts that work against the articulation of the power of labour (as in Pannekoek's discussion of crisis, for example); and many of those who have made important theoretical contributions to theorising working class power have adopted often ambivalent political positions in practice (Adorno, Bloch, for example). The crisis of the regimes of Eastern Europe is, or can be, a liberation of Marxism from much of the baggage acquired over the last century, but it is very important to try to be clear about the foundations of this liberated Marxism.

The most obvious point to be made about a theory of struggle is that its basis is uncertainty. If the world is to be understood in terms of struggle, then there is no room for determinism of any kind. Struggle, by definition, is uncertain, open, and the categories which conceptualise it must be understood as open too. The determinism of Marx's more triumphalist moments (such as the end of Section 1 of the *Communist Manifesto,* Chapter 32 of Vol. 1 of *Capital,* or the 1859 "Preface" which is so important for the "orthodox" Marxist tradition) must go, as must any idea of historical necessity, and any suggestion of a final inevitable victory of socialism. As Adorno put it, after the experience of fascism, it is no longer possible (if it ever was) to think of a smooth dialectical progression ending with communism as the resolution of conflict, the inevitable negation of the negation. We can only think of the dialectic as being a negative dialectic, a dialectic of negation with no certain synthesis. In a world of untruth, the only concept of truth that we can have is negative. There is no certainty in Marxism: its only claim to truth is the force of its attack on untruth. This leads perhaps to a dizzy, dizzying vision of the world (cf Adorno 1990, 31), but the dizziness lies not in the vision but in the reality of a world hurtling who knows where.

The dialectic of negation is the struggle of the working class. In a world of struggle, there is no neutrality. The perspective is the perspective of our struggle. As Tronti put it in an article which provided one of the starting points for the theory of *autonomia* in Italy: "We too had a conception of capitalism that put capital in first place and the workers in second. That was a mistake. And now we must reverse the polarity and start again from the beginning. And the beginning is the class struggle of the working class" (1964, 1979, 1). The beginning is the struggle, our struggle, our scream, the scream of negation. As Rosa Luxemburg put it, "The secret of Marx's theory of value ... was that he looked at capitalism from the point of view of its transcendence, from a socialist point of view" (1973, 40). It is only from the standpoint of negation that Marx's categories make any sense at all: without that, they are quite literally meaningless. That is why there cannot be any continuity between bourgeois theory and Marxist theory: the basic presuppositions which underlie their categories are totally incompatible. Underlying bourgeois theory is an assumption about the stability of capitalism, the power of capital to retain control of society indefinitely. The basis of Marxist theory is just the opposite: the instability of capitalism, the power of labour to overthrow capitalism.

It is essential to retain the idea that the starting point must be the struggle of the working class. Linton Kwesi Johnson has a wonderful expression when he describes the violent reaction of a group of blacks to police harassment: "the bile of oppression was vomited" (*Five Nights of Bleeding*). If we are to avoid the structural-functionalism that characterises so much of Marxist theory, it is important to think of our work in those terms: as a vomiting of the bile of oppression.

However, there is a difficulty here, and it is a difficulty presented by a lot of left theory. The focus on the struggle of the working class leads very easily to a conception of the working class as purely external to capital. From (correctly) emphasising the subjectivity of labour and the antagonism between labour and capital as the starting point, such approaches easily move to simply counterposing the subjectivity of labour to the objectivity of capital, thus reproducing the concept of the objectivity of capital. The one-sided emphasis on subjectivity (voluntarism), although it appears to be the opposite of objectivism (determinism), is actually its logical complement. Both operate with the assumption that there is a distinction between class struggle and the laws of economic development: the difference lies only in the primacy attached to one or the other. Alternatively, all notion of the "logic of capital" is abandoned and capital is seen as a purely external subject, manipulating and controlling labour. Class struggle is then seen as the clash of two opposing armies, as a battle that goes back and forth, to and fro. At this level there is no history, or rather history is a formless thing, without shape, without tendency.

Marx's conception is different: in the clash of the two opposing armies of capital and labour, there is something that gives direction and shape to the struggle. That is the fact that the two sides are not in fact external to each other: capital is nothing other than alienated labour, the objectivity of the "real world" is nothing than our own alienated subjectivity. The basis of both sides of the class struggle is the same: the power of labour. Capital is nothing other than alienated labour. This is the basis of the labour theory of value, which was seen even before Marx, by both the radical Ricardians and their critics, as an assertion of the power of labour. At its most basic, the power of labour is the power to create, and therefore also the power to destroy. When Marx distinguished between the worst architect and the best bee by saying that the former plans the construction before executing it, he might also have added that the architect is also more likely to fail in the construction. The power of labour is the power of uncertain creation, the power of that which is not, the power of non-identity (Adorno), of the Not Yet (Bloch), of the working class No (Tronti).

When labour and capital confront each other, this is not an external confrontation. The power of labour meets the power of labour, but in the form of its antithesis. Contradiction is "non-identity under the aspect of identity"

(Adorno), negativity under the aspect of positivity, labour under the aspect of capital. The substance of capital is the power of labour; the power of labour exists under the aspect of capital: it assumes the form of capital, the fetishised form of capital. Once the relation between capital and labour is seen as an internal relation, then the question of form becomes crucial. Unlike the Ricardians, who were content to show that the substance of value was labour, Marx was concerned with the form of value, with the question why the product of labour took the form of value — and indeed he saw the question of form as being the crucial dividing line between his theory and bourgeois theory, for which the question of form is meaningless (*Capital* I, 80). The whole of Marx's *Capital* is a study of the (more and more fetishised) forms of the power of labour. The "pivot" for an understanding of the different forms of social relations is the dual existence of labour as concrete and abstract labour, the fact that concrete, useful labour takes the form of abstract labour, the fact that useful, creative labour confronts itself in meaningless, alienated form.

If capital cannot be understood as external to labour, it cannot be understood as something economic. The movement of capital can only be understood as the movement of the contradiction (internal to capital itself) between capital and labour, the movement of struggle. The notion of "Marxist economics," one of the most unfortunate creations of the "orthodox" Marxist tradition, in so far as it suggests a separation of capital from struggle, must be abandoned. But if the movement of capital can only be understood as the movement of struggle, the movement of struggle can only be understood as a movement in-and-against capital. The notion that you can understand the movement of struggle or of society in abstraction from the particular form which it takes, the notion that underlies the concept of "Marxist sociology" must also be abandoned. (The absurd notion of a Marxist political science, an idea raised by Poulantzas, need not even be mentioned.)

Discussions of form (or form analysis) often appear to be very far removed from any political concern, so it is important to emphasise why the concept of form is important for developing Marxism as a theory of struggle. The central issue is the articulation and recognition of the power of labour. A concept that emphasises struggle, but sees struggle as being external to capital, recognises only one aspect of the power of labour. It hears the scream but is deaf to the resonance of the scream within capital itself. It sees the power of labour in strikes, in demonstrations, in armed struggle, but does not see it in the contradiction between productive and money capital, in the inadequacies of technology or in the internal disorder of the state. It sees the power of labour in the response of the state to overt struggles, but does not see it in the very existence of value as an uncontrollable chaos at the heart of capital. It is the presence of the power of labour within capital that makes it ineradicably crisis-ridden, and that allows us to speak, not of laws of capitalist development, but of certain rhythms and tendencies in the development of struggle.

It is important, however, to see that the concept of form here implies contradiction, instability. The power of labour appears in the form of its antithesis, the power of capital. Class struggle takes the form of relations or "things" (value, money, profit, etc) which appear to be neither class relations nor antagonistic. Class "exists in the mode of being denied" (Gunn). As forms of class struggle which deny their own substance, the social forms of value, money, state etc are inevitably characterised by a constant tension between form and content. The content is not contained within the form, but constantly breaks its banks and overflows. To quote Adorno again: "The name of dialectics says no more, to begin with, than that objects do not go into their concepts without leaving a remainder, that they come to contradict the traditional norm of adequacy" (1990, 5). The power of labour is not contained within the forms of capital, it constantly overflows and forces these forms to reconstitute themselves, to re-form, in order to contain the uncontainable. Fetishism in other words is not an established fact, but a constant process of fetishisation.

This distinction between fetishism and fetishisation is crucial for the way that we understand society and the way that we understand Marxism. If fetishism is total, if class antagonism is completely contained within its form, then revolution as the self-organisation of the working class becomes theoretically impossible. If fetishism is total and the working class cannot see through the forms in which class struggle presents itself (as neutral things), then there are only two possibilities: either one sees the working class within the structures of capitalism and gives up hope of revolution — the understandable but destructive pessimism of the Frankfurt School — or else one sees the only possibility of revolution as lying in the intervention of a deus ex machina, a vanguard party who will come from the outside. But there is no outside, just as there is no inside: there is only an inside-outside, an overflowing, an in-against-and-beyond. The only possible way of resolving this dilemma, the dilemma common to Leninism and the Frankfurt School theory, is to see that fetishism is not total. It is not an established fact, but a constant process of fetishisation. Labour does not simply exist in the form of capital: it exists in-against-and-beyond the form of capital. Class struggle does not simply exist in the form of value, money, state, etc: it exists in-against-and-beyond those forms. The forms of value, money, state, etc., are better thought of as form-processes, as processes of valorization, monetisation, stratification.

The state, to take an example, is not an institution in the sense of a thing that is outside us, nor is it simply a form of social relations in the sense of a link in the chain of capitalist reproduction: it is rather a form-process, an active process of forming social relations and therefore social struggles in a certain way. It is not just an aspect of fetishism (the neutral state) but, as part of the general struggle of capital against labour, an active process of fetishisation that systematically channels class struggles into non-class forms, into struggles on behalf of citizens, struggles for democracy, for human rights, etc — forms which systematically deny the existence of class and therefore promote the dis-articulation of the power of labour.

Or money, to take another example, is not simply a fetishised form of social relations. It is a process of monetising life, of subjecting human existence to the command of money, which implies a constant and violent struggle. The intensity of that struggle is reflected, for example, in all the conflicts surrounding the unprecedented expansion of debt throughout the world, and in the equally unprecedented rise in theft and "crimes" against property.

Or, to make the point more generally, if the dual existence of labour as concrete and abstract labour "is the pivot on which the comprehension of political economy turns," then it is important to see the abstraction of labour (the "imposition of work" as it is sometimes referred to) as a process, as a struggle which permeates not only the workplace, but the whole of society — a point emphasised but without differentiation in the concept of the "social factory."

Capital's reproduction depends on fetishisation, on the containment of a struggle that always goes beyond it. The relation between labour and capital is neither external nor internal: it is both, but with no clear dividing line. Labour does not simply exist within capital; it exists in-against-and-beyond capital (again with no clear dividing line between in, against and beyond, and therefore no clear distinction between class-in-itself and class-for-itself). Labour overflows from capital. Capital is not simply the form of labour; it is the process of forming labour, it is the constant process of self-reconstitution to contain labour. Class struggle is the movement of the overflowing-and-containment, or, in other words, class struggle is the movement of fetishisation / defetishisation. This is not to say that class struggle is theoretical, although theoretical reflection is clearly part of it. The process of fetishisation / defetishisation is a practical one. Fetishisation is the process by which social interconnections are broken down and become impenetrable. It is the decomposition of the working class. Defetishisation is the opposite movement: the movement by which, through struggle and the theoretical reflection that is part of it, interconnections are established and the working class is recomposed. Fetishisation is the containment of the power of labour, defetishisation is the overflowing of the power of labour, the scream of negativity. Fetishisation is the smothering of the scream, the assurance that "things are so." Defetishisation is the unleashing of the scream, the awareness that the only truth is that things are not so, that truth is not yet, or simply not.

Marxism is defetishisation, the theory of the power of labour in-against-and-beyond capital, the theory of the scream which shows that the scream does not exist only in overt militancy (in what is usually called "class struggle"), but that it is much, much more powerful than that because it reverberates in the very concepts of capital, because it reverberates in the deepest silence of everyday life. As Linton Kwesi Johnson puts it:

> Inside our ears are the many wailing cries of misery,
> Inside our bodies, the internal bleeding of stifled volcanoes,
> Inside our heads, the erupting thoughts of rebellion.
> How can there be calm when the storm is yet to come?
> ("Two Sides of Silence")

The "internal bleeding of stifled volcanoes" inside our bodies, the "erupting thoughts of rebellion" inside our heads, the existence of non-identity under the aspect of identity, the presence of the Not-yet in the Now, the power of labour in-against-and-beyond capital are the instability of capital, its constant tendency to crisis. Crisis is the manifestation of that power and for that reason the central concept of Marxism,. Crisis is the eruption of the power of labour.

ENDNOTES

Adorno, T.W. (1990). *Negative Dialectics* (Routledge, London).

Gunn, R. (1987). "Marxism and Mediation," *Common Sense,* no 2.

Hall, S. (1985). "Realignment for What?," *Marxism Today,* December.

Johnson, L. K. (1975). *Dread Beat and Blood* (Bogle L'Ouverture Publications, London).

Marx, L. (1965). *Capital,* Volume 1, (Progress Publishers, Moscow).

Editor's Preface to Johannes Agnoli's "Destruction as the Determination of the Scholar in Miserable Times"

Johannes Agnoli's contribution first appeared in German in 1990. Against the background of the fall of the Berlin Wall, the context of Agnoli's argument is the institutionalisation through parliamentary politics of the so-called new social movements of the 1970s during the 1980s. This "normalisation" and "responsibilisation" of the new (West-)German Left was accompanied by what at first sight appears to belong to a different area of controversy: the Historians Dispute of the 1980s. This dispute was provoked by Habermas' reaction to neo-conservative attempts at normalising German fascism. According to them, fascism was justified as a defence of the European middle classes against Bolshevism and the extermination of millions merely a copy-cat of the original Gulag. Habermas reacted against this "asiatic" interpretation of German fascism and proposed that, in contract to the neo-conservative attempt of providing a new basis for national pride and love of the German fatherland, that the only patriotism possible in German is constitutional patriotism — the love of the constitution. The institutionalisation of the previously unruly new social movements and the historians dispute connect in Habermas' idea of a constitutional patriotism, that is the espousal of the liberal-democratic state and its values of equality, justice, and freedom, as the best of all world. Instead of criticising the constitutional liberal-democratic state for what it is, the acceptance of the "political game" entailed and entails the acceptance of the values upon which it is based, transforming the critique of the state into a constructive criticism that while aiming to better the state, leads to the strengthening of the structures of power. Agnoli contrasts and compares the constructive attempts of the erstwhile new social movements to better the state with system theory's stern conception of how to contain and integrate new social forces into the structures of power — this not to change but rather to strengthen them. The essay shows the integrative force that the norm "responsibility" entails and explains why conflict is seen by the proponents of state power as a useful resource for stabilising the structures of power.

Agnoli concludes his essay by saying that it was written for German readers. Indeed, the essay deals with German conditions. But it does so in a systematic way and this means that his argument reveals theoretical insights of much wider importance. In fact, the essay is essentially about the relationship between the Left and the form of the state. He argues his case by contrasting constructive critique (and constructive conflict) to destructive critique (and destructive conflict). He stands firmly on the side of destructive critique and demands that it has to be restored to its rightful place: to destroy horrors. In contrast, he shows that honest and well-meaning constructive critique is forced to accept the very conditions through which horror subsists. The implication of Agnoli's argument is that the Left, if it takes itself seriously, has to be a destructive Left and that is, a Left that stands firmly on the side of human emancipation. Such emancipation entails that the Left abandons its illusions about the state as a means of liberation. The world to win is a world where humans are a purpose and not a resource, a world of human dignity.

Human dignity does not come cheap. It involves courage. More importantly, it requires patience and irony.

The first publication of Agnoli's essay in English in *Common Sense* no. 12, was translated by Werner Bonefeld and Byrt Klammack. It contained a number of errors that have been corrected in the present translation. The re-translation benefited from the publication of a revised German edition of the essay published in his *Der Staat des Kapitals und weitere Schriften zur Kritik der Politik*, Ça ira, Freiburg, 1995. The article appeared first in *Konkret* no. 2, February 1990.

2

Destruction as the Determination of the Scholar in Miserable Times

Johannes Agnoli

The determination of scholarly work as destruction originated with Johann Gottlieb Fichte; Hölderlin drew attention to the misery of the period. Fichte's determination was based on the belief in the emergence of a new era; Hölderlin, in contrast, found the period to be one of such misery that he asked himself what role, if any, was left for a poet.

In our time, misery remains strangely hidden and appears alien. Everywhere conformist constructions prevail. We witness the reconstruction of values, the dignity of nature is unearthed together with its flora and fauna. Although there are many ruptures, these are seen to be confined to other regions of the world. This then leads to the self-satisfied and contented view about our never ending wave of progress. To put it differently: an historical end is still proclaimed and this proclamation comes from the United States. In contrast to Marx's dream of the beginning of human history, it announces the final victory of the Western order. It celebrates the blessings of accumulation and praises the achievements of the liberal-democratic *Rechtsstaat* (state of law-and-order) as history's finest and final accomplishment.[1] The scholarly world, that is those sciences that do not deal with pure chemicals or with physical quantities but, rather, with human affairs, conditions, and troubles, does not remain on the sidelines. On the contrary, it contributes forcefully to the stabilization of the institutional structures, the system of liberal normative values, and the communicative systems of interaction; and it is powerfully engaged in the creation of news forms of citizenship, of life-styles and life-worlds, and the establishment of new forms of functionality. Certainly, as never before, the true mission of the scholar is seen to consist in constructive work. Reason is set to work, in part to simplify the world of things through systemic reductions (the so-called "reduction of complexity"), in part to advance placid forms of communication (the philosophical endeavour to mimic the data-processing of informatic studies),[2] and in part, in a complete reversal of reason, to attack reason. Because of an affectionate feeling of discontent, the attack on reason goes hand-in-hand with cheerful leaps into the spiritual, the mush of the soul.[3] The latter is not worth discussing. It is however disturbing that the new proponents of the enlightenment deny reason its historic role of, at any given time, provoking insubordination and destroying horrors, whether it be from church, state, despotism — or any other form of rule, as Voltaire liked to say.

It is not the case that the scholarly world accepts the seeming lack of ruptures uncritically. Nolte has criticised historiography and its failure to interpret German fascism in asiatic terms; Habermas criticised Nolte and his discarding of reason; Tugendhat criticised — in constructive terms according to the *Frankfurter Rundschau* — Habermas' friendly critique of Nolte.[4] Nevertheless, a constructive mood dominates and trust in the established order is widespread. Those who do mistrust especially the existing relations of constituted power and engage reason's historic role to lead humanity to emancipation,[5] and who do not make positive proposals and shun a constructive engagement with politics, find themselves, quite unintentionally, in conflict with the stipulated norms of the Constitution according to which scholarly work has to project constitutional values (see below).

The misery of our time that the successfully stabilized structures of power crystallize at all levels — even those engaged in alternative social projects have become becalmed from self-content — this misery demands destruction. The "system of order" has to be dismantled, trust has to be undone; and, instead, the explosive power of doubt has once again to be restored to its rightful place so that at last the soothing image of a faultless world changes, and that, in the face of current dramatic developments, the symbols of the positive, the good and the pretty vanish. Meanwhile, Germany (fortunately recently only West-Germany) seems to remain a country where critique blossoms always in constructive terms.[6] Is this the German culture? Is this a continuous, uninterrupted German intellectual tradition?

The Classics

The greatest of the German proponents of the Enlightenment teaches us something different. Kant, it is true, regarded according to tradition and his own statements, duty as a noble endeavour, the moral code in our hearts as a useful institution, and he admired the star-studded sky. Anything else, however, that came to his mind he demolished: the metaphysical unity of the world, the objectivity of space and time, the immortality of the soul, the indisputable existence of God. Admittedly, he let God, or what Goethe refereed to as the "old man," return through the backdoor that he conveniently constructed. This he did, however, only to install a sort of moral authority to ensure good behaviour in our daily life — better: as a "postulate" so that we all live decent lives and regard humanity as a purpose, not as resource as in, for example, the realization of profits or the achievement of parliamentary majorities.

Heinrich Heine, whom Goebbels declared a *Destruktiver,* a "force of decomposition," held Kant as a more resolute and decisive revolutionary than the French Jacobins. And Giosui Carducci (Nobel Prize 1906) took up Heine's contention: *"Decapitaron Emanuele Kant Iddio, Massimiliano Robespierre il Re"* — which is to say: Kant decapitated God, Robespierre decapitated the king. Whereby Kant holds first place among the destructive figures of history.

Kant, however, was not satisfied with doing away with God. He did worse: he decapitated the impartial head of science and replaced it by reason and that is, the principle of partiality, of social obligation. According to Kant, only that science is true which helps the common individual to dignity (Hartenstein, *Nachlaß,* p. 625).[7] He added an even more destructive element. In 1794, on the 12th of October, he received a "special order" from his Majesty the King to cease his philosophic "distortion and degradation of Christianity." (Note that if one replaces Christianity by the liberal-democratic ground order of the German constitution, the King's order amounted to the first conception of an anti-radical law).[8] Under this type of pressure, Kant began to understand the character of the constituted political order and started a dispute with the constitutional scholars. In his *Conflicts of the Faculties,* he developed the principle of partiality in its entirety. The constitutional scholars, he argued, might allow themselves to work positively within the existing constituted political system and affirm existing conditions. However, philosophy has a more important role: it is the role of philosophy to enlighten the population about the "true character" of the constitution in spite of orders to conceal it. What did Kant understand by the "true character?" Kant in no way meant the well-known gap between constitutional norms and constitutional reality whereby it would be the obligation on the part of politicians and scholars to restore the damage. Kant did not differentiate between "good constitutional norms" and "bad constitutional reality." Kant's emphasis on the true character of the constitution focused negatively on the rottenness of the norms themselves. He vindicated the right of philosophy to destroy all constitutional illusions and expose the fiction of a representative body as, in fact, a reality of domination [*Herrschaft*]. He called all affirmations of the constitution by one name: "Deceitful publicity" (*Conflicts of the Faculties,* Königsberg, 1798).

Kant's conception of the determination of the scholar did not remain without consequences. The destructive element found its way into Hegel's conception of negation as the dynamic force of the consciousness of freedom — even though the ageing Hegel (in contrast to Kant, who became wiser with age) subsumed negation under a general reconciliation with the state. Hegel was a poor master who, however, had a much better student. The good student followed Kant's "critical project" and pushed aside Hegel's reconciliation. Marx wanted neither to construct or affirm. He wanted primarily to negate. Like Heine, he was tradition-bound to the historic duty of decomposition. He went, however, several steps further: into the depth and into the basis of society. Marx was not satisfied with merely exposing the true character of the constitution. Beyond the recognition of the constituted deceitfulness of the constitutional state and after exposing its true character, the reality of its essence, and that is its function, had to be revealed. He destroyed the illusion of the pretty form of the state, a form that hides and yet organizes an ugly content. In this way, the absurdity of a mode of production on which bourgeois purposive-rationality, profitability, and respectability feed, was exposed. It stood naked. All who live from their labour and the sale of their labour power "find themselves directly opposed to the form in which, hitherto, the individuals, of which society consists, have given themselves as individuals, they must overthrow the state." Bakunin on Asia? No: Marx and Germany (*German Ideology*, MEW 3, p. 77).

Negation and destruction are therefore not missing form the German scholarly tradition. On the contrary, it has its classics. Their destructive reason has representatives even where common wisdom and the educated middle classes would least expect. Only a few in this country know, for example, who this Benimm-Knigge really was: "free Mister" Knigge was a radical Jacobin who understood the *terreur* and who, thinking about "Ça ira," criticised the German condition, lamenting that in Germany, "the nice lampposts are standing all so unused."[9]

Some Edifying Notes

Is this tradition really that of the "other Germany" which has historically been pushed aside by mainstream, constructive Germany?

In reassurance: Knigge's lampposts — whether pretty or not — are still quite properly providing light only for the streets. For the scholar, on the other hand, there still remains the Kantian duty and the Marxian project and that is, to continue the philosophical-political destruction of this powerfully protected misery that is blessed by consensus. By continuing this project, however, the scholars are likely to be forced to live in the shadows. General goodwill is removed from them and they make themselves suspect. But they must accept that danger if they are to take their determination and themselves seriously. This then means that against all official orders (*Basic Law,* Art. 5, 3),[10] scholars are left with no alternative but to reveal the fiction of freedom that the "Palace" (as the ancient Egyptians referred to the structure of power) posits and to disclose the fragility of its existence. When scholars orientate themselves on Kant, then they appropriate Kant's wisdom (see his answer to the special order of the King) and deal with the constituted liberal-democratic order and the structures of power in a two-fold and rightly famous manner. They will attempt to conceal the true character of the constitution and thereby bring their work into line with the *Zeitgeist.*[11]

The *Zeitgeist* creeps in fact away from the correct determination of scholarly work, and chooses instead to participate in the building of consensus: if one affirms existing conditions and norms, then the deplorable state of affairs loses its reality and transforms into correctable accidents. The responsibility for overcoming these rests with the so-called self-regulating capacity of the market, of power, and of parliament.

The first manifestation of the *Zeitgeist* undoubtedly understands itself as critical, but does not recognise its negative determination which is above all and principally "de omnibus dubitandum" (doubt everything). The critical dimension of the *Zeitgeist* is characterized by the painstaking quest for the good; that is, justice, equality and freedom. The good is supposed to be constitutionally guaranteed, despite various weaknesses. But the comforting conviction that the liberal-democratic ground order is basically sound despite the occasional infiltration of bad political practices which can be coped with whenever necessary, renders philosophy a pure work of edification, of state building. In spite of all enlightened proclamations, and in opposition to a programme that is admirably devoted to rationality, these new ideas of state building discover the universal element through which all political interactions first realize their human character: LOVE. But even love can have, within itself, the rationality of destruction (see Goethe's *Marienbader Elegie*). Rescued from such danger, caught on the edge of the abyss, and drawn into the positive, love becomes transcendental if, through edification, it is offered an object of desire that lies beyond all critique. Such transcendental love remains shielded from all adverse experiences and can therefore be loved for its own sake and that is, because of and for itself.

The initial enlightenment can not be denied. Love is given a rationally defined object that prevents any stumbles into the emotional-barbaric, and guarantees instead something of good quality. Besides, love of the fatherland — patriotism, the original sense of the word, has run its course — brings to the fore unpleasant things: heavy indigestible stuff that is well past its sell-by date. On this point, philosophy remains philosophical and that is, it maintains its destructiveness. But as love enters the phase of edification and reaches its object, it becomes harmless, observable, and worthy of affirmation: edification brushes away the love of the fatherland and proclaims, instead, its love of the constitution.[12] In this respect Friedrich Engels' observation is confirmed: in the rest of the world, political power explicitly insists on the rule of law and on the compliance with the constitutional order. In Germany, however, obedience to law, order and constitution is not sufficient — one is also required to love them.

For fear of undermining the political culture and of raising new uncertainties about proven institutions, reason, once free and probing, becomes pure affection and dissolves in a two-fold manner: first in general and second in love. In the late middle ages, philosophy had freed itself from servitude — due in part to the destructive force of nominalism. Philosophy did no longer want to remain in the role of an *ancilla theologiae* and regained its autonomy. Now, its constructive manifestations drag philosophy back into the role of a social servant: *ancilla constitutionis*. By refusing the possibility of a destructive autonomy within society that searches for emancipation, and by refusing to observe the institutional norms — these are norms of power and domination — with suspicion, philosophy affirms existing conditions and its defence of the constitutional order provides the office for the protection of the constitution, that is the security service, with the much desired ideological legitimation. This development is in stark contrast to a not-so-distant past when there was intellectual scolding of this office. However, when dealing with supposed or real enemies of the constitution, the security service's institutional love inspires quite different activities compared with the activities of those whose love of the state holds honest constructive intentions. The revolutionary tragedy of the Jacobin terror has long since been transformed into a constitutional comedy — to use a famous phrase (cf. Robespierre's speech on the 12th of December 1793, with German *Basic Law*, Article 18).[13] In the meantime, love has become a satyr's game: the new Chauvin[14] stands grinning at the Celler hole.[15]

In this manner, Kant has been stood on his head: the true character of the constitution lies in the fact that the constitution is true. Consequently, any further thoughts about it, any critical pronouncements, any destruction of the structure of power become superfluous. For constitutional patriotism, the destructive scholar is a scandal.

SYSTEMIC CONSIDERATIONS[16]

Constructive endeavours are widely accepted and edification approves itself. The other positive manifestation of the *Zeitgeist* has some misgivings about this. Does a dynamic state form not need the conflict of opinions and interests between groups and social partners? Does it not require the pluralist competition between interests? Cianetti who was Italy's Minister of Corporations in 1943, already saw the necessity of the social conflict.[17] But he also declared that conflicts must be contained within the limits of the system; in general: they must be regulated through law, not provoked. This clever notion achieved constructive endorsement in system theory which emphasises the constructive nature of conflicts and the consolidating quality of strikes. Besides, the German constitution provides guarantees for clashes of interest and seeks to support them as long is they are confined within the boundaries of the constitution.

Here it is not love which is seen as the most secure foundation of the political form. Rather it is *CONFLICT*. Conflict is accepted as a stabilizing force of the system, providing it with structures and securing its success. However, wherever conflict manifests itself in constructive or functional forms, the critical element does not remain absent. Conflicts without critical ideas amount to mere shadow-boxing and so lose their functionality. Critique seems, then, to be a systemic condition of political stability. But this presupposes a particular, much praised and emphasised quality of critique — critique has to abandon its negativity: it must refrain from destruction and operate constructively. Constructive critique — yet another tautology of the *Zeitgeist* — constantly makes positive proposals and seeks to improve and consolidate existing conditions. In so far as constructive critique opposes any attempt at demolishing existing conditions which is the aim of destructive critique, constructive critique is also a critique of destructive critique.[18] Destructive critique — looked at from the lenses of systemic thought — lacks the functionality of the positive.

System theory focuses with great care on the positive elements of conflict, for the positive is the yardstick against which anything new is measured. A theory which is devoted to the state and sees the state as "Being" or "Subject," must analyse new forces that enter the political arena not only with love but also with severity. This is because, as we know, within the system all fields, processes, movements, facts and persons not only interact with one another, they also, and importantly, constitute a finely meshed network that is susceptible to disturbances and ruptures. Should one mesh fail, and thereby allowing a dysfunctional conflict, an unknown intention, or an autonomous social power to slip into the network, then the complex relations between function and system can destabilize and destruction may assert itself.

System theory has much more reliable means of protecting the state against such destructive possibilities than any chatter that sees itself to operate in spaces where power does not exist.[19] This means is the norm that facilitates integration. It was first conceived by Max Weber. It is not called love. It is called responsibility. New social forces are subsumed under the obligation of responsibility. Only when new social forces enter the structures of power on the basis of responsibility and not merely on the basis of conviction, do they show their "political capacity" [*'Fähigkeit zur Politik'*]. If they act responsibly, they leave behind all its subversive, insurrectionary potential and contribute instead to the consolidation and extension of political power, rendering it fully accepted as a legitimate group. First it gains the capacity to act as opposition [*oppositionsfähig*], then it gains the capacity to enter into coalitions [*koalitionsfähig*], and lastly it gains the capacity to govern [*regierungsfähig*]. Absorbed by the norms, rules and limitations of liberal-democratic parliamentary democracy, its previously unruly character dissolves and it becomes a firm constituent element of constituted power. In other words, the representatives of the new social forces transform into functionaries of representation and thereby perform the systemic function of stabilization. In the end, neither the nice A. Vollmer nor the destructive J. Ditfurth can withdraw from this mechanism of integration that is so much stronger than the power of constitutional love.[20]

Who would deny that system theory deals with its object (the constitutional state) in as critical a manner as the heirs of critical theory — that is: critical but constructive.[21] Occasionally, it even displays mistrust but it does so only for the sake of form. For its declared intention is precisely the opposite. Its aim is not to generate mistrust but to create new relations of trust and loyalty. In this endeavour, it is very much served by a logic of argumentation that is as complex as it is rich with associations. It detests destructive critique and is suspicious of any mistrust since it, like a mole digging underfoot, undermines the belief in the correctness of conditions. In essence, system theory without knowing or intending it, finds its political consummation in the German constitutional guarantee of the continuity of power: in the "constructive vote of no-confidence."[22]

I do not know whether the founders of the German constitution were aware of the etymological humour of this monstrous idiom. Nevertheless, system theory finds in it its belated justification. The vote to remove an existing Chancellor by a new one during a parliamentary term results from a conflict situation and, in this way, symbolizes precisely the type of conflict that serves stability. Constructively handled distrust — such as the constructive vote of no-confidence — grows out of a trust in the continuity of power. The work of the scholar, in contrast, should be concerned with the demise of power.

But since love is the basis of trust, edifying and systemic work find themselves together again in the end, and both contribute to the creation of a new theodicy of the state. Love of the constitution is not misled by the evil of the political world; and system theory supplies the means for the functional integration of love. The systemically achieved edification is realized in a constitutionally protected high level of tolerance: the neo-Leibnizian proof of a secularised theodicy. But this theodicy does not lack its malicious element — just as in the original. For in his time, God certainly loved the best of all possible world — but he also watched very carefully the haphazard evil of man-kind in order to make corrections and mete out final punishment. A love that protects the constitution cannot do without control. It is for this simple reason that all those who are lovingly tolerated are also systematically kept under surveillance.

SOMETHING SUBVERSIVE

In the end, there should be some constructiveness after all. "Where is the positive?" In the misery of our time, we find it only in negation, in the nowhere — the so-called Utopia. In fact, the utopia that emerges from the destruction of all structures of inequality, subordination and power — this utopia is today the only possible way out from the impending obliteration that looms on the horizon. For the scholar, this means that social conflict must be freed from its systemic, stablilizing function, and it must be released from all constitutional love. Its historic dignity as a force of destabilization has to be restored. The defence of destabilization is identical with the defence and realisation of freedom. "Who claims earnestly to want freedom but simultaneously battles all destabilizing activities, contradicts himself" (Geymonat).[23]

POSTSCRIPT

Doubt comes to the fore: I have written this for German readers and German readers are earnest people whom one must take seriously. Hence the concluding problem: how can we achieve enlightenment with respect of destruction as the determination of the scholar without the furor teutonicus [*teutonic furore*] playing the accompaniment? The melody that will entice the ossified relations to dance, needs the basso continuo of irony — that is the most secure defence against the tortuous and misguided path of constructive thought.

TRANSLATED BY WERNER BONEFELD

ENDNOTES

These notes have been compiled by the editor. They are meant to guide the reader through Agnoli's argument and to suggest further reading.

1 For a detailed assessment see Agnoli's "The Market, the State and the End of History," in Bonefeld, W. and K. Psychopedis (eds) *The Politics of Change,* Palgrave, London, 2000.

2 Agnoli refers here to the regressive transformation of consciousness into forms of technological and that is functional rationality.

3 Agnoli refers here to the growth of occultism, spiritualism and esoterism during the 1980s.

4 Agnoli refers here to the Historians Dispute of the 1980s. The *Frankfurter Rundschau* is a national liberal-left newspaper. See also Agnoli's *Faschismus ohne Revision,* Ça ira, Freiburg, 1997, for an analysis of fascism and critique of attempts, including Nolte's, at normalising fascism and of according blame for fascism to the working class. An introduction of his book to an English readership can be found in Bonefeld "On Fascism," *Common Sense* no. 24. See also Bologna's "Nazism and the Working Class," published in *Common Sense,* no. 16.

5 See Kant's definition of the Enlightenment as humanity's exodus from self-imposed immaturity.

6 Note that the article was first published in February 1990 when the upheaval in East Germany was at its peak.

7 Kant, I. (1868) "Nachlaß," in *Sämmtliche Werke,* G. Hartenstein edition, vol. 8, Leopold Voss, Leipzig.

8 Agnoli refers here to the *Radikalenerlaß* of 1972. This *Erlaß* barred people with supposedly anti-constitutional opinions from employment in the civil service, including teachers and postmen. See also footnote 10.

9 Adolf Freiherr von Knigge, 1752 to 1796, was the author of a book on how to behave. "Benimm-Knigge" translates as "Behave-Knigge."

10 Art and science, research and teaching, shall be free. Freedom of scholarly work shall not absolve from loyalty to the constitution" (*Basic Law,* Art. 5, 3). By the late 1970s, at the height of the new social movements, University Professors were, under pressure of dismissal, forced to sign statements declaring their loyalty to the state. Unless scholarly work accepts the constitutional order, it would otherwise place itself in legal jeopardy and be subjected to police surveillance and persecution. The following quote from a Constitutional Court judgement of the early 1970s might clarify this: "The normative right to free speech and free expression of opinion is restricted if

the expression of opinion is in opposition to the liberal democratic ground order. The legally protected right to express the opinion that there is no freedom of opinion in the Federal Republic of Germany casts doubt on the validity of the constitutional value of the liberal democratic ground order. Because of this, the opinion that there is no freedom of opinion in Germany is not protected by the basic right of free opinion" (quoted in Preuß, *Legalität und Pluralismus*, Suhrkamp, Frankfurt, 1973, p. 24). On Agnoli's conceptualisation of the *Rechtsstaat* and liberal-democracy, see his *Die Transformation der Demokratie und andere Schriften zur Kritik der Politik*, Ça ira, Freiburg, 1990. For an introduction of this book to an English readership see, Bonefeld "Constitutional Norm versus Constitutional Reality in Germany," *Capital & Class* no. 46, 1992.

11 Kant's reply is published in his *Conflicts of the Faculty*. In his reply to the King's order to abstain from denigrating Christianity, Kant argues that since he did not provide an appreciation of Christendom, he could therefore not be accused of degrading Christendom. His reply, in fact, emphasises the importance of Christendom because of its moral force to secure good and honest behaviour. In short, Kant's reply agrees with the King and it does so in such a way that makes the ossified relations dance. Kant replies with irony, determination and praises the existing powers in a careful way. Praise of existing powers is not a punishable offence. Yet, like never ending applause, it can work like a destructive force.

12 Agnoli is referring here to Habermas' notion of a constitutional patriotism that he offered as an alternative rational source of national identity and as a means of securing the liberal-democratic values of justice, equality and freedom.

13 Article 18 of the German Constitution declares that those who make an unconstitutional use of the basic liberal rights enshrined in the Constitution, lose their basic rights. See also footnote 10.

14 The term chauvinism derives from a French comedy in which the character of Nicolas Chauvin plays the role of an ardent veteran of Napoleon's. Chauvin's absurdly extravagant national pride and sense of national duty repeats itself as a comedy in the activities of the security service against supposed enemies within (see footnote 15).

15 Agnoli refers here to the activities of the security service in the federal state of Lower Saxony. It became known in 1986 that a bomb that had exploded outside the walls of a prison in the town of Celle, where persons convicted of terrorist offences were held, was not detonated by a terrorist group as it was alleged, but by the security service itself. The person responsible for the bombing was a convicted murder who had been

released from prison. The bomb attack was used as a means of intensifying the search for terrorists and of infiltrating the convict into the terrorist scene as a contact. The constitutional comedy, referred to by Agnoli, entails, then, the new Chauvin as an ardent follower of law and order of a constitutional status quo based on state terrorism.

16 This section analyses the contribution of system theory to the stabilisation of political power. The important proponents are Luhman and Parsons. Parsons' work plays a significant part in Habermas' reconstruction of critical theory. For a destructive critique of Habermas, see Reichelt, "Jürgen Habermas' Reconstruction of Historical Materialism," in Bonefeld, W. and K. Psychopedis (eds.) *The Politics of Change,* Palgrave, London, 2000.

17 On Italian fascism's acceptance of social conflict as a constructive force that supports the stability of political power, see chapter 8 of his *Faschismus ohne Revision,* op. cit.

18 In order to clarify this point, see for example the current debate on globalisation where well-meaning commentators argue that globalisation leads to new forms of barbarism if its logic cannot be arrested through the creation of new forms of liberal-democratic intervention at the national and transnational level. This argument charges that the Left has to abandon its negative critique of capital and its state because the misery created by globalisation requires urgent action and intervention of a radical reformist kind. Globalisation is said to have rendered obsolete the ability of anti-systemic opposition to effect change. In order to avoid the dreadful consequences of globalisation, the Left is called upon to make positive constructive proposals. In short, destructive critique of capital and its state is rejected as socially irresponsible. It provides no positive proposals for the avoidance of barbarism and for this reason, by implication, is seen to be complicit in capital's project of neo-liberal globalisation. For a detailed discussion, see Bonefeld "Globalisation and Democracy," in *Common Sense,* no. 22, 1997.

19 The idea of communicative action in spaces defined by the absence of power is Habermas'. For critique see, Reichelt (op. cit.).

20 Vollmer and Ditfurth were representatives of the German Green's realist (Vollmer) and fundamentalist (Ditfurth) factions. The realist faction called for a policy of ecological realism and favoured to join the Social Democratic Party in a coalition government. The fundamentalist faction represented a more comprehensive rejection of the established party system and were reluctant to enter into government with the Social Democratic Party. Note that Agnoli's essay was first published in 1990 Many member of the fundamentalist faction left the Green Party in 1991. The Greens are currently the

junior partner of a coalition government led by the Social Democratic Party.

21 Agnoli refers here to Habermas and Offe, the two best known representatives of the second generation of critical theory.

22 "The federal parliament can only pass a vote of no-confidence in the Federal Chancellor by the election, with an absolute majority, of his successor" (*Basic Law*, Article 7, 1).

23 Agnoli quotes here from Geymonat's *La Liberta*. Geymonat is professor of philosophy at the University of Turin, Italy.

3

Marxian Categories, the Crisis of Capital, and the Constitution of Social Subjectivity Today

Harry Cleaver

Introduction

This article does two things. First, against post-Marxism and postmodernism, it recognizes the crisis of Marxist theory posed by the crises of capitalism and socialism but argues both that Marxist theory remains essential in the struggle against domination and for liberation and that at least one tradition of Marxism has developed in such a manner as to be useful for these purposes. Not only does the theory of that tradition grasp the globality of the problem and provide the means to understand the separations and connections which account for our weaknesses and our strengths, it also provides a framework within which we can recognize and analyze the emergence and autonomy of new social subjects supposedly beyond the purview of Marxist theory. Second, the paper discusses the limits to the ability of Marxist theory to conceptualize and provide positive theories appropriate to those emerging social subjects and therefore the need to develop revolutionary theory by taking account of the autonomous development of ideas within the struggles of emerging social subjects. As an example of the kind of assessment we need to do, the second part of the paper examines, with a view to discovering common ground as well as identifying differences, one feminist attempt to construct a theoretical alternative to the Marxist theory of labor.

The Continuing Relevance and Limits of Marxist Theory

The intellectual challenge posed to Marxist theory by the recent evolution of critical social thought, i.e., the proliferation of post-modernism and post-

Marxism, is an ideological moment of the more profound historical challenge posed by the crisis of capitalism (including the crisis of the traditional workers' movement and of socialism). It is also a moment of the associated formation of new social subjectivities which are not only undermining the domination of capital but crafting new, alternative projects of social constitution. Retrospectively, every historical crisis of capital, brought on by the political recomposition of the working class, has involved a crisis for Marxist theory in the sense that it has implied transformations in the qualitative organization of the capital relation and thus the need to rethink the scope and redefine the content of Marxist categories so that their interpretation remains adequate to understanding changes in the dynamics of the enemy and to the elaboration of working class strategy.

But prior to such processes of theoretical adaptation, within the crisis the very contingency of the confrontation with all of its rupture and possibility of social mutation, Marxist theory has always faced both its verification and its limits. The verification can be seen in the crisis brought on by our struggles. The limits can be found in the theory's ability to grasp their new directions of movement. On the basis of an approach which rejects the abstract generalization of Marx's analysis of the dialectic of capital into a cosmology (dialectical materialism),[1] we must recognize that the social transcendence of capital also involves a transcendence of Marxism. In other words, in so far as our struggles go beyond our efforts as workers against capital to the elaboration of alternative ways of being, i.e., to become processes of "self- valorization," to that degree we must develop new theory beyond Marx's theory of capitalism.

Moreover, if communism is not a future social order beyond capital but just such on-going processes of self-valorization, then we should be looking for new ways of thinking and "theorizing" in the present. Simultaneously, of course, as the history of past struggles shows, we may also find innovative efforts being recuperated within the capitalist dialectic, and thus aborted in their autonomy. Thus, we have *a research agenda* that involves two interlocking projects: first (I) to continue the adaptation of Marxist theory in order to understand the changing strategies of our common enemy (and the best ways to fight it) in terms of our own self-activity, and second (II) to seek out and critically evaluate new, alternative categories of analysis. The former project requires the study of the current content of the class struggle and of the adequacy of our current interpretations of Marxist theory. The later project requires the exploration of the constituent power (and limits) of emerging processes of self-valorization — and their self-conceptualizations. These projects, of course, are not completely separate because understanding capital's efforts at domination requires understanding the working class' efforts at liberation and these latter involve not merely the positive creation of alternative ways of being but also the resistance to domination.

I

One thing is certain: in spite of justifiable post-modern objections to master narratives, simple self-defense requires that for any critical social theory to be useful in the struggle for liberation, it must recognize and comprehend not only different forms of domination but the world-wide and totalizing character of the capitalist form. We can recognize how capital seeks the totalization of society within itself without attempting to replicate such tendencies in either social relations or theory. After all, one aspect of our struggles which tend to rupture such attempted totalizations is our theory which can be as diverse as other aspects of our projects of self-valorization. Contemporary developments of Marxist theory must provide a methodology which grasps the totality of capital's project without reductionism and with appreciation of the complex particularities (including theories) that resist the totalization.

Globality and Particularity: The Theory of Class Composition

In the past, of course, there have been various Marxist efforts to grasp the totality of capital as well as efforts to recognize and analyze the particularities that oppose it. Three examples have been: (1) the Hobson-Bukharin-Leninist *theory of imperialism* which visualized capitalism in terms of a world conquered, divided and redivided by competing national blocks of capital; (2) *dependency theory* which similarly sought to understand the global order of capital in terms of a hierarchy of development and underdevelopment; and (3) *world-systems theory* which has focused on the global interconnections through which capital has knit the world into its own kind of totality. Unfortunately, in all three cases the manner in which the theories were developed — starting from a focus on capitalist totalization — led to the displacement of the analysis from class conflict to nation-state conflict and the relative neglect of the particularities of class conflict. In all three cases there was a failure to grasp the totality of capital as an attempted internalization of a diversity of class conflicts whose dynamics account both for the form of the relationship and the direction of its movement. Because of the top-down orientation of these projects, nowhere has there been an attempt to grasp the logic of capitalist development in terms of the autonomous self-activity of the people struggling against it. It has been this failure that has left these theories open to the "master narrative" critiques characteristic of the post-modern emphasis on the diversity and differences among social movements.

Yet, surely, despite the validity of such critiques, such theories must retain a certain appeal because the globality of the class relationships of capitalism has never been clearer than it is in the wake of the overthrow of socialism in Eastern Europe and the Soviet Union. Today, global capitalism spearheaded by the International Monetary Fund (IMF) is transforming the institutional structures of the ex-socialist countries into variations of familiar Western types. Simultaneously, and at the root of both the collapse and the current efforts at transformation, the similarities between the struggles of the working classes of Central Europe and those of the West are becoming more and more obvious. We now see them more clearly and recognize the parallels not only because their institutional framework is becoming more familiar, but because with the collapse of the traditional barriers to East-West communication their struggles and ours are joining. As hitherto barely visible reservoirs of resistance and self-valorization link with their Western counterparts through face-to-face encounters (e.g., of environmental activists) and autonomous computer networks (e.g., Glasnet — Peacenet, etc.) the commonalties of struggle resonate and new common directions are being elaborated. Thus, ironically, just as the ideologies of post-modernism have trumpeted the radical incomparability of contemporary social conflicts and have demoted the Marxist analysis of class and class conflict to the status of one-issue-among-others, the development of those very social conflicts — East and West — have produced such an unmistakable unification of the institutions of capitalist power that no matter how autonomous the social conflicts the omnipresent menace of *capitalist* repression must force the recognition of a common enemy and of the continuing usefulness of Marxist analysis. Perhaps, with apologies to Marx, this character of the crisis "will drum the salience of class into the heads of the upstarts of post-modernism."

However, at the same time, the criticisms do highlight the failures to grasp the particular in such Marxist attempts to theorize the whole. Nor is it just a question of developing an analysis of the particular to complement the analysis of the whole — as the evolution of the debate over dependency and world-systems theory shows.[2] Rather what is required is an ability to grasp simultaneously: the nature of the totality/globality that capital has sought to impose, the diversity of self-activity which has resisted that totality and the evolution of each in terms of the other. Moreover, what we need is a theory that articulates all this from the point of view of the resistance to capital's totalization (as opposed to what we might call bourgeois theory which deals with these things from the point of view of capital) and of the effort to move beyond it. The question then is whether there are any traditions or developments within Marxism that provide such a theory, or important elements of such a theory.

There is a tradition of Marxist theory — one which I call "autonomist Marxism" — which has evolved in such a way as to answer the post-modern demand for the recognition of difference and the Marxist insistence on the totalizing character of capital. This is a tradition which long ago abandoned the simple reductionism of that deterministic orthodoxy which post-Marxism usually takes for its rhetorical target. In place of a narrow conception of the working class (as the waged industrial proletariat) which ignored or sought to subordinate other oppressed segments of society, we have had for several decades a complex *theory of class composition* explicitly designed to grasp, without reduction, the divisions and power relationships within and among the diverse populations on which capital seeks to maintain its dominion of work throughout the social factory — understood as including not only the traditional factory but also life outside of it which capital has sought to shape for the reproduction of labor power.[3] This is a theory which inverts, from a working class perspective, Marx's analysis of the composition of capital and constructs a theory of the changing "composition" of working class power.[4] Thus the concept of working class is seen to include all those lives capital has been able (to one degree or another) to subordinate to its own logic while, at the same time, appreciating the differences and conflicts among them. This theory explores how various sectors of the working class, through the circulation of their struggles, "recompose" the relations among them to increase their ability to rupture the dialectic of capital and to achieve their own ends. In response, over time and according to the dynamics of that recomposition, capital is forced to seek a restructuring "decomposition" of the class — which may involve the repression and/or the internalization of self-activity — to restore its control. Such analysis has involved the systematic reworking of all concepts within the changing historical context and has generated a comprehensive analysis of the evolution of Twentieth Century capitalism.

One central example of the recasting of key Marxian concepts in the light of changes in the class relations of capitalism has been that of Marx's concept of the "collective worker" elaborated in *Capital*, Volume I. Historical examination of the shift from skilled craft labor to relatively unskilled mass production labor led to the theory of the "mass worker" in the Fordist-Keynesian period.[5] That reworking produced analyses of the complexity of a new constitution of the working class in ways which have brought out both the autonomy and interconnectedness (complementarities *and* conflicts) among sectors of the class — including the various parts of the waged proletariat as well as groups traditionally defined as outside that class such as unwaged housewives, students, peasants and urban "marginals."[6] Such recognition and analysis of diversity has continued through the crisis of the Fordist-Keynesian period into the current phase of the crisis of capitalism.[7] Such analysis has provided the tools necessary to reveal the weaknesses and strengths of our struggles as well as the success and limits of capital's efforts to restore its power of command.

For the period beginning with the crisis of Fordist-Keynesian style command, the Marxist theory of class composition has provided an historical analysis of the crisis of the class relations of capitalism that we have been experiencing for the last 25 years in terms of two phases: (1) a complex and interrelated insurgency of a broadly defined working class which, through a process of political recomposition of the structure of class power, ruptured the sinews of capitalist command, and (2) a capitalist counterattack which has sought to decompose that power in order to restore its own ability to subordinate society. In both phases the key issue has been the ability of diverse sectors of the working class to overcome their isolation and differences and circulate their struggles among themselves and to other sectors.[8] Where they have succeeded they have gained ground in the class war; where they have failed capital has been successful in its counterattacks.

To begin with, the "class composition" analysis of the late 1960s and early 1970s demonstrated how the crisis of capital (which is at the heart of the violence of its reaction) was precipitated by a cycle of various interconnected struggles (including those of peasants, students, women, industrial workers, state workers, etc.) which succeeded in rupturing the post-WWII structures of global capitalist power, i.e., Fordism-Keynesianism-Pax-Americana. In other words, those working within this framework have shown how these struggles constituted a political recomposition of *class* power at the same time they were moving more or less autonomously in their own directions.[9] Subsequently, in response to the variety of capitalist counterattacks launched in the 1970s and 1980s, from the reorganization of international money through the use of inflation and deflation to industrial and social restructuring, the theory of class composition has delineated both our failures to cope and the sources of our continuing strength.

On the negative side of our weaknesses, analyses based on this theory have shown how the defeats we have suffered over the past two decades of crisis have been in large part due to our inability to avoid being divided and conquered, i.e., to avoid the successful decomposition of our power. *At a global level,* capital's ability to impose localized hunger, disease and starvation in the 1970s and 1980s (especially the famines of Africa), through its ability to impose austerity (unemployment and falling real income) and police repression (e.g., Mexico, Brazil, Mozambique, the American rust belt, the ghettos of

Washington and Los Angeles), to its ability to impose war and devastation (e.g., Panama, the Persian Gulf), the success of these terribly destructive counterattacks have depended on preventing the mobilization of outside support through the isolation of the targeted populations — in part through the manipulation of circuits of information and communication.[10] *In the U.S.*, counterattacks against particular sectors, especially those whose demands and struggles cut transversally across numerous other conflicts (e.g., the women's movement, "minority" movements, and immigrant self-mobilization) have involved fueling the most vitriolic ideologies of human division — sexism, racism and ethnic jingoism.[11] The objective of such ideological attacks being to mobilize support for juridical and legislative attacks on gender rights, for similar attacks on racial rights as well as welfare cuts and Drug Wars aimed at already ghettoized minority populations and for the overt repression of the circulation of immigrant autonomy. Such official state violence, of course, has sanctioned an expansion of private violence accelerating the incidence of rape, gay bashing and skinhead attacks on minorities and immigrants.

On the positive side, the theory has helped locate our ability to resist such attacks in capital's inability to destroy or control existing connections or to prevent the further formation of linkages among those of us engaged both in destructuring the mechanisms of capitalist command and in pursuing our own autonomous purposes. Subsequent work on the failures of capital's counter-offensives have sought to understand the transformations through which people have been able to resist capitalist assault and continue to build their own autonomy.[12]

Internationally, the power of the Nicaraguan revolutionaries or of the Palestinian intifada to assert and defend their own programs has depended in obvious ways on international networks of relationships which inhibited both the American and Israeli governments in pursuing their proclivities toward military repression. The extremely rapid diffusion of information through such networks, which have evolved from newsprint into cyberspace, has been essential in the mobilization of mass opposition to the deployment of American troops against the Sandinistas (thus the recourse to the contras and economic blockade) and to the brutality of Israeli repression of Palestinian struggles. Similarly, the amazingly rapid mobilization of a movement against the possibility of a Gulf War which took place in the Autumn of 1990 — despite its failure to prevent the war — was based on the ability of those opposed to the military build-up to utilize global systems of computer communication (especially Peacenet) to diffuse counterinformation that was used for local organization. On a smaller scale, but more persistently, the ability of the South African liberation movement to break out of its isolation and mobilize a world-wide antiracist movement against apartheid (imposing boycotts and disinvestment) was fundamental to its ability to force all of the recent changes which have widened the possibilities of its struggles. Perhaps most dramatically, the instantaneous circulation of the images of revolt from country to country, played a fundamental role in the wildfire-like spread of political revolution against Soviet-style communism in Central Europe.

In the U.S. such linkages have been multiplied a thousand fold and account for both the power of resistance and the power of constitution in arena after arena of social conflict. The resistance of American women to the "backlash" against their progress toward liberation and autonomy, that of the old to the attack on social security and healthcare, that of the gay community to the neglect of the AIDS epidemic and that of parents, students and the poor to reductions in school lunch programmes and food stamps are examples of struggles which stymied the Reagan White House's "social agenda" in the 1980s and forced it sometimes to abandon its efforts, sometimes to have recourse to private or local initiatives (e.g. the attack on abortion rights, state legislation, media ridicule of feminism and exposés of welfare cheats and street crime in the ghettos, the push for privatization of public schools) or even to make further concessions against its will (e.g., more money for AIDS research and outreach, more money for food stamps).[13]

The persistence of pro-active struggles (beyond mere resistance) among such groups can be seen in the continuing drive by women, gays and racial minorities to extend the spaces and opportunities for self-development in spheres such as education where as students and professors they have forced the creation of courses and whole programs of study to provide opportunity and time for the elaboration of new kinds of self-understanding and autonomous projects — from the exploration of the hidden history of women and sexual diversity to that of Afrocentrism. It has been the strength of such struggles, the pervasiveness of the critiques of contemporary society which they have produced, together with their success in pushing forward their autonomous agendae that has produced an audience for the emphasis on difference characteristic of postmodernism as well as the most recent ideological backlash against "political correctness," diversity and multiculturalism.

The Autonomy of New Social Subjects and Self-Valorization

The theory of class composition insists that patterns of these evolving conflicts are materially rooted in the character of the class relations as they have evolved through these struggles. Among the most interesting aspects of the analysis of the current character of class struggle (as well as the movement beyond it) are the efforts to grasp the way in which the constitution of the working class has become increasingly autonomous of capital.

I have used the term "autonomist" Marxism to designate a tradition within which there has always been a tendency to recognize and valorize the ability of workers not only to resist capitalist exploitation and domination but to act in their own interests. In terms of the theory of the working class the main implications of this orientation has been to recognize and theorize both the self-activity of workers vis-à-vis capital and the self-activity of various sectors of the class vis-à-vis other sectors, e.g., of women vis-à-vis men, of blacks vis-à-vis whites. The study of skilled craft workers emphasized, in part, the autonomy of those workers in the control of the production process. The study of mass workers emphasized, in part, the autonomy of those workers from the labor process itself. The study of the cycle of struggles that ruptured the Fordist-Keynesian period emphasized the struggle against the capitalist imposition of work in all its forms, from the factory floor, through the rice paddy to the schoolroom and single-family dwelling. The theory of class composition has explored many areas of the "social factory" to reveal the particularities of domination and those of resistance and subversion. Thus, Mariarosa Della Costa, Selma James, Silvia Federici and others have examined the hidden fabric of gender relations that convert the daily lives of women into housework for capital, i.e., into the production and reproduction of life as labor power. At the same time, they sought to identify the sources of strength through which women have developed the power to resist such work and explode the capitalist subordination of daily life. In all of these cases, the degree and quality of that autonomy, it is suggested, not only explains the crisis of capital and the quality of its reaction (both its specificity and its violence) but also the concrete possibilities for liberation.

In the course of attempting to grasp the connection between autonomous character of workers' struggles and those possibilities of liberation, some of those working in this area began to differentiate between those struggles (or those aspects of struggles) which resisted capitalist exploitation and those that sought to move in new directions beyond it. One way of conceptualizing the latter movement is in terms of the autonomy and self-liberation of desire — of the sort analyzed by Gilles Deleuze and Félix Guattari in their two volumes on capitalism and schizophrenia.[14] Another way of conceptualizing such movement is embodied in the term "self-valorization" as it developed within the Italian New Left. Whereas Marx often used the term interchangeably with capitalist valorization, referring to the self-expanding character of capital, Antonio Negri suggested that the term be used instead to designate the self- determination of the working class. Thus Negri's *auto-valorizzazione* refers to the ways in which workers act as autonomous subjects crafting their own existence, not only against capital, but for themselves. Although it is in practice often difficult to separate out the two moments of resistance and self-valorization, the distinction is fundamental to the notion that the working class becomes a revolutionary subject, not merely reacting to domination but constituting a new world through its self-activity.

Because the term has been developed in a way that conceptualizes working class self-valorization not as unified but as diverse, it provides a theoretical articulation of the tradition within "autonomist Marxism" of recognizing the autonomy not merely of the working class but of various sectors of it. To both recognize and accept diversity of self-valorization, rooted like all other activity in the diversity of the peoples capital seeks to dominate, implies a whole politics — one which rejects traditional socialist notions of post-capitalist unity and redefines the "transition" from capitalism to communism in terms of the elaboration from the present into the future of existing forms of self-valorization.[15]

In this recognition of the autonomy of the newly emerging social subjects, and of the diverse paths of self-valorization that may be followed, the theory of class composition differs radically from other Marxist efforts to understand the contemporary development of class relations — efforts such as those of the sociologists of the labor process or of the economists of "regulation theory." In both cases, the perception of fundamental change is clear enough but the focus is on the *capitalist* manipulation of change and the reorganization of its command. In terms of the contemporary crisis of capitalism, the sociologists are preoccupied with the increasingly flexible ways capital seeks to organize and exploit labor, while the regulation theorists retain their on-going fascination with regimes of accumulation and modes of capitalist regulation. Both think of the changes in terms of a movement from "Fordism" to "Post-Fordism" — a choice of terms which bespeaks their focus on capital. The difference in perspective of the Marxist theories of class composition and self-valorization is immediately apparent in its very inverse focus on the characteristics of the working class subject active at the heart of these different social dynamics.[16]

With respect to the current period of crisis and restructuring, the emphasis on the autonomy of peoples' self-activity within, against and beyond the mechanisms of capitalist domination has led some Italian and French theorists of working class composition to suggest that at the heart of the crisis of "Fordism" and at the core of capitalist efforts to construct a "post-Fordist" form of control is a new kind of working class subjectivity which has emerged out of that of the mass worker. They suggest that only by understanding the positive characteristics of that subjectivity, which ruptured capitalist control and continues to defy its present efforts at subordination, can we understand either those efforts or the emergent possibilities of liberation. One early characterization of this new subjectivity (which is actually seen as a diversity of subjectivities) was given by Sergio Bologna in the 1970s who identified a new "tribe of moles" — a loose tribe of highly mobile drop-outs, part-time workers, part-time students, participants in the underground economy, creators of temporary and ever-changing autonomous zones of social life that forced a fragmentation of and crisis in the mass-worker organization of the social factory.[17] Another characterization has been that of Antonio Negri, who used the term "socialized worker" to focus on how the crisis of the social factory has been generated precisely by a subject whose self-activity in all moments of life challenges the fabric of capitalist control.[18]

In recent years, in collaboration with a variety of French and Italian Marxists, Negri has sought to identify the evolving characteristics of this "socialized worker." Typical of the work of the theorists of working class composition, he and his co-workers have sought to go beyond the sociological analyses of the newest forms of capitalist command, to discover the newest forms of working class self-activity. As in the previous period of the mass worker or of the tribe of moles, the object is to identify the possibilities of liberation inherent within the capacities of self-activity. Thus within the interpersonal interactions and exchanges of information that the theorists of post-Fordism associate with the "computer and informational society," Negri and company believe to have identified an increasingly collective appropriation of (i.e., control over) "communication."

The analysis runs as follows: whereas the period of mass production was characterized by radical divisions between and within mental and manual labor (both within and outside of the factory) that limited daily participation in any kind of collective system of interactive communication to a small minority of skilled workers (e.g., engineers and scientists), the dynamics of the class struggle has increasingly forced a spatial and temporal recomposition of work that is undermining that division. On the one hand, automation has been dramatically reducing the role of simple manual labor — increasingly in the "service" sector as well as in manufacturing. At the same time, the needs of global coordination and continuous innovation have expanded not only the role of mental labor but its collective character, creating ever more jobs that require the manipulation of information flows, intelligent and informed decision making within production, independent initiative, creativity and the coordination of complex networks of cooperation.[19] The two forces of automation and communication have even contributed to the breakdown of this traditional distinction between mental and manual — especially, but not uniquely, in sectors of the "informational society."[20] The essential point is that at a social level, these developments embody the adaptation of capitalist command to the emergence of an increasingly independent collective subject — "the socialized worker" — whose self-organization of essentially intellectual work and play repeatedly outruns capital's ability to limit and control it.

The analysis of this emerging collective subject has suggested that it has begun to impose its hegemony on the class composition as a whole, much in the way the "mass worker" dominated the prior "Fordist" period of capitalist development. In other words, while during the period of the "mass worker" (Fordism) neither all nor even most workers were employed in factories on assembly lines, nevertheless they formed the paradigmatic core whose organization influenced all others. The argument is that, in the present period, not only are the new attributes of this collective subject (interlinked intellectual cooperation, appropriation of social communication, constituent of differentiated communities with new values, rejection of traditional politics and labor organization) increasingly coming to characterize the class as a whole but that subject has taken on, more and more, the political role of igniting, solidifying and linking social struggles. This grounding of the collective processes of constitution in communication, it is argued, is a common characteristic in the development of an array of "new social movements" which have been widely seen to be the most important components of social confrontation in this period. Let us look at some examples.

The Autumn 1986 French "student movement" has provided Negri with one concrete case of the appearance of the "socialized worker" and one in which the "'truth' of the new class composition appears most transparently."[21] That students are involved in cooperative networks of "intellectual work" is obvious.[22] That their collective work has been increasingly disciplined by a labor market which demands "productive" education, and that such "productive" intellectual activity (in the university as well as in later waged jobs) has become increasingly central to the organization of the global work machine is fairly widely recognized.[23] The degree to which capital succeeds in disciplining and expropriating that activity versus the degree to which students (and sometimes their professors) succeed in autonomously determining the direction of their own development was not only the central issue that provoked the Fall explosion, but has become the on-going central issue of "education" not only in France but throughout the world — East and West, North and South.

A subsequent study of student struggles in Italy, demonstrated not only the similar character of the conflict but the ways in which students organized themselves as a fighting collective subject through the use and manipulation of various means of communication.[24] Recent American studies of IMF plans for "restructuring" education in Africa, also show clearly how the fundamental aim is the repression of the autonomy of students and professors and the reduction of education to the production of labor power.[25]

To these examples, we can add the well known "democracy" movement in China in 1990 which was also clearly spearheaded by those who seem to fit the analysis of the new socialized worker: students and communication workers from Chinese universities, radio and television. (Traditional factory workers followed, not led, the movement.) Not only did these lead the movement into the streets but their formation into a movement and the circulation of their struggles were achieved precisely through the mobilization of those characteristics attributed to the "socialized worker." Traditional forms of organization such as mass meetings and strikes were complemented, in close collaboration with their counterparts in other countries, by the masterful utilization of virtually every technology of communication available, i.e., the tools of their trades: telephone, fax, radio, television, and computer networks — not only to mobilize international support but to build and circulate their struggles within the country. The state resorted to repressive and bloody violence only after repeated failures to cut the communicative sinews of the movement (e.g., the movement circumvented the state tactic of cutting intercity phone lines by linking cities via fax through third countries).

Outside the academy (although partly within as well), we can identify another set of self-constituting communities of "intellectual workers" at the core of "communication" as those working in or through the electronic world of computer networks. Originally constructed and operated to facilitate the development of technology at the service of capital (ARPANET), contemporary networks (e.g. INTERNET, BITNET) have not only, in fact, been largely constructed by the collectivities which use them — and retain the material stamp of that autonomy in their uncentralized and fluid technical organization — but constitute a terrain of constant conflict between capitalist attempts at reappropriation and the fierce allegiance of most users to freedom of use and "movement" throughout the "cyber" space they have created and constantly recreate. The most visible evidence of this autonomy, and of the class character of the confrontation involved, is the conflict between the "hackers" — who repeatedly break down the barriers to free movement created by capital in its attempt to harness and control these networks — and the state. They mostly became visible in the U.S. as a result of the recent wave of inept state actions aimed at disrupting and repressing their activities.[26] Less visible but more important are the myriad participants of the networks who, operating from personal or institutional (academic, corporate, or state) entry points, utilize the technology not only for their "official" work but in the pursuit of their (and their friends') own interests. What has been striking over the last few years has been the constitution of a proliferating network of networks almost totally devoted both to the subversion of the current order and to the elaboration of autonomous communities of like-minded people connected in non-hierarchical, rhizomatic fashion purely by the commonalty of their desires. Examples include not only independent networks like PeaceNet, EcoNet, or the European Counter Network, but also radical nets within official nets, such as Pen-L (the Progressive Economist Network) and Activ-L (the Activist Mailing List) within Listserv on BITNET.

What needs to be emphasized here is that these networks are not constituted merely by "computer nerds" — those who like to play with computers — but by far the greater number of participants in these collectivities are workers in a diverse array of institutions. While some networks such as the Progressive Economist Network may be constituted mainly by academics, others such as PeaceNet or the European Counter Network involve people in all kinds of activity and all kinds of struggle.

The social character of the "socialized worker" derives not primarily from the way in which capital has annexed and integrated the sphere of reproduction (school, community, family, etc.) with the sphere of production (factory, office, etc.)[27] but mainly from how new subjectivities have redefined and restructured themselves in such a way as to undermine such distinctions. Women within the home and community and students of both sexes within the schooling system have come to recognize how their activities in those locations are supposed to be subordinated to the accumulation of capital. Simultaneously, they have sought to maintain or craft a subversive autonomy in those activities which undermines their role in the creation and reproduction of labor power and contributes to the constitution of new kinds of personal and social being, as discussed below. Similarly, waged workers have subordinated the tools of their trade to the realization of more broadly defined objectives and thus transformed to some degree the activities in the work place into liberated activity, often directly related to other spheres of life.

What has been remarkable about the proliferation of the "personal" computer in the U.S. (which is more extensive than anywhere else) has been the way it has rapidly evolved into a gateway of communication and mobilization linking otherwise isolated people and movements. In striking contrast to the first generation of arcade-style computer games, which were widely interpreted as contributing (like television) to the collapse of social being into screen-glued and purely reactive protoplasm, the modem and the spread of communication nets are providing the sinew of a growth of collective social being in dramatic ways.

Stepping back from this analysis of new social subjectivities which might be classed as variations of the "socialized worker," we must keep in mind that they are developing within a global population whose subordination to capitalist work continues through forms the most ancient as well as the most recent. Despite the emergence of new subjectivities within the most "high tech" parts of the social factory, vast numbers of people are still struggling against exploitation through more traditional forms, from the Fordist assembly line and state taxation to patriarchal slavery within the family and therefore seek to escape their life sentences at hard labor through all means possible. Processes of self-valorization, of the elaboration of new social projects, occur under the most diverse of circumstances — not just on the cutting edge of high tech. As work on the struggles of peasants and urban marginals has shown, it flowers in rural villages and urban barrios as well as university campuses and high-rise office buildings.[28] Yet, there can be no doubt that although some, at very different positions of the international wage hierarchy, have the power to push forward their own projects of self-valorization, others are being crushed by capitalist austerity and repression and struggle barely to survive. What we need today, in an age where capitalist strategy and policy are increasingly global, is to build, piece by piece, a comprehensive analysis of the international class composition and the processes of political recomposition which grasps the interactions among all sectors of the class, identifying those being beaten down as well as those on the move, those subject to the most abject exploitation as well as those capable of launching new initiatives.

With respect to the kinds of examples just cited, and to the analysis of them which has been carried out to date, it seems to me that we can see how the kind of Marxist theory which I have described is in the process of elaborating such an understanding of contemporary social conflict. The openness of the theoretical and political project to a kind of class analysis on all levels, from global configurations to the individual psyche, and to seizing not only the interconnected determinations of various kinds of domination but the positive diversity of collective self-valorization, provides an appealing framework for thinking about emancipation from repression and processes of liberation.

II

As suggested at the outset, however, no matter how appealing the theories of class composition and self-valorization, they have their limits. The theory of class composition is a theory of *class*, a theory of the relationships within and between the classes of capitalist society. It was neither designed for nor is it adapted to the theorization of the emergence of post-capitalist social relations. Like other aspects of Marxist theory, it *can* help us understand something about the social forces at work undermining capitalism. It *can* focus our attention on the diversity of autonomous movements within the working class and thus suggest the need for a politics of alliance against capital by various movements headed in different directions. But, it does *not* provide us with an understanding of the positive content of those movements, of the new directions or patterns being developed. Similarly, the theory of self-valorization *can* concentrate our attention on the self-activity of the working class, on how, for example, living labor may be evolving into a revolutionary subject capable of casting off the constraints of capitalism, freeing itself from the vampirism of dead labor. But, it does *not*, in itself, give us more than very general concepts of this movement: of its autonomy, of its diversity. When we begin to explore the diversity of self-valorization in detail what we find are a variety of social relations under creation which by escaping capitalism also escape our Marxism.

Where are we to find useful understandings of such social relations, if not in Marxism? In the spirit of Marxism (as opposed to the spirit of all universalizing philosophies), I would say that we must look within the emerging movements themselves.[29] Just as new movements of the working class have generated new adaptations of capital and the need for new conceptualizations, so any movement which is struggling to craft social relations different from those of capitalism may generate new conceptualizations more or less consistent with its own character.[30] Where there are a multiplicity of movements, we may expect to find a multiplicity of concepts, quite different from their analogs in Marxist theory.

The need to be open to such possibilities is not merely intellectual but immanently political. The theory of molecular autonomy and the diversity of self-valorization implies a politics of alliance, as Guattari and Negri have argued: "the task of organizing new proletarian forms must be concerned with a plurality of relations within a multiplicity of singularities — a plurality... [which] develops toward... a functional multicentrism."[31] Whatever "machines of struggle" can be constructed on the basis of such plurality, they argue, must involve "the totally free movement of each of its components, and in absolute respect of their own times — time for comprehending or refusing to comprehend, time to be unified or to be autonomous, time of identification or of the most exacerbated differences."[32] As they recognize, such a politics cannot depend on any kind of "ideological unification" — including consensus around the meaning or importance of theoretical categories.[33] It seems obvious that working out the terms and dynamics of such alliances requires a direct confrontation with the diversity of ideas and values that proliferate within their constituent parts. It would also seem clear that those ideas requiring the most urgent attention are those which are central to the conceptual world views of the various autonomous movements with which one would most like to establish links and build political alliances. Thus, once again, a double agenda: the working out of one's own analysis and the critical exploration of "neighboring" activities, values and ideas.

If what we are looking for in such a confrontation are new ideas that articulate new realities transcending those of capital, then we have two tasks: first, to juxtapose the new ideas being investigated with the (Marxist) ones we have already developed for the social relations of capitalism — to see if the new ideas are really new, and second, to the degree that they appear to be, to investigate the social movements which have given rise to those ideas in order to better understand what is new about the struggles involved (in order to decide how we want to relate to them).[34]

Theories of Work, Marxist and Feminist

As an example or contribution to such efforts, I want to comment briefly on the feminist critique of the Marxist concept of work by Maria Mies and on her attempt to sketch an alternative feminist theory of work in her book *Patriarchy and Accumulation on a World Scale*.[35] In terms of the two tasks just mentioned, I will limit my comments here to the first, namely to see whether and to what degree her work really does go beyond the concepts of Marxism and illuminates new kinds of social relations.

Mies' work is not only interesting but has been widely influential in the feminist movement in Western Europe, in the Third World and in building links between autonomous movements in both. Confronting her arguments can be done in a relatively straightforward manner for two reasons. First, she accepts the importance of thinking about feminist issues and politics in relation to global capitalism and on the basis of the autonomy of the various struggles against it.[36] Second, she came to these positions, in part, through the study of Marxist texts. In that study she shares with the theorists of class composition and self-valorization a common source of inspiration in the work of Italian Marxist feminists.

According to Mies' own account she, and a number of other German feminists with whom she collaborated, drew on the theoretical work of Mariarosa Dalla Costa and Selma James dealing with the relationship between housework and capital and critiquing traditional Marxist positions. Dalla Costa and James' writings, beginning with "The Power of Women and the Subversion of the Community," attacked concepts of housework as "unproductive" and of the only fruitful place for women's struggles being in the waged labor force.[37] On the basis of a detailed analysis of how women's activities in the family, home and community create and reproduce labor power (i.e., how they constitute work for capital), she argued the fundamental importance of that work in accumulation, the importance of recognizing how women's lives are exploited by it and the necessary autonomy of women's struggles over unwaged work. All this, and the subsequent "debate over domestic labor," Mies considers to have been "an important contribution to a feminist theory of work."[38] Concerning these aspects of work under capitalism, there is considerable agreement between Mies' feminism and the theories of autonomist Marxism.

Disagreement begins over the concept of work that she sees as prevalent in all capitalist and socialist countries — one she believes is shared by Marx.[39] In her view that virtually omnipresent concept is one of work as "a necessary burden . . . which has to be reduced, as far as possible, by the development of productive forces or technology. Freedom, human happiness, the realization of our creative capacities, friendly unalienated relations to other human beings, the enjoyment of nature, of children's play, etc., all these are excluded from the realm of work and are possible only in the realm of non- work, that is, in leisure time."[40] The source of this formulation is obvious and she soon makes it clear by quoting the passages on the realm of necessity and the realm of freedom in the third volume of *Capital*. She also cites or quotes various passages from the *1844 Manuscripts*, the *Grundrisse* and *The German Ideology*. It soon becomes clear that her view of Marx's reasoning is one she draws from, or shares with, Alfred Schmidt who had previously interpreted the *Grundrisse* as a paean to the possibility of total automation.[41] For her, the epitome of the dead-end to which such a concept leads are the hallucinations of Andre Gorz for whom, as she puts it, the time has already arrived "for a straight march into the Marxist paradise because, with micro-electronics, computers and automation, necessary labor can almost be reduced to zero."[42]

There are two problems immediately apparent about this interpretation. First, it completely ignores the quite contrary orthodox Marxist arguments that the realization of socialism and communism would fully realize human potential not by eliminating work but by making everyone into a worker — precisely the ideology that has justified the brutal socialist imposition of work. Second, it also ignores the theory of the very positive, creative role of work in both Marx and the theory of self-valorization. However, not only can we read the passages on necessity and freedom as not excluding human fulfillment through work, but the (only partly) implicit analysis of unalienated work in the *1844 Manuscripts* (also mentioned above) demonstrates an appreciation of the potentiality of work to be a source of human self-realization, not something which has to be abolished. The argument in *Capital* does say that the "realm of freedom" only begins where necessary labor ends.[43] However, not only might the sphere of freedom (or disposable time) include work freely undertaken, but there is nothing in Marx to suggest why work in the realm of necessity cannot also be fulfilling, i.e., an integral part of autonomous self-constitution. The endless "wrestling with nature" that Marx foresaw, even under communism, need not be interpreted negatively as a limitation on human development — especially when Marx's own description of how this can take place evokes "conditions most worthy and appropriate for their human nature." Just as wrestling between humans may contribute to their mutual development (depending on the context), so may such interaction with nature be organized within human constitution. In the *1844 Manuscripts,* Marx reflected on the content of the alienation of work under capitalism and provided, partly by implication, a sketch of what "unalienated" labor might be like: work as a life-giving objectification of the worker's personality and desires,[44] collective work which builds positive social relations among individuals, the sharing of the results of work as constitutive of social bonds, work as one link between individual and "being" of our species. In his subsequent analysis of the development of labor and working class subjectivity, Marx never returned to such a detailed discussion of how that development might transform the character of "liberated" labor. Nevertheless, as Negri has shown, the *Grundrisse* contains a whole line of (mostly abstract) argument of how such development becomes an increasingly autonomous process of "self-valorization." In fact, as we will see, some elements of this analysis are very close to Mies' own attempts to formulate a feminist theory of labor. Even the well known passage she quotes from *The German Ideology* about how communist society will "make it possible for me to do one thing today and another tomorrow, to hunt in the morning, fish in the afternoon, rear cattle in the evening, criticize after dinner, just as I have a mind," evokes self-realization through several kinds of work. Hunting, fishing and husbandry are all forms of work according to Marx's definition, only "criticism" resembles a "purely leisure activity."

The confusion in the kind of interpretation Mies attacks, of the sort typified in Schmidt and in Gorz, is rooted in an inability to relate the quantitative dimension of workers' struggles against capitalist work, their attempts to reduce their exploitation by working less, to the qualitative transformation of work and of the relations between work and non-work activities. It is not that workers have sought the delusion of a total elimination of work, but rather it has been success in the reduction of working time, which has not only forced increases in productivity, but facilitated qualitative struggles to transform the character of work and the relations between work and non-work. It was the strategy of the refusal of (capitalist) work in the 1960s which forced the qualitative changes that have tended to displace the "mass worker" by the "socialized worker" who has more direct control over work and more possibility to either appropriate it or change it into non-work. At the same time, it is also true that, as Mies points out, the reduction in official working time (weekly hours, age of retirement, etc.) has rarely led to the reduction of unwaged domestic labor.[45] In fact, she might also have argued that historically speaking the achievement of such reduction along with the liberation/exclusion of children and women from long factory hours was what led to the capitalist colonization of "free time," the creation of generalized schooling, home economics and most of the other 20th Century institutions to guarantee the imposition of unwaged labor.

However, in consequence, the struggle for the reduction of work was generalized as unwaged workers also came to refuse work, i.e., to liberate their daily activities from the real subordination to capital. Women have refused the work of procreation and other forms of housework, students have refused to subordinate their learning to job training, peasants have refused to work for the commodity market, or to join the labor market, and so on. The theory of the mass worker evolved into a theory of the *social* factory and it was recognized, in part thanks to feminists like Dalla Costa and Selma James, that more workers in that factory were unwaged and engaged in the work of reproducing labor power than in producing other commodities on Fordist assembly lines.[46] At the same time, those struggles to refuse the work of reproduction clearly involved not merely, or even mainly, less activity (e.g. fewer babies, less schoolwork, less time dealing with crop marketing agencies) but rather changes in the kinds of activities: from work for capital to self-activity of other kinds, both work and non-work (e.g., developing new kinds of gender relations, self-directed studying, experimenting with innovations in traditional techniques). However, it is also true that vast numbers, especially of the unwaged and especially unwaged women, being on the bottom of the capitalist income/power hierarchy, benefited less from the changes we have been analyzing and have been more vulnerable to capitalist counterattack. While not all of those working within the tradition of the Marxist theory of class composition have concentrated their work on the "underside of paradise," enough have to demonstrate that this kind of Marxist theory is not susceptible to the critique Mies directs at Marx and at Gorz.[47] On the contrary, there is a lot of common terrain, I would argue, on the basis of which we can understand each other well enough to work together.

To further explore the degree of commonality and difference, let us look at Mies' alternative, *feminist theory of work* which she elaborates, in part, in direct opposition to her interpretation of Marx. To begin with, it is important to recognize that Mies' "feminist concept of labor" is not primarily intended, as Marx's theory was, to be a critique of work under capitalism (in which we can, with effort, identify tendencies which point toward communism). In her book, and elsewhere, Mies has written a great deal about women's work within capitalism but her "feminist concept of labor" is primarily a theory of the kind of work women should fight for (and what elements of current labor processes are worth preserving) and only derivatively an analysis of what is wrong with current work practices.

Rather than the industrial wage worker whom Marx took as his paradigm, or the housewife who was the focus of Italian Marxist feminist research, Mies takes the *mother* as her model.[48] For the mother, she argues, work is never just a burden but also "a source of enjoyment, self-fulfillment and happiness."[49] Similarly, she argues that for unwaged *peasants*, especially peasant women, "whose production is not yet totally subsumed under commodity production and the compulsions of the market" work has this same dual character of burdensome toil and occasion for enjoyment and creative social interaction. Drawing on her experience in Germany and India, she evokes scenes of singing and dancing during periods of intense collective labor. What makes these work processes different from alienated factory labor, she argues, is that they are "all connected with the direct production of life or of use values." Therefore, she concludes, "*a feminist concept of labour has to be oriented towards the production of life* as the goal of work and not the production of things and wealth" (my emphasis).

As should be clear from the earlier discussion of alternative readings of Marx, this proposition contradicts neither Marx's analysis in the *1844 Manuscripts* of how self-determined work can be life-creating, even within necessary labor, nor the theory of self-valorization which Negri has discovered in the *Grundrisse*. On the contrary, this kind of Marxist theory provides precisely a conceptual framework to make the distinctions Mies wants: between life-destroying work and life-giving work. In the case of mothers as in the case of peasants (and indeed to some degree in the case of almost everyone within capitalism) daily life is rarely a case of either/or; it is more commonly full of tensions between the kind of alienation associated with capitalist command, and peoples' efforts, both as individuals and collectively, to reappropriate their activities. Mothers, for instance, may — when they have the energy — seek to interact with their children in reciprocally life-giving (self-valorizing) ways but they also, all too frequently, experience the life-destroying pressure of capital on that interaction in the form of school demands that they police their kids' stultifying homework or of husband demands (sometimes violent) for work reproducing his labor power. Peasants live similar contradictions between individual and collective attempts at autonomy (e.g., the kinds of intimate human relationships Mies describes) and the pressures of agribusiness or state repression that drain both their energy and their time. Which brings us to the second aspect of Mies' feminist theory of labor.

A feminist concept of labor, she argues, must have *a different concept of time* — by which she means that time should not be divided (either in the world or in theory) into burdensome work time and pleasurable leisure time. Although she presents the alternative to such a division as the alternation and interspersion of "times of work and times of rest and enjoyment" (which seems to retain the distinction she is arguing against) her previous argument about how work can and should be rewarding suggests a better formulation. Namely, that if various kinds of work along with other sorts of activity are organized so as to be rewarding in themselves then the question of how much time one spends working at this or that can become one of personal and collective choice among an array of alternative kinds of self-valorization requiring varying degrees and kinds of effort. This was clearly the kind of thing Marx had in mind when he wrote the passage in *The German Ideology* about cattle rearing, fishing, hunting and criticism quoted above. If he had known more about peasants he might have mentioned singing, dancing or story-telling as well.[50]

The third and fourth aspects of Mies' feminist theory of labor focus *the importance of work being sensuousness*, of the way it can provide a "direct and sensual interaction with nature, with organic matter and living organisms." Clearly drawing on her exemplar of the mother as worker, and of the subsistence peasant working the land, she attacks the elimination of such interaction between workers and organic nature which has come with the development of the machine and modern automated production methods. This development, which she thinks Marx embraces wholeheartedly, has reached its nadir, according to her, with the appearance of the computer technology which is "destroying all productive human power, all understanding of nature and, in particular, all capacity for sensual enjoyment." Against this she argues that only through labor processes which involve such interaction can we retain a healthy physical capacity for "enjoyment, for sensuality and for erotic and sexual satisfaction." On the basis of this argument she explains, in part, the pathological mystification's involved in men's fascination with the female body and the tendential increase in violence against women. Against arguments that athletic sports and hobbies could provide an antidote for such estrangement and its pathologies, she reasons that they cannot because unlike work they lack the "sense of purpose," a "character of being useful and necessary" and do not produce products which are "useful and necessary."

The parts of this argument which insist on the value of sensuously healthy work and of working having a sense of purpose is completely parallel to Marxist analysis and by no means its contrary. Marx deplored, like others before him, e.g., Adam Smith, the destructive character of work under capitalism: especially the way the division of labor leads to a crippling deskilling of workers and how the imposition of capitalist purpose is one aspect of labor which alienates them from it. The implication of such Marxian analysis, as I have already indicated, is that to the degree that workers are able to take command over their work and their lives more generally, they transform the organization of labor so as to overcome such destructive organization. The uncritical embrace by socialist managers of capitalist work organization (e.g., of Taylorism in the Soviet Union) may have required the studied neglect of Marx's analyses of these matters but it is there and, once again, it is in harmony with Mies' own arguments.

Her arguments about the results of such estrangement of workers from positive forms of sensuousness are interesting and useful contributions to the analysis of the relationship between the divisions of labor and divisions of gender. They complement Jungian theories of individuals' quest for missing gender traits while emphasizing the increasingly important element of violence which accompanies the desperation of such alienation.[51] They are also very consistent with the Marxist tradition of analyzing the nefarious effects of alienated work conditions. Whereas Marx tended to spend more time writing about such physical effects as poisoning and exhaustion, many contemporary Marxist theorists have focused on the analysis of psychological damage. The intersection of Marxian and various strains of psychoanalytic thought has not always been fruitful but it has deepened our awareness of the links between capitalism and psychological phenomena. Within the development of the theory of class composition and that of self-valorization the most important such intersection occurred with the schizoanalytic thought of Gilles Deleuze and Félix Guattari.[52] The result has been lines of analysis highly sensitive to the kind of problem Mies has identified. In discussing the women's movement, Guattari and Negri have acknowledged the importance of the insistence on body politics: "The corporeality of liberation became primary. Insurrection of bodies as an expression of subjectivity, as incarnating the materiality of desires and of needs, as promising in the future the impossibility of separating the collective character of economic development from the singularities of its ends."[53] On the basis of such recognition that accepts and also attempts to theorize exactly the kind of issues Mies sees as being at the heart of her theory of labor, there would seem to be considerable grounds for the exploration of common concerns.

The final theoretical point which Mies considers essential for a feminist theory of labor concerns the reduction or abolition of the division and distance between production and consumption. This, she proposes, is necessary to achieve "the sense of usefulness, necessity and purpose with regard to work and its products." Only understanding the entire material circuit of products from production to consumption can guarantee progress towards creating the kind of work she has described. Not surprisingly, this approach leads her to an embrace of considerable community and regional self-sufficiency.

In this last point and in her focus on mothering and on subsistence agriculture, Mies seems very much a part of the "small is beautiful" movement which tends to valorize small scale, autonomous, traditional agrarian communities and the immediacy of social relations, i.e., the refusal of mediation — especially of the market, of capitalist managers and of the state. These last characteristics have also been prominent in the "workers autonomy" movement out of which the Marxist theory of class composition and constitution have grown. The points of reference for the latter have tended to be urban and large scale rather than rural and small scale but appreciation of autonomy and the refusal of mediation are similar.

Mies' critique of the computer which contrasts with the more positive Marxist assessment of its role in the development of subjectivity would seem to derive in part from this difference in scale as well as from the historical gender specificity of computer use. There is no doubt that women have been more obviously exploited by computers than men and more alienated from them.[54] The scale of their interaction has tended to be limited to woman-machine (e.g., secretarial word processing and data entry) where part of the machine's capability (i.e., the ability to keep track of key-strokes per minute) is being used to impose an increased, indeed crippling, intensity of labor or where women have been put to work assembling computers also in crippling fashion (e.g., soldering connections under a microscope). Whereas men have been more likely to have been involved in the very collective and interactive design of computers or their utilization as tools in research and vehicles of the kind of play and communication mentioned above. It is only recently that some women have begun to reverse their relations to such machines and to incorporate them into their own autonomous struggles. For example, feminist computer networks explicitly for the circulation of experience and political discussion have been proliferating, e.g., Femecon-L, Wmst-L, Gender, Systers. Both kinds of relationships between women and computers must be taken into account. Changes in women's assessments of the appropriability of such technology as well as the ways in which such appropriation occurs are developments which will change the texture of the "socialized worker" and need to be taken into account if the concept is to help us and have meaning.

To sum up, close examination of Mies' "feminist" theory of labor reveals enormous overlap with Marxist theory rather than the dramatic opposition which she asserts to have established. If there is any point where her analysis goes beyond Marxist theory to articulate feminist projects of self-reconstruction, it would seem to be in her desire to reconceptualize the relationship between humans and the rest of nature — for which she seems to feel the woman-nature nexus is key. In this desire, which she shares with a variety of other eco-feminists, there is an attempt to overcome the human/active-subject — nature/passive-object dichotomy which Marx takes over from Hegel and shares with most of the enlightenment.[55] A feminist theory of labor, as she says elsewhere, must "replace the predatory economic relationship of Man to 'nature' by a cooperative [or reciprocal] one."[56] Such attempts to rethink the human-nature relationship are extremely interesting and have been one of the most thought provoking aspects of both feminist and environmental movements. Unfortunately, neither in her book nor in the article just cited is there any substance offered for the meaning of a "cooperative [or reciprocal]" relationship beyond a lack of exploitation. Both terms "cooperative" and "reciprocal" imply the existence of different beings who come together and act together in mutually beneficial ways. But in what sense can we say non-human nature *acts*? In Hegel and Marx humans are thought to be differentiated from other life forms by having a "will." In Chapter 13 of Volume I of *Capital,* Marx analyzes the meaning of "cooperation" in the context of human work but does not extend the concept to the relationship between humans and the rest of nature. Today many persons, including scientists as well as animal rights activists and ecologists, are willing to identify a greater or lesser "will" in other kinds of life. But what does "cooperation" mean in such an interspecial context? How do humans "cooperate" with great apes, with whales, with dogs and cats, with rats and mice? And beyond animals there is the issue of the whole ecosystem of animals, plants, rivers, winds, rocks and oceans. Many ecologists have thought about what "less exploitative" relations between humans and their environment might mean. Perhaps more of this might be brought to bear in our collective efforts to reconceptualize and to change the nature of work.

Moreover, I would argue that we should question the very concept of "work" or "labor" itself and not just the adjectives we attach to it. "Work" is an abstraction from a wide variety of concrete activities — an abstraction that only makes sense in a capitalist world of commodity production. Capitalism, by its very nature, turns all human activity into the "production" of objects as its fundamental mechanism of social control. Part of the processes of self-valorization through which we liberate ourselves from such a world would seem to involve reconcretization of activities we now call work — a new "embedding," to use Polanyi's term, within new contexts of meaning and social relationships. Growing food, for example, instead of being just one more form of capitalist work through which workers and nature are exploited and a commodity is produced, can be one element in a social pattern of non-exploitative human interaction and meaning as well as a collective human interaction with the rest of nature, e.g., part of a (cooperative?) metabolic process regenerating a complex ecosystem within which humans situate themselves as participating moments. Mothering, for example, instead of being the work of producing labor power can be one kind of mutually supportive and reinforcing relationship between the young and the old and between the old themselves — for there is no a priori reason to conceive of "mothering" as limited to the activities of an individual mother.

In her research and activism, Mies has had considerable experience both in India and in Germany. She might add substance to her attempts to redefine work by analysing the new meanings and new social relationships crafted by women in India and Germany as part of their struggles to create better lives. Mies' evocations of their lives suggests the existence of such creativity, but she does not tell us enough to reveal what it has generated that transforms their activities into something richer than the concept of work in Marxist theory.

Despite the limitations of Mies' analysis, however, I think that her work, as well as that of others who have sought ways out of the alienations of capitalist labor, deserve the closest attention from all of us interested in the transcendence of capitalism. Ultimately, it is only amongst such creative efforts that paths forward can be found.

Conclusion

What all of the forgoing suggests, it seems to me, is that the ability to understand emerging possibilities of liberation through attention to the newest forms of "class" recomposition and of collective constitution (beyond class) requires the closest study of the diverse directions different subjectivities may pursue and theoretico-political interaction among them over their different ideas and projects. Only such a politics of alliance can minimize the possibilities for capital to divide and conquer by accentuating antagonisms (e.g., aggravating gender, racist or ethnic divisions). Only such a politics can make it possible for the constitution of Marxist categories to keep up with the developments of our struggles and for us to explore the limits of their ability to grasp the emergence of new ways of social being.[57]

Endnotes

1 This approach, which is far from common among Marxists, is based on an assessment of Marx's own work and has received considerable elaboration. Besides being based on an interpretation of the content of his theory of capitalism as class struggle, we can also point to Marx's own reply to

Mikhailovski in which he denied having produced a general philosophical theory of all of history. See: Letter to the Editor of *Otechestvennye Zapiski* (St. Petersburg), of November 1877, in S.K. Padover, *Letters of Karl Marx*, Englewood Cliffs: Prentice-Hall, 1979, p. 321–322. The contemporary elaboration of an explicitly anti-dialectical Marxist theory of the working class has included the work of Gilles Deleuze, Félix Guattari, Antonio Negri, Jean-Marie Vincent and others around the Parisian journal *Futur Antérieur.* The basic thrust of such theory not only sees capitalist society as a social order of class conflict but grasps the dialectic as the totalization capital seeks to impose on working class antagonism in order to convert it into mere useful contradiction. Within this perspective, that antagonism appears as a force which repeatedly ruptures the dialectic and has the potentiality of exploding it once and for all.

2 One of the earliest and most telling Marxist reproaches to dependency and world-system theory was that its focus on the sphere of circulation neglected the sphere of production, especially the existence of different "modes of production" in the Third World. Such was the argument, for example, that Ernesto Laclau made against the work of Andre Gundar Frank. But as the subsequent evolution of Laclau's work makes clear, the neglect of difference could not be remedied simply by paying attention to it. Once one does pay attention the whole theory — including the theory of the whole — must be reworked. Laclau's inability to figure out how to do this within Marxism led him to post-Marxism. Others, however, have shown how this can be done as I sketch below.

3 For an overview of the development of that theory, some of whose themes began to appear in anarcho-communism and council communism, which began to take on its modern form in the U.S. and France in the 1940s and was elaborated and polished in Italy in the 1960s, see the introduction to my book *Reading Capital Politically*. From insights of C.L.R. James, Raya Dunayevskaya and the editors of *Socialisme ou Barbarie* into the need to grasp not only the autonomy of the working class but also the concrete particularities of specific sectors of that class through the work of Raniero Panzieri, Romano Alquati, Mario Tronti, and Mariarosa Dalla Costa in systematizing the analysis in Marxian theory and practice to more recent American and French elaborations by the editors and friends of the journals *Zerowork*, *Midnight Notes* and *Futur Antérieur*, the theory of class composition has received both intensive development and extensive application.

4 For more detail on methodological aspects of this "inversion" see H. Cleaver, "The Inversion of Class Perspective in Marxist Theory, from Valorization to Self-Valorization," in W. Bonefeld, R. Gunn and K. Psychopedis (eds.)

Open Marxism, Vol II, London: Pluto Press, 1992. There appear to be some parallels between the theory of class composition and what Michael Lebowitz has in mind when he calls, in his book *Beyond Capital*, for the development of a "political economy of wage labor" to complement Marx's analysis of capital.

5 The development of the theory of the "mass worker" has recently been traced and analysed by Sergio Bologna. See his "Theory and History of the Mass Worker" in *Common Sense*, no. 11 and no. 12.

6 Key moments in the adaptation of Marxist theory to the ever more inclusive character of the working class were Mario Tronti's theorization of capitalist reproduction as social factory and Mariarosa Dalla Costa's work on the role of housework within capitalism. See: Mario Tronti, *Operai e Capitale*, Torino: Einaudi, 1964 (a central chapter of which is available as "Social Capital" in *Telos*, no. 17) and Mariarosa Dalla Costa and Selma James "Women and the Subversion of the Community" 1972. Subsequent work on the capitalist character of the work of peasants and urban "marginals" has been done by Selma James, myself, Ann Lucas de Roufignac, Gustavo Esteva and others.

7 The crisis is thus located in the insurgency of the working class which occurred as it transformed itself into something no longer compatible with the Fordist organization of accumulation and the Keynesian role of state management.

8 The term "sectors" is used loosely here to designate various subdivisions of the working class which have mobilized themselves autonomously vis-‡-vis the rest of the class, e.g., women, blacks, students, black students, black women, and so on.

9 Although earlier European centered analyses of this process appeared in Italy in the late 1960s and early 1970s (scattered pieces of which appeared in translation in the journals *Radical America* and *Telos*), the first detailed American elaboration of this analysis appeared in the first issue of the journal *Zerowork* in December 1975. The bulk of that first issue has been reissued as part of *Midnight Oil: Work, Energy, War, 1973–1992* (Brooklyn: Autonomedia, 1992) by the Midnight Notes Collective. Watered down versions of this analysis, stripped of revolutionary politics, have appeared in the form of French theories of "regulation" and of American theories of "social structures of accumulation" — theories which have, as their titles imply, shifted the focus of analysis from working class power to the requirements of capitalist command.

10 The flagrant state manipulation of the news media during the Gulf War to prevent the barbarous reality of the war from becoming apparent to the

world — which has produced an outpouring of critical articles in the U.S. — provided an important public lesson on the day to day limitation and distortion of communication which prevents particular groups of people from recognizing the commonality of their situation with others.

11 This fueling has been propagated from the highest political levels, e.g., in the case of racism, from the thinly veiled racism of a George Bush or Giscard d'Estaing to the more overt racism of David Duke, Jean-Marie Le Pen, Jörg Haider or Neo-Nazis in Germany.

12 In the U.S. this historical research has mainly been carried out by the contributers to, and those influenced by, the two journals *Zerowork* (in the 1970s) and *Midnight Notes* (in the 1980s and 1990s).

13 H. Cleaver, "Reaganism et rapports de classe aux Ètats-Unis," in M-B Tahon and A. Corten, *L'Italie: le philosophe et le gendarme*, Montréal: VLB, 1986.

14 Gilles Deleuze and Félix Guattari, *L'anti-Oedipe*, Paris: Editions de Minuit, 1972 and *Milles Plateaux*, Paris: Editions de Minuit, 1980.

15 On the reformulation of the transition from capitalism to communism and on the limits of the concept of socialism, see "Lesson 8" in Antonio Negri, *Marx Beyond Marx*, Brooklyn: Autonomedia, 1991 and Harry Cleaver, "Socialism" in Wolfgang Sachs (ed), *The Development Dictionary: A Guide to Knowledge as Power*, London: Zed Books, 1992.

16 This tendency of regulation theory to adopt the perspective of capitalist control rather than the perspective of the working class subject has been emphasized by Yann Moulier, "Les Theories Américaines de la ´segmentation du marché du travail' et italiennes de la 'composition de classe' à travers le priseme des lectures françaises," *Babylone* no. 0, 1981–1982; W. Bonefeld, "Reformulation of State Theory," *Capital & Class* 33, 1987; J. Holloway, "The Great Bear, Post-Fordism and Class Struggle," *Capital & Class* 36, 1988 (reprinted in Bonefeld & Holloway (eds.), *Post-Fordism & Social Form*, London: Macmillan, 1991); and G. Cocco and C. Vercellone, "Les Paradigmes Sociaux du Post-Fordisme," *Future Antérieur* no. 4, 1990. Given the evidence of early regulation theorist familiarity with the theory of class composition, this choice has been quite conscious and symptomatic of its very different political orientation. See the discussion of "l'opéraïsme" in A. Lipietz, *Crise et Inflation, Pourquoi?* Paris: Maspero, 1979.

17 Sergio Bologna, "La tribù delle talpe," *Primo Maggio* no. 8, 1977. In English as "The Tribe of Moles" in Red Notes & the CSE, *Working Class Autonomy and the Crisis*, 1979. The term "temporary autonomous zone" is taken not from Bologna but from Hakim Bey's book *T.A.Z.: The Temporary Autonomous Zone, Ontological Anarchy, Poetic Terrorism*, Brooklyn: Autonomedia 1991.

18 The term "socialized worker" (*operaio sociale*) was coined by Romano Alquati and adopted by Toni Negri in the late 1970s. See R. Alquati, N. Negri and A. Sormano *Università di ceto medio e proletariato intellectuale,* Turin: Stampatori (1976) and A. Negri *Dall'Operaio Massa All'Operaio Sociale* (1979) and his "Archeologia e proggetto: L'operaio massa e l'operaio sociale" in *Macchina Tempo* (1982). This last is also available in English as "Archaeology and Project: The Mass Worker and the Social Worker," in *Revolution Retrieved: Selected Writings of Toni Negri,* London: Red Notes, 1988.

19 See: B. Coriat, *L'Atelier et le robot,* Paris: Christian Bourgois, 1990; and M. Lazzarato, "Les caprices du flux, les mutations technologiques du point de vue de ceux qui les vivent," *Future Antérieur,* no. 4, 1990.

20 This analysis has been partly based on a study of working class self-activity in the Italian and French garment industry carried out by Negri, Maurizio Lazzarato and Giancarlo Santilli, *Beneton et Sentier: L'Entreprise Politique et la Nouvelle Cooperation Productive Sur L'Espace Europeen,* 1990.

21 M. Lazzarato and A. Negri, "Travail immatériel et subjectivité," *Future Antérieur,* no. 6, 1991, p. 92. Also see the earlier essay by A. Negri in *The Politics of Subversion,* op.cit., "Paris 1986, 26 November–10 December."

22 Obvious at least since the 1960s when the student movement provoked Marxists to begin to analyze schooling in terms of the production of labor power. (Just as the women's movement gave rise to a parallel analysis of housework.)

23 In the U.S. this tendency — involving a dramatic expansion of "professional" training (e.g. engineering, sciences and business administration at the university level, lower level technical training within junior colleges and trade schools) at the expense of traditional "liberal arts" — has been widely recognized and lamented by humanist defenders of the latter fields. Yet the same expansion of "professional" training has also occurred within the liberal arts (especially in the social sciences) and constitutes a response to successful student struggles to expand the spaces and opportunities for critical analysis and self-valorization and to the crisis more generally. See below.

24 Especially the use of faxes and control of media reporting of the university occupations. M. Lazzarato, "La 'Panthère' et la communication," *Future Antérieur,* no. 2, 1990.

25 Committee for Academic Freedom in Africa, "The World Bank and Education in Africa," *Newsletter* no. 2, 1991.

26 Other state interventions have occurred through juridical and police intervention in defense of "intellectual property rights" (i.e., the control over the reproduction of software) against the pervasive "pirating" and sharing of

programs. The communist character of such free redistribution of innovation is apparant and has taken legal form in the proliferation of "shareware" and "freeware" widely available for downloading from computer networks.

27 Such integration was already recognized in the analysis of the "mass worker" and the "social factory."

28 See the work of Cleaver, de Roufignac and Esteva mentioned above. Wolfgang Sachs, (ed.), *The Development Dictionary*, op. cit., brings together a variety of authors whose work focuses on the conflicts between various paths to self-valorization (although most of the authors would not use this term) and capitalist development.

29 This suggestion should even appeal to those die-hard dialectical or historical materialists who believe that it is impossible to escape the dialectic. The only problem, of course, is the likelihood that no matter what they find, they will impute to it a "dialectical" logic that will blind them to the existence of other kinds of relationships.

30 I say "more or less consistent" because it is clear, from the history of the workers' movement, that a whole range of concepts may be generated standing in quite different relationships to the dynamics of that movement. Not only have the meanings of "socialism" and "communism" varied widely, but so have those of all the other oppositional concepts thrown up by the struggles.

31 F. Guattari and A. Negri, *Communists Like Us*, Brooklyn: Autonomedia, 1990, p. 107.

32 Ibid., p. 120.

33 Ibid., p. 108.

34 This formulation obviously derives from the intellectual/political project of this paper. Clearly, the politics of autonomy mandates the study of other struggles and the investigation of the possibilities of complementary action regardless of whether those struggles have thrown up interesting new ideas or are based on old familiar ones.

35 Maria Mies, *Patriarchy and Accumulation on a World Scale*, London: Zed Books, 1986.

36 Ibid., all of these themes are discussed in the first chapter of the book. Her conception of autonomy is as thoroughgoing as that of any autonomist Marxist. With respect to the need for autonomy *within* the feminist movement, she writes: "As there is no centre, no hierarchy, no official and unified ideology, no formal leadership, the autonomy of the various initiatives, groups, collectives is the only principle that can maintain the dynamism, the diversity, as well as the truly humanist perspective, of the movement." p. 41.

37 Mariarosa Dalla Costa and Selma James, *Potere femminile e sovversione sociale,* (*The Power of Women and the Subversion of the Community*), Padova: Marsilio, 1972. First published in English in *Radical America,* Jan.–Feb. 1972 then by Falling Wall Press in England.

38 Ibid., p. 33.

39 Without going into detail, it should be said that her views on the fundamental similarities of 20th-century socialism and capitalism are shared by autonomist Marxists.

40 Ibid., p. 212.

41 Mies quotes approvingly from Schmidt's book *The Concept of Nature in Marx,* London: New Left Books, 1973.

42 She is referring to Gorz's 1983 book *Les chemins du paradis* — a book which draws, mostly in an unacknowledged fashion, on autonomist Marxist thought but twists it around to Gorz's own purposes. See also Cocco and Vercellone, "Les Paradigmes Sociaux du Post-Fordisme," op. cit., pp. 90-91.

43 *Capital,* Vol. III, Chapter 48 on the trinity formula. See below for a feminist critique of this division and a response.

44 Because it is important in the discussion of feminist theory below, let us note that Marx's view of the "life-giving" character of human labor by no means disappeared in his later writings which focused more on evolving forms of capitalist exploitation. His oft repeated use of the vampire metaphor to characterize capital's relation to living labor is dramatic evidence of his view of that labor as a kind of "social life blood." This view was rooted in the very anthropocentric view which he shared with Hegel of what made humans different from the rest of nature: their imagination and will which allowed them to create/give-birth to newness in the world.

45 Mies, *Patriarchy and Accumulation on a World Scale,* op. cit., p. 217.

46 This evolution occurred in Italy in tandem with the development of the struggles. Tronti's early, but fairly bare bones, recognition of the social character of the factory was only given flesh when the explosion of autonomous women's and student struggles focused theory on the real life content of the "reproduction of labor power." Compare Tronti's "La fabbrica e la societ‡, *Quaderni Rossi* no. 2, 1962 and "Il piano del Capitale," *Quaderni Rossi,* no. 3, 1963 with Dalla Costa's and James' "Power of Women" cited earlier.

47 In the first place, I should say that I include Dalla Costa and James within the Marxist tradition of the analysis of "class composition" — Dalla Costa's own thinking developed within the space of *autonomia* (or workers' autonomy) in Italy and James' work was rooted in earlier related activities of the

American Johnson-Forest Tendency and its offshoots. In the second place, much of the research some of us have done on various sectors of the unwaged has built directly on their work, especially work on peasants and students.

48 This is an interesting choice given the history of feminist rejections of the mother as the appropriate paradigm for thinking about women and of women's struggles to have the right to refuse to be mothers!

49 The section of Mies' book from which this and the material which follows is drawn, is that on "Towards a feminist concept of labor" in the last chapter, pp. 216-219.

50 What this description evokes is the inversion of the tendency of capitalism to convert all activities including those that take place during "leisure" into alientaed work. Here we imagine unalienated work as a moment of an unaliened life.

51 The parallels are striking between Mies' argument and that of the Jungian analyst Robert Johnson in his recent book *Ecstasy*, dealing with the absense of joy (Dionysios) and the destructiv additions it produces.

52 Deleuze and Guattari, *Anti-Oedipe* (1972) and *Milles Plateaux* (1980) op. cit.

53 Guattari and Negri, op.cit., p. 44.

54 In the workshop on computer networks in the circulation of struggles, held as part of the "International Meeting" of some 2,000 grassroots activists in Venice in June 1991, the vast majority of partipants were men. They noted the absense of women but had little of use to say about it.

55 This orientation of Marx's seems to have been constant in his work, from the early *1844 Manuscripts* to the later volumes of *Capital* — compare his dicussion in "Estranged Labor" where the human works on passive nature to give it life by incorporating it into the human world and that in chapter 7 of Volume I on the "labor process" where the three elements are human labor, tools and raw materials, with the latter treated as inert and passive.

56 See her interview with Ariel Sallah, "Patriarchy & Progress: A Critique of Technological Domination," *The Fifth Estate*, Vol. 26, No. 3, Issue 338, 1992, pp. 8-9, 17.

57 [Editor's Footnote] Since Cleaver's article first appeared in *Common Sense* no. 14, significant publications have appeared on the topic of his article: Hardt, M. and A. Negri (2000) *Empire*; D. Dyer-Withford (1999) *Cyper-Marx*, see also Negri's and Dalla Costa's contributions to this volume. Cleaver refers extensively to the French journal *Futur Anterieur*. This journal is now defunct and its concerns have been taken up by *Multitudes* in France and *Posse* in Italy. Further work by Cleaver on cyber space can be found in Holloway, J. and E. Pelaez (eds) (1998) *Zapatista* and in his on-line papers on this topic

on his web-site <http://www.eco.utexas.edu/facstaff/Cleaver/index2.html>. See also his "Subersion of Money-as-Command in the Current Crisis" and Marrazi's "Money in the World Crisis" [both published in Bonefeld, W. and J. Holloway, (eds.), (1995) *Global Capital, National State and the Politics of Money*] for autonomist Marxist assessments of global money and class de- and re-composition.

4

Human Practice and Perversion: Beyond Autonomy and Structure

Werner Bonefeld

Introduction

Marxists agree amongst themselves that class struggle is the motor of history. However, there are sharp divisions as to the "status" of class struggle vis-à-vis capital. For example, class struggle can be seen, as in structuralist approaches associated with Althusser, Poulantzas as well as Hirsch and Jessop, as a struggle which unfolds within the framework of the capitalist structures. Or, as in autonomist approaches associated with Negri, Tronti and others, class struggle can be conceived of as an ongoing struggle by capital to decompose labour's revolutionary existence. These distinct conceptions of class struggle are founded on the differentiation between, on the one hand, the objective character of "capital," and, on the other, the subjective character of class struggle. This paper assesses structuralist and autonomist approaches to class struggle. The assessment is founded upon an understanding of the *internal* relationship between structure and struggle. I shall discuss this internal relation by emphasising "labour" as a constitutive power. This emphasis is developed in terms of a dialectical relationship between integration and transcendence. These two terms connote the revolutionary power of labour (transcendence) and its mode of existence within the perverted form of capital (integration).

The Problem

Structuralist approaches accept the economics-politics separation inscribed in bourgeois society (see Poulantzas, 1973; Jessop, 1985; and Hirsch, 1978) and propose an analysis of each of these fragmented spheres as distinct regions of social existence. Subsequent historical concrete analysis has to introduce, as exemplified by the post-fordist debate, the historically specific combination between different regions so as to show the modalities of their interaction.[1] By taking for granted the fragmented character of bourgeois society, these theories neglect questions of the social constitution of the fragmented character of society and strain to integrate class struggle into their analysis. As Aglietta (1979, p. 67) sees it, class struggle is beyond "any law." "Capital" is not conceived as a social relation in and through labour. Instead, "capital" is seen as an entity which has its own logic, a logic which stands above class relations. Thus "capital" is not class struggle because "capital is the subject" (Jessop, 1991, p. 150). Class struggle is expelled from the analysis insofar as a proper understanding of the concrete, empirical, conditions of class struggle needs to be based on a specification of the capitalist framework within which class struggle obtains and unfolds. Consequently, structuralism emphasises the objective lines of capitalist development. Structures are the only subject recognised by structuralism. Class struggle is treated as a derivative of structural development. The dynamic of capitalist development is located in capital itself. Contradiction is seen as internal to capital, and capitalist development is a result of these contradictions.

Unlike the theoretical suppression of class struggle in structuralist approaches, autonomist approaches place at their centre the self-activity of the working class. Class struggle is seen as primary. The emphasis is on labour's revolutionary power. Autonomist approaches take as their starting point the Marxian notion that all social relations are essentially practical. In that emphasis lies an important difference from structure-centred approaches. The difficulty inherent in "autonomist" approaches is not that "labour" is seen as being primary but that this notion is not developed to its radical solution.

Approaches predicated on the notion of labour's self-activity tend to divide social existence into distinct spheres of, on the one hand, a machine-like logic of capital and the transcendental power of social practice, on the other. The emphasis on "labour's self-activity" is founded on the "inversion" of the class perspective.[2] This inversion was advocated by Tronti who argued that rather than focusing on capitalist development, the emphasis should be on the struggle of the working class. As Tronti (1965/1979, p. 10) put it, capital uses exploitation as a means of escaping "its de facto subordination to the class of worker-producers." Such a formulation contradicts the insight that labour is a constitutive power. This is because capital is conceived as a subject in its own right: "capital" is construed as something which not only reacts to the self-activity of labour but which also "lives" by cajoling labour's self-activity into serving the capitalist cause. In other words, the inversion of the class perspective is dependent upon two "subjects": there is the self-activity of labour and capital's cajoling power. The emphasis on "inversion" does not raise the issue that "labour" is the producer of perverted forms. Instead, labour tends to be seen as a power which exists external to its own perverted social world: the constitutive power of labour stands external to its own perversion. This perversion is called "capital." Labour is seen as a self-determining power at the same time as which capital is a perverted power by virtue of its "cajoling capacity." Thus Negri's (1992) emphasis on capital as a "bewitching power." The emphasis on the struggle component of the relation between structure and struggle cannot overcome their theoretical separation. The question why does human practice exist in the perverted form of capitalist domination is not raised. Minus an interrogation of question of form, i.e. the specification of the social form in and through which the constitutive power of labour subsists in a contradictory way, notions of labour's autonomy from capital can amount only to a romantic invocation of the revolutionary subject's immediacy (see Bonefeld/Gunn, 1991). Merely invoking labour's revolutionary immediacy tends to externalise structure from subject, so leading to a subjectivist conception which is the other side of structuralism's coin. Unlike structuralist approaches, the emphasis is on class struggle, a struggle which remains, however, external to its object. Capital remains construed in terms of a logic which lies solely within itself and whose inconsistencies, alone, and in abstraction from the contradictions which are constitutive of the capital-labour relation, provide points of purchase for revolutionary autonomisation. The capital-labour relation is understood merely in terms of a repressive systemic logic counterposed to subjective forces in a dualist and external way.

Structuralist and autonomist approaches understand the contradictory constitution of capitalism in terms of two externally related things: in structuralism the contradiction obtains in the form of structural inadequacies and/or dysfunctionalities as between different regions such as the "economic" and "political"; in autonomism the contradiction obtains between the autonomy of the revolutionary subject and the capitalist system. Neither autonomism nor structuralism see the contradictory character of capital in and through the constitutive power of labour, a constitutive power which exists in and against and beyond capital. Both the theoretical suppression of labour, as in structuralist approaches, and the theoretical subjectification of labour, as in autonomist approaches, fail to reconcile objectivity with subjectivity and vice versa.

Labour and Capital

Contrary to structuralist approaches and to those invoking the immediacy of the revolutionary subject, the task is to trace out "the inner connexion" (Marx 1983, p. 28) between social phenomena, so as to establish the "inner nature" (cf. Marx) of their relation. To trace out the inner connection between social phenomena is to theorise the human content which constitutes their social reality as interconnected, as complex forms different from, but united in, each other. In order to theorise this interconnection, the theoretical approach has to specify the constitutive power that makes social phenomena different from each other in unity. Different phenomena exist in and through each other; each phenomenon is the presupposition of the other. This means that one cannot differentiate between an abstract construction of, for example, an economic logic and a political logic, and an existence of these "logics" (cf. Jessop, 1985) in a real world, a world merely mediated by class struggle. Nor can one divide the social whole into capital logic and subjective power. Structure and struggle involve each other as moments of one process. Diverse phenomena, such as structure and struggle, do not exist as externally related entities one of which is determining and/or dominating the other, but as forms of existence of the relation which constitutes them. The notion of social objectivity can be comprehended, as argued by Backhaus (1969), only when objectivity is seen as an existing abstraction — an abstraction which exists in practice (*daseiende Abstraktion*). Social relations are practical relations. The notion that social relations are founded in and through practice implies a quite different starting point from that taken by those who advocate notions of a fragmented social world. The starting point is the social constitution of the historical movement of labour. The historical development of labour holds the key to the history of society. This key is contained in the abstraction; the human content which, in capitalist society, exists in a mode of being denied.

In every society human beings play the role of producers. However, in capitalist society, the simplest category, i.e. labour, takes on a mystifying character because the material elements of wealth transform from products of labour into properties of commodities and still more pronouncedly they transform the production relation itself into a relation between things. The productive power of social labour exists in the "perverted" form of value. The "objective," or factual, existence of "capital" can thus not be taken as a conceptual starting point. This is because that which asserts itself to the economic mind as "objectivity," or "objective logic," or "objective being" is, in Marx, understood as alienated subjectivity (as specified in Backhaus, 1992). Labour is an alienated subject by virtue of its social existence as a producer of a perverted world. This means that the practical-critical activity of labour exists *against itself as itself* in the form of the fetishised world of capitalism. "The constitution of the world occurs behind the backs of the individuals; yet it is their work" (Marcuse, 1937/1988, p. 151). In other words, the reality in which humans move day in and day out has no invariant character, that is, something which exists independently from them. It is the social practice of labour which constitutes, suffuses and contradicts the perverted world of capitalism. Labour does not exist "external" to perverted forms. Rather, "perverted form," including capital's "cajoling power," exist in and through labour's social practice. Thus "subject and object do not statically oppose each other, but rather are caught up in an "ongoing process" of the "inversion of subjectivity into objectivity, and vice versa" (Backhaus, 1992, p. 60). Understanding the constitution of perverted forms in this way makes it possible to see the generic as inherent in the specific, and the abstract as inherent in the concrete (see Marx, 1973, Intro.). This view involves a way of thinking which moves within the object (i.e. the social-historical form of human relations) of its thinking. Dialectics does not proceed to its object from outside but from inside. Dialectical thinking attempts to appropriate conceptually the contradictory mode of existence constituted by, and constitutive of, social practice. Dialectical thinking conceptualises itself within, and as a moment of, its object (Gunn, 1989, 1992). Such a conceptualisation of social existence seeks an understanding of the apparently isolated facts of life as comprising a mode of existence of social relations. Dialectics emphasises the unity-in-difference as between structure and struggle. It does so on the basis of the understanding that "all social relations are essentially practical" and that these social relations comprise the constitutive practical-critical activity of labour.

Any conceptualisation of "capital" which focuses on its seemingly formal logic (as in structuralism) disregards the distinctiveness of Marx's theory and espouses, instead, the reified world of capitalism as the object and purpose of theory. Further, any conceptualisation which focuses merely on labour's autonomy from capital disregards the historically specific form of labour's existence and espouses, instead, an ontological constitution of being, a constitution that can be found — apparently — in the subjectivity of being which has escaped the grasp, and which threatens a revolutionary disposal of "capital." It is the contradictory unity of the relation between human practice as commodified work in and through class which constitutes society in terms of a continuous displacement and reconstitution of the "enchanted and perverted world" of capitalism (Marx, 1966, p. 830). The constitution of social practice as capitalist reproduction presents the concrete substance of class antagonism. The removal of "capital" into the museum of history can go forward only through the revolutionising of labour's existence as the alienated subject which produces capital.

The social relation which constitutes the mode of existence/movement of labour in capitalist society is the relation between necessary labour and surplus labour, that is, the class antagonism of capital and labour which constitutes the social working day. The capitalist mode of existence of labour is characterised by the continuous compulsion to revolutionise the relation between necessary and surplus labour in order to increase the latter. However, surplus labour exists only in antithesis to necessary labour. "Capital" exists only through living labour as substance of value, and hence surplus value. The antagonistic tendency of the social form of labour compels capital towards the elimination of necessary labour which undermines the existence of capital as existing only in and through labour. "Capital" can not autonomise itself from living labour; the only autonomisation possible is on labour's side. Labour is not external to "capital." Labour exists in and against capital, while capital, however, exists only in and through labour. The contradictory existence of labour is manifest in its antithesis to capital's command and in its existence as a producer of capital: labour is value creating. In other words, labour exists against itself as a labouring commodity. The social practice of labour exists against capital and, also, as a moment of the latter's existence. The constitutive power of labour's social practice attains a contradictory existence as the movement of transcendence and integration. This movement is founded upon the asymmetrical constitution of class antagonism. Transcendence and integration do not exist separately, but as the movement of one process — extreme poles of a dialectical continuum that social practice represents. As extreme poles of a dialectical continuum, transcendence and integration constitute a contradictory process that is open to the process of struggle itself. Understanding class antagonism as a movement of contradiction between dependence and separation and conceptualising social phenomena as the mode of existence and mode of motion of class antagonism, it follows that labour is neither internal nor external to capital. Labour exists in and against capital.

In and Against

The term *in and against* seeks to overcome the danger of subjectivism inherent in approaches which stress the primacy of labour's self-activity. Contemporary elaboration of such approaches can be found in the development of thought which invokes the revolutionary subject's *immediacy*. The subjectivism is contained in the understanding of labour as a self-constitutive power. "Capital" is no longer seen as a mode of existence of labour. Rather, it is seen as an entity which is confronted by its own substance. This dualism between capital and labour is founded on the notion that value is being "deconstructed" through labour's refusal to participate in capital's own project (see Negri, 1992). The notion of "alienated subjectivity" is thus destroyed and replaced by the notion of labour as a self-constituting revolutionary subject. Capital becomes merely a "hypnotising, bewitching force" and as such a counterrevolutionary "phantasm, an idol: around it revolve the radically autonomous processes of auto-valorization and only political power can succeed in forcing them, with the carrot and with the stick, to begin to be moulded into capital form" (ibid., p. 89). "Auto-valorization," for Negri, means the concrete existence of the subjective power.[3] This power creates and safeguards the space for the values which belong to the exploited classes. In sum, auto-valorization is the production and reproduction of labour as the subject (see Negri, 1989). This approach presupposes that there are spaces in society which are external to the class relations and in which experiments in "authentic subjectivity" challenge and provoke capital's disenchanted world. This approach neglects the forms in and through which labour exists in capitalism. The essentialisation of the subject remains abstract insofar as its social existence obtains outside society. This is because the notion of "labour's autonomy" presupposes the existence of a space already liberated from capital. There is thus a dualism as between two presuppositions which stand external to each other at the same time as each of these presupposition is supposed to render its contrasting term coherent. The two presuppositions are: the presupposed freedom of the social subject and the presupposed logic of the capitalist system. No answer can be provided as to the constitution of both labour's self-activity and capital's cajoling power. The only answer possible is the denunciation of capital as subordinating labour's autonomy and a study of the changing composition of labour's revolutionary subjectivity which is seen as being in opposition to a presupposed logic of capital.

In sum, the internal relation between capital and labour is transformed into a relation of mere opposition, thus reducing the internal relation between form and materiality to a simple juxtaposition of opposition. Thereby, labour is taken as a one-sided abstraction. At the same time, the essentialisation of the subject goes hand-in-hand with the fetishisation of capital as a "bewitching power." Contrary to seeing the relation between capital and labour as a social relation *qua* contradiction in and through the forms constituted by this relation itself, the insistence on labour as merely "against" capital dismisses dialectics as a concept that moves within, and is a moment of, its object. As was reported above, the understanding of labour as existing *against* capital involves a conceptualisation of capital as a machine-like entity. Capital becomes a logic, defined by certain laws whose irrationality provides oppositional space for insurrection. The relationship between structure and struggle is merely conceived of as a relation of cause and effect: i.e. the disruptive and revolutionary power of the working class causes disruption and crisis to which, in turn, capital responds by reimposing its domination over labour (see Negri, 1979). Such a view undercuts the internal relation between structure and struggle and replaces it by a sociological investigation into insurrectionary forms of being which exploit the inconsistencies of the capitalist system. The notion of the presence of labour in and against capital effectively says that labour does not exist outside capital. The class struggle exists only in and against the forms in and through which the constitutive power of labour exists *qua* contradiction. Of course in a sense the class struggle exists in the form of revolutionary separation, but it so exists only as one extreme pole of the dialectical continuum of transcendence and integration, the development of which is open to the class struggle itself. Autonomist approaches disentangle the internal relation between transcendence and integration by construing social practice solely in terms of transcendence.

On the other hand, approaches which stress that labour exists merely "in" capital dismiss the antagonistic character of capitalism, neglecting the contradictory relation between transcendence and integration. Instead, capital is conceived of as a one-sided abstraction at the same time as social practice is sacrificed on the altar of scientism. These approaches are structuralist-functionalist because what for them really counts are the inescapable lines of tendency and direction established by capital's projects. Labour no longer exists in opposition to capital but is, rather, a part of capital's own project. Structuralist approaches contend that the reproduction of capital is not simply given by the logic of capital. Capitalist reproduction goes forward through class struggle. Structurally predetermined views of social development entail a conception of the subject as merely (but at least) the bearer — *Träger* — of social categories. The subject who bears categories must, at the same time, be the subject who transforms them. But on a structuralist approach, he or she can transform them only by reproducing them. The contradictory logic of capital requires "human agency."

The conception of human practice in terms of "human agency" is based on the notion that the abstract nature of capitalist laws stands above class relations. Class struggle transforms thus from a struggle for human emancipation into a sociological category of capitalist reproduction. Capital is seen as an autonomous subject and labour exists solely within capital. Class struggle becomes subordinate to the internal logic of different social structures such as the political and economic, leading on to a conception of class only via voluntarism. Structuralism asserts the subjective in the form of a voluntarist conception of class, i.e. a conception of class as a structure-reproducing agency. For example, in Jessop's approach, class conflict "does not as such create the totality nor does it give rise to [capitalism's] dynamic trajectory" (Jessop, 1991, p. 154). This is because the "conceptual identity of classes is given by the capital relation itself rather than being constrained by classes which shape the capital relation" (ibid.). In other words, Jessop conceives of "capital" as a self-relation whose internal logic structures the class struggle in the "real" world. In other words, class struggle is firmly located within the framework established by the internal logic of capital.[4] Hence, "capital" is seen as some-thing which determines social relations and the class struggle is treated as a derivative of this "thing." The importance of class struggle lies in the circumstance that the institutional logic and dynamic of capitalism needs to be overdetermined by an "economic class struggle in which the balance of class forces is moulded by many factors beyond the value form itself" (Jessop, 1983, p. 90). In other words, the value form defines the coherence of the capitalist mode of production, a coherence which is achieved, in practice, through the contingent forces of conflict in the "real" world. Structuralism and voluntarism are complementary (see Bonefeld, 1993). Structuralism depends on a distinction between structure and struggle — each of which, however, is supposed to render its contrasting term coherent. Structure is seen as escaping determinism because it is qualified by agency and agency is seen as escaping voluntarism because it is qualified by "structural constraints." However, the intelligibility of structure is seen as deriving from agency and vice versa. The dualism between structure and struggle is thus sustained only through a tautological movement of thought. Adding together, eclectically, two fallacious positions hardly amounts to a theoretisation wherein either one of them can be redeemed.

In sum, the problem of autonomism and/or structuralism arises from a conceptualisation that sees labour as existing either merely *against* capital (autonomism) or merely *in* capital (structuralism). Structuralist and autonomist approaches are complementary because both depend on the notion of "capital" as a logical entity. While structuralist approaches emphasise capital as an autonomous subject, autonomist approaches emphasise capital as a machine-like thing. Both approaches depend on a determinist view of capital inasmuch as capital is perceived fetishistically as an extra-human thing.

The notion of labour as existing in and against capital does not provide simply a middle way out of the problem as, for example, implied by the notion of "objective laws but also class struggle." This notion, which is central to the post-fordist debate, construes capital as a one-sided abstraction whose development causes societal effects in terms of social conflict. This view sees the concrete as providing "empirical indicators" of underlying (i.e. general) tendencies. In this view, the concrete is seen as an expression of more fundamental laws whose existence is logically presupposed. In other words, a distinction is made between the supposedly inner logic of capital and the historical analysis of capitalism. Human practice stands external to the fundamental laws of capital. Unity between structure and struggle is realised not on the fundamental level of the formation of abstract concepts but on the contingent level of historical development within the framework of objective laws. In contrast to such an understanding, the notion of labour as existing in and against capital stresses the internal relation between materiality and social form. The presence of labour in and against capital is understood as labour's constitutive power that exists in a mode of being denied in the capitalist form of social reproduction. The notion "mode of being denied" stresses the social constitution of what asserts itself over social relations as mere thinghood; a contradictory unity through the presence of labour which is also a presence in and against capital. The notion of labour as existing in and against capital makes it possible to understand the contradictory mode of existence of social phenomena and to conceive the movement of this contradiction as one of the transformative power of human practice. In other words, the notion "in and against" does not entail an externality between two complementary perspectives: in "and" against. Rather, it emphasises the circumstance that objectivity and subjectivity engage with each other in an internal, nonetheless contradictory, way. I offered the notion of "alienated subjectivity" to emphasise this point. This notion means that, in capitalism, human relations exist, contradictorily, in the form of relations between things. The critique of political economy amounts to a critique of "economic categories" *ad hominem*. In other words, the critique of fetishism does not entail a division of a social world into appearance (fetishistic forms) and essence (human content). Rather, human relations subsist in and through these forms. They do so in a contradictory way. I offered the notion of an asymmetrical constitution of the capitalist class antagonism to emphasise this point.

Conclusion

Structuralism finishes up by invoking precisely the romanticised subject celebrated in approaches which counterpose the virtues of subjectivity to the alleged fetishism of structures. Equally, approaches predicated on the notion of "labour's autonomy" finish up by invoking precisely the untheorised object celebrated by structuralist approaches which counterpose the virtue of structure to the alleged existence of class struggle outside any law. Whereas the structuralist version of the subject entails the inescapability of capitalist reproduction as it merely seeks an empirical testing of preformed categories, the notion of "labour's autonomy," *minus* the idea of an internal relation between structure and struggle, entails the revolutionary testing of a reality which it is unable to comprehend. Both approaches beg the question of the objectivity of subjectivity and, conversely, the subjectivity of objectivity. If one were to integrate form and content, one would be able to analyse the asymmetrical relation between capital and labour (i.e the notion of capital depending on labour but labour not depending on capital) as a relation of class struggle, a struggle which is constitutive of social reality, which is a constituted social presupposition and at the same time a constituting social practice.

I offered the terms "integration" and "transcendence" so as to conceptualise the asymmetrical relation between capital and labour. The dialectical continuum of integration and transcendence emphasises the idea of a practical world in which the integration of labour into the capital-relation and the revolutionary transcendence of capital are neither logically presupposed nor historically determined. The notion of "integration/transcendence" connotes the idea that structure and struggle stand to each other in a relation of difference-in-unity. Neither are structures identical with labour's constitutive practice nor do structures exist separately from labour. The dialectical continuum of "integration" and "transcendence" is founded upon the notion of a "perverted" world in which the constitutive power of social practice exists — as itself — contradictorily. It exists in a mode of being denied.

In sum, structuralist approaches see society as an organism which develops according to its own immanent laws. Labour is seen merely as an aspect of this organism. Structuralism sees social practice as a sociological category, so treating human activity in the fetishised form of a commodity. Structuralism presents an apologetic theory of capitalism. Structuralism and autonomism, while complementary to each other, stand to each other in an asymmetrical way. Structuralism depends on a voluntarist understanding of social practice as a structure-reproducing entity. Autonomism depends on a revolutionary understanding of social practice as a structure transforming human activity. Autonomist approaches emphasise the transformative role of human praxis. The emphasis is on "transcendence," i.e. the revolutionary transformation of a society in which humans exist as commodities. Therein lies an important difference from structuralist approaches. Indeed, autonomist approaches are much more alive to the contradictory unity that obtains between "integration and transcendence." The emphasis on "revolutionary subjectivity" supplies an "anticipatory perspective" of the revolutionary transformation. Thus, autonomist approaches focus on the revolutionary liberation of "transcendence" from "integration." Rather than conceptualising the dialectic between integration and transcendence, they pose the question of political power (*Macht*). They do so, however, in a way which contradicts their own critical perspective. As was argued above, in autonomist approaches, the subject is perceived as a power which stands external to its own perverted world. However, the critique of political economy can be made manifest in practice only when it has seized the masses; when, in other words, the masses are seized by the understanding that it is their own labour, their own social practice, that produces a world that oppresses them (cf. Marx, 1975, p. 182). Rather than presupposing the revolutionary immediacy of the social subject, autonomist approaches need thus to be deepened into a critique of the social existence of labour as a power which constitutes, suffuses and contradicts perverted forms.

ENDNOTES

1 On the post-fordist debate see the volume edited by Bonefeld/Holloway (1991) and Gambino's contribution to this volume.
2 On this "inversion" see, Cleaver (1992) and his contribution to this volume.
3 See Moulier (1989) on this interpretation of Negri's work.
4 See Clarke (1991) for a similar critique of Hirsch's approach. For a similar critique of Poulantzas, see Clarke (1977/1991).

REFERENCES

Aglietta, M. (1979), *A Theory of Capitalist Reproduction,* Verso, London.
Backhaus, HG. (1969), "Zur Dialektik der Wertform," in Schmidt, A. (ed.), *Beiträge zur marxistischen Erkenntnistheorie,* Suhrkamp, Frankfurt.
Backhaus, HG. (1992), "Between Philosophy and Science," in Bonefeld, W., Gunn R. and K. Psychopedis (eds.), *Open Marxism* Vol I, Pluto, London.
Bonefeld, W. (1993), "Crisis of Theory," *Capital & Class,* no 50.
Bonefeld, W. and R. Gunn (1991), "La constitution et sa signification," *Futur Antérieur,* no 8.
Bonefeld, W. and J. Holloway (eds.) (1991), *Post-Fordism and Social Form,* Macmillan, London.
Clarke, S. (1977/1991), "Marxism, Sociology and Poulantzas's Theory of the State," in Clarke, S. (ed.), *The State Debate,* Macmillan, London.
Clarke, S. (1991), "The State Debate," in Clarke, S. (ed.) *The State Debate,* Macmillan, London.
Cleaver, H. (1992), "The Inversion of Class Perspective in Marx's Theory," in Bonefeld, W., Gunn, R. and K. Psychopedis (eds.) *Open Marxism* Vol II, Pluto, London.
Gunn, R. (1989), "Marxism and Philosophy," *Capital & Class,* no 37.
Gunn, R. (1992), "Against Historical Materialism," in Bonefeld, W., Gunn, R. and K. Psychopedis (eds.), *Open Marxism* Vol. I, Pluto, London.
Hirsch, J. (1978), "The State Apparatus and Social Reproduction," in Holloway, J. and S. Picciotto (eds.) *State and Capital,* Arnold, London.
Jessop, B. (1985), *Nicos Poulantzas: Marxist Theory and Political Strategy,* Macmillan, London.
Jessop, B. (1991), "Polar Bears and Class Struggle," in Bonefeld, W. and J. Holloway (eds.) *Post-Fordism and Social Form,* Macmillan, London.

Marcuse, H. (1937/1988), "Philosophy and Critical Theory," in Marcuse, H. *Negations,* Free Association Press, London.

Marx, K. (1966), *Capital* Vol. III, Lawrence & Wishart, London.

Marx, K. (1973), *Grundrisse,* Penguin, Harmondsworth.

Marx, K. (1975), "Contribution to Critique of Hegel's Philosophy of Law. Introduction," *Collected Works,* vol. 3, Lawrence & Wishart, London.

Marx, K. (1983), *Capital* Vol. I, Lawrence & Wishart, London.

Moulier, Y. (1989), "Introduction" to Negri 1989.

Negri, A. (1979), "Capitalist Domination and Working Class Sabotage," in *Working Class Autonomy and Crisis,* Red Notes–CSE, London.

Negri, A. (1989), *The Politics of Subversion,* Polity, Cambridge.

Negri, A. (1992), "Interpretation of the Class Situation Today," in Bonefeld, W., Gunn. R. and K. Psychopedis (eds.), *Open Marxism* Vol. II, Pluto, London.

Poulantzas, N. (1973), *Political Power and Social Classes,* New Left Books, London.

Tronti, M. (1965/1979), "The Strategy of Refusual," in *Working Class Autonomy and Crisis,* Red Notes–CSE, London.

Part Two

The Insurrection of Labor and Global Capital

5

A Critique of the Fordism of the Regulation School

Ferruccio Gambino

Introduction

Some of the categories that people have used in recent years to describe the changes taking place in the world of production, such as Fordism, post-Fordism and immaterial production, have shown themselves to be rather blunt instruments.[1] Here I intend to deal with the use of the concepts "Fordism" and "post-Fordism" by the regulation school, which has given a particular twist to the former term, and which coined *ex novo* the latter. The aim of my article is to help break the conflict-excluding spell under which the regulation school has succeeded in casting Fordism and post-Fordism.

From midway through the 1970s, as a result of the writings of Michel Aglietta[2] and then of other exponents of the regulation school, including Boyer, Coriat and Lipietz, Fordism began to take on a neutral meaning, due in part to a degree of slipshod historiography, but also to the reduction of movements of social classes into mere abstraction.[3]

When they use the term Fordism, the regulation school are referring essentially to a system of production based on the assembly line, which is capable of relatively high industrial productivity.[4] The regulationists' attention is directed not so much to the well-documented inflexibility of the Fordist process of production, to the necessary deskilling of the workforce, to the rigidity of Fordism's structure of command and its productive and social hierarchy, nor to the forms and contents of industrial conflict generated within it, but to the regulation of relations of production by the state, operating as a locus of mediation and institutional reconciliation between social forces. *I shall call this interpretation "regulationist Fordism," and shall use "pre-trade union Fordism" to refer to the sense in which Fordism was generally understood in Europe from the early 1920s to the 1960s.*[5]

Regulationist Fordism

In what follows I shall outline briefly the periodisation which the inventors of the regulationist notion of Fordism have given their idea, because this is crucial if we are to understand the ways in which it is semantically distinct from pre-trade union Fordism; I shall then sketch the basic characteristics of the latter.

According to the regulation school, Fordism penetrated the vital ganglia of the US engineering industry and became its catalysing force in a period that is undefined, but presumably in the 1920s, delivering high wages and acting as the cutting edge of the mass consumption of consumer durables. Having passed through the mill of the Great Depression and the Second World War, Fordism then provided the basis for the expansion of Keynesian effective demand in the United States, where it provided the underpinning for a "welfare" regime, and thus for a stable global social reproduction, presumably from the end of the 1940s onwards. In the 1950s, this system of production is seen as reaching out from the United States towards the countries of Western Europe, and Japan. According to the regulationist periodisation, therefore, the high season of Fordism actually turns out to be rather brief, since it converges — albeit only on paper — with Keynesianism at about the end of the 1930s; then it becomes a concrete reality at the start of the 1950s, and lasts through to the end of the 1960s, when it goes into irreversible crisis. In their view, that point sees the opening of the period — through which we are still passing — of post-Fordism.

The regulation school can justifiably claim credit for the interpretation which associates transformations in the processes of valorization with changes taking place in the socio-political sphere, and vice-versa. It was to make this position its own, and developed it with contributions on the state apparatus and its relations with modern and contemporary capital, in the writings of Hirsch and Roth in Germany and Jessop in Britain.[6] According to Jessop, the regulation school comprises four principal directions of research.[7]

The first direction, initiated by Aglietta, studies regimes of accumulation and models of growth according to their economic determinations, and it applied its first interpretative schema to the United States. Other studies looked at state economic formations — sometimes to examine the spread of Fordism in a given context, and sometimes to follow the particular circumstances of its development — independently from the question of the insertion or otherwise of those states within the international economic circuit.

The second direction concentrates on the international economic dimensions of regulation. It studies the various particular models of international regulation, as well as the form and extent of the complementarity between different national models of growth. This involves examining subjects such as the inclusion and/or exclusion of state and regional formations from the economic order, and the tendencies to autarchic closure and/or internationalistic openness of given countries.

The third direction analyses the overall models of the social structures of accumulation at national level. Reproduction of society depends on an ensemble of institutionally mediated practices which guarantee at least a degree of correspondence between different structures and a balance of compromise between social forces. This strand of regulationism devotes particular attention to the categories of state and hegemony, which it considers to be central elements of social regulation.

The fourth strand, the least developed of the four, studies the interdependences of emerging international structures, and various attempts to lay the basis of a world order through international institutions (which the regulationists call "regimes") aimed at establishing or re-establishing an international order.

Now, even from this summary listing of the regulation school's principal themes it becomes obvious that the centre of gravity of its interests lies in the analysis not so much of the social relations of production, but rather of the economic/state institutions which oversee them. *In short, the regulation school stresses the permanence of structures, and tends to overlook human subjects, their changes and what is happening to them with the disorganisation and reorganisation of social relations.*

From the start regulationism has been fascinated by the staying power of US capital post-1968, despite the United States' defeat in Vietnam. According to the regulationists, in the period after World War II one has to grant the US "the dominant imperialist position":[8] it therefore becomes necessary to understand how, *and thanks to what institutions* its structures and those of its allied industrial countries maintained their stability. Within this hypothesis there is an underlying assumption, in which Western institutions are seen as remaining solid (extremely solid in the case of the US), while not only the institutions of the labour movement, but also living labour power as a whole appear as inescapably subjugated to the unstoppable march of accumulation: in short, in the medium and long term capital's stately progress is destined to continue, while its aporias melt on the horizon. Thus it becomes a question of studying the laws by which Western capital has succeeded in perpetuating itself. It was from within this framework that Michel Aglietta's book[9] emerged, in the year following the first oil price shock, which was also the year of Washington's political and military defeat in Vietnam.

The Uncertain Contours of Regulationist Post-Fordism

For the regulation school, post-Fordism is like a crystal ball in which, "leaving aside the still not completely foreseeable consequences of molecular and genetic technology" it is possible to read some signs of the future. Particularly in the new information technology, in telecommunications and in data processing technologies, all of which could become the basis for a "hyperindustrialisation," they see a potential for revolution in the world of production. Radically transforming work and fragmenting the "Taylorist mass worker," the "electronic revolution" restratifies labour power and divides it into a relatively restricted upper level of the super-skilled, and a massive lower level of ordinary post-Fordist doers and executors. In short, it separates and divides labour power hierarchically and spatially and ends by breaking the framework of collective bargaining.[10] As a result the rhythm of accumulation becomes more intense, and there opens a perspective of a long period of capitalism without opposition — a *turbo-capitalism* — with a political stability that is preserved intact. The post-Fordist worker of the regulation school appears as an individual who is atomised, flexibilised, increasingly non-union, kept on low wages and inescapably in jobs that are always precarious. The state no longer guarantees to cover the material costs of reproduction of labour power, and oversees a contraction of workers' consumption. In the opinion of the regulation school it would be hard to imagine a more complete overturning of so-called Fordist consumerism, within which, it is claimed, the workforce was allegedly put into conditions of wage employment which would enable them to buy the consumer durables that they created.

If we then look at the discontinuity between Fordism and post-Fordism, it seems to derive from the failure of two essential conditions: the mode of capitalist accumulation and the failure to adjust mass consumption to the increase in productivity generated by intense accumulation.[11] In the "golden years" following the Second World War, these two conditions had been satisfied. Fordism mobilised industrial capacities at both the extremes of high skilled and low skilled labour, without the system being destabilised by this polarisation; satisfactory profits were produced from mass consumption, which kept pace with growing investments.[12] As from the 1960s, these twin conditions were no longer given, because investments in the commodity-producing sector in the industrialised countries grew more than productivity, generating a crisis which capital then attempted to resolve by seeking out production options and market outlets in the Third World.

According to the regulationists the consequences at the social level are enormous. The influence of the state is reduced in society; the state is pared back; the majority sector of the non-privileged cuts back on its standard of living in order to organise its own survival; there is no sign of new aggregations arising out of the ashes of the old organisations and capable of expressing a collective solidarity. For the regulationists, strikes, campaigns and conflicts at the point of production are seen in terms of a pre-political spectrum which ranges between interesting curiosities (to which university research cannot be expected to pay attention) and residual phenomena.

THE TOYOTOPHILE VARIANT

The proponents of the advent of post-Fordism discovered Toyotism as a variant of post-Fordism towards the end of the 1980s.[13] In the 1960s, the West began belatedly to take account of the expansion of Japanese capitalism.[14] At that time it was understood as a phenomenon which combined shrewd commercial strategies with an endemic conformism and inadequate social policies.[15] On the Left there were some who — correctly, and before their time — saw in Japanese expansion new hegemonic temptations for Japan in East Asia.[16] Some years later, an admirer of the country's rate of economic growth drew attention to the regular increase in Japan's standard of living and the way in which the Japanese absorbed the oil price "shocks" of the 1960s.[17] There were also those who issued warnings about the regimentation of Japanese society, and about its incipient refusal of the rules dictated by the West.[18] Meanwhile there was something of a fashion for Japanese authors who supplied the West with dubious but easy explanations of the rise of Japan on the basis of its cultural and religious ways of life.[19]

In the 1980s the debate entered the public domain with the publication of a number of important works on Japan's economic structures, despite the growing hostility of Western commercial interests and subsequent gratuitous attacks on the Japanese industrial system in the media.[20] However, still in the 1980s, a number of studies by Japanese economists and sociologists that had been translated into English went almost unobserved.[21] Even the book by the main inventor and propagator of the word "Toyotism," Tai'ichi Ohno,[22] was only translated and distributed in the West at the end of the 1980s, at a point when the world of Japanese industry was becoming one of the key focuses for discussions of industrial productivity.

In the early 1990s, thanks principally to the book by Coriat,[23] in continental Europe too the focus of the debate on Japanese industry shifted from cultural motivations to business strategies; other earlier and worthwhile contributions had aroused less interest. According to Coriat, the lessons emanating from the Toyota factories introduced a new paradigm of productivity, whose importance was comparable to those of Taylorism and Fordism in their time. *Thus Toyotism comes into the limelight in the guise of a post-Fordism that is complete and by now inevitable.* Toyotism is seen as the fulfilment of a tendency to a new form of rationalisation, a rationalisation which had certainly dawned with the category of post-Fordism, but which, in the West, had appeared vague, not yet taking concrete form in a specific form of production and a consolidated social space. In Toyotism however, we are told by Coriat, post-Fordism is realised not only as an ensemble of attempts to rationalise and reduce production costs, but also as a major experiment in new and more advanced relations of production — in fact of a new sociality which might prefigure new forms of industrial democracy. In Coriat's book the West remains in the background, but if we transferred our attention from the delicate balance of productivity in Japan to its European variant, the diffuse factory, we would find an informal Toyotism already operating there, based on individual work contracts. For example, in the celebrated Italian industrial districts, we would find the employers in the "diffuse factory" attempting to set up individual relationships with their workers in order to break down systems of collective bargaining.

According to the Toyotist vulgate, the new system of productivity emerged principally as a result of endogenous demand factors during and after the boom of the Korean War (1950–53), as "just-in-time" production, and thus in large part as an attempt to reduce lead times and cut the workforce.[24]

What is new about Toyotism is essentially the elements of "just-in-time" production and prompt reaction to market requirements; the imposition of multi-jobbing on workers employed on several machines, either simultaneously or sequentially; quality control throughout the entire flow of production; real-time information on the progress of production in the factory; information which is both capillary and filtered in an authoritarian sense, in such a way as to create social embarrassment and drama in the event of incidents which are harmful to production. Production can be interrupted at any moment, thus calling to account a given work-team, or department, or even the whole factory. Any worker who shows a waged-worker's indifference to the company's productivity requirements, and therefore decides not to join "quality control" groups etc, is stigmatised and encouraged to leave. From Coriat we learn that in the interplay of "democracy" and "ostracism," the group may enjoy a measure of democracy, but the person stigmatised will certainly enjoy ostracism. In the interests of comprehensiveness, in his description of the wonders of Toyotism Coriat[25] devotes a laconic note to Satochi Kamata, the writer who went to work in Toyota in 1972 and whose experiences were reflected in the title of his book: *Toyota, the Factory of Despair*.[26]

Toyotism has a number of advantages for the regulation school as regards Western managerial perspectives, even though the Japanese advantage in productivity is showing itself to be tenuous, despite the propagandistic aura that has surrounded it in the West.[27] First of all, it is an experiment that is geographically remote and commercially successful, inasmuch as it defines a route to accumulation (albeit in conjunctures that are both pre-war and war-based, and not at all in conditions of peace, as the enthusiasts of Toyotism would like to have us believe). In the second place, Toyotist methods seem to contradict the growing process of individualisation, which is often given as the reason for the endemic resistance from Western workforces to massification and regimentation. Thirdly, Toyotism is the bearer of a programme of tertiarisation of the workforce, the so-called "whitening" of the blue-collar worker, which, while it actually only involves a rather limited minority of workers, nonetheless converges with the prognosis for a dualistic restratification of the workforce which the post-Fordists consider inevitable.

Pre-trade union Fordism

What was the reality of Fordism for those workers who experienced it at first hand? Put briefly, Fordism is an authoritarian system of production imposed "objectively" by the assembly line, operating on wages and working conditions which the workforce is not in a position to negotiate collectively. Pre-trade union Fordism, with its use of speed-up, armed security guards, physical intimidation in the workplace and external propaganda, in the 1920s and 1930s was *one of the key elements in the slow construction of the world of concentration camps* which put out its claws initially in Stalin's Soviet Union and which would soon put out claws in Nazi Germany too. By the opposite token, even during the Depression, the US witnessed a continued, and even strengthened, democratic grass-roots way of doing things which aimed at the building of the industrial union, and which laid siege to Fordism, and brought it down. In the twenty years preceding the unionisation of Ford in 1941, the company's managers and goon squads conducted anti-worker repression, with beatings, sackings and public relations operations. One day perhaps we will be able to be more detailed than Irving Bernstein when, speaking of the main Ford plant of that period, he wrote: "The River Rouge...was a gigantic concentration camp founded on fear and physical assault."[28] The fact is that the Fordist mania for breaking down the rhythms of human activity in order to crib and confine it within a rigid plan at the worldwide level was defeated in the United States, but in the meantime it had already made its way across to a Europe that was in flames. One could argue that in the twentieth century the assembly line is, together with totalitarian state systems and racist nationalism, one of the originating structures which broadly explain the concentration-camp crimes perpetrated on an industrial scale. By this I mean that in pre-trade union Fordism, and in Taylorism before it, there was not already contained in potentiality its opposite: not the superiority of work "to capital" as in Abraham Lincoln; nor the construction of the CIO industrial union; nor the fall of the racism and male dominated division of labour; nor even less the right to strike. Fascism and Nazism were not in their origins the losing versions of Fordism, but were forced to become such thanks to the social and working-class struggles of the 1930s in the United States — struggles which had already stopped a ruling class that was set on a course of corporatist solutions at the time of the formation of the first Roosevelt government in 1932–33.

As we know, in the United States the assembly line dates from way back. The process of series production of durable goods in the twentieth century was built on the American System of Manufactures, the method of production by interchangeable parts which was already operating in US industry in the nineteenth century.[29] Ford's experiment in his factories is a crucial moment in this series production, inasmuch as it applies it to a consumer durable, the motor car, which had been a luxury object in the early years of the last century, even in the United States. By so doing, Ford structured an increasingly broad-based and pressing consumer demand, which in its turn legitimated among public opinion the authoritarian measures so typical of the Ford factories in the period stretching from the early part of the century to the eve of World War II.

I use the word "authoritarian" advisedly to describe the Ford experiment, because in its way it was both more authoritarian and — especially — more grounded than the proposals that had been advanced by F.W. Taylor twenty years previously. The worker who works for Ford is an individual who produces the means for a multiplication of the points of contact between individuals,[30] but paradoxically he produces it precisely thanks to his own imprisonment for hours on end at the point of production, where he is deprived of the right of movement to an extent hitherto unheard of, just as the woman employed on his daily reproduction is bound to the rhythms of industrial production while at the same time confined to the social twilight of domestic labour. The worker is also deprived of the right of speech, because — in this respect Fordist disciplining goes one stage further than Taylorism — the rhythm of his working day is set not so much by direct verbal orders from a superior, as by a pre-ordained tempo set by the factory's machinery. Communication and contact with his peers was minimised and the worker was expected simply to respond automatically and monotonously to the pace set by a totalitarian productive system. By no means the least of these factors of isolation were the linguistic barriers which immigrant workers brought as a gift to Ford, and which the company maintained and deliberately exacerbated for four decades on end, fomenting bitter incomprehensions and divisions. These were lessened only with the passing of time, by daily contact between workers, by the effects of the Depression, and by the organisational efforts — apparently defeated from the start, but nevertheless unstinting — of the minority who fought for industrial unionism during the 1920s and 1930s.

As we know, right from its establishment in 1903, the Ford Motor Company would not tolerate the presence of trade unions: not only the craft unions or industrial unions, but even "yellow" or company unions. Trade unions remained outside the gates of Ford–USA right up till 1941. Wages became relatively high for a period with the famous "five-dollar day" in January 1914, but only for those workers whom Ford's Sociological Department approved after a minute inspection of the intimate details of their personal and family lives — and then only in boom periods, when Ford was pressurised by the urgent need to stabilise a workforce which was quitting its factories because of the murderous levels of speed-up.[31] The plan for total control of workers and their families went into crisis after America's entry into the war in 1917; thereupon surveillance began the more detailed use of spies on the shop floor. In the recession following on World War I, the wages of the other companies were tending to catch up with wages at Ford, and Ford set about dismantling the forms of welfare adopted in the 1910s. In February 1921, more than 30 per cent of Ford workers were sacked, and those who remained had to be content with an inflation-hit six dollars a day and further speed-ups.

Ford's supremacy in the auto sector began to crack halfway through the 1920s, when the managers at General Motors (in large part refugees from Ford and its authoritarian methods), definitively snatched primacy in the world of auto production. Rather than pursuing undifferentiated production for the "multitudes," as Henry Ford called them, General Motors won the battle *in the name of distinctiveness and individuation,* broadening its range of products, diversifying, and introducing new models on a yearly basis. From the end of the 1920s, and up till unionisation in 1941, the Ford Motor Company was to be notorious for its wages, which were lower even than the already low wages in the auto sector in general.[32]

The fact of the company having been overtaken by General Motors, and Ford's financial difficulties, were not sufficient to break pre-trade union Fordism in the United States: it took, first, the working-class revolts and the factory sit-ins of the 1930s, and then the unionisation of heavy industry, to bring about the political encirclement of the other auto manufacturers, and, finally, of Ford, to the point where it eventually capitulated to the United Auto Workers union following the big strike in the Spring of 1941. Pre-trade union

Fordism dissolved at the point when, faced with attacks by the company's armed security guards, the picketing strikers instead of backing down increased in numbers and saw them off. It was a moment worth recalling with the words of Emil Mazey, one of the main UAW organisers: "It was like seeing men who had been half-dead suddenly come to life."[33]

With the signing of the first union contract in 1941, not only did Ford line up with the other two majors in the auto industry, General Motors and Chrysler, but it even outdid them in concessions to the UAW. Ford was then saved from bankruptcy a second time only thanks to war orders from the government. Already in the course of the Second World War it had been attempting to strengthen the trade union apparatus in the factory, to bring it into line with the company's objectives. As from 1946, a new Ford management set about a long-term strategy to coopt the UAW and turn it into an instrument of company integration. Thus was Fordism buried. If, by Fordism, we mean an authoritarian system of series production based on the assembly line, with wages and conditions of work which the workforce is not in a position to negotiate by trade union means — Fordism as it was generally understood by labour sociologists in the 1920s and 1930s — then *Fordism was eliminated* thanks to the struggles for industrial unionism in the United States in the 1930s, which were crowned by the imposition of collective bargaining at Ford in 1941. As for the dictatorial tendency to deny the workforce discretionality in the setting of work speeds, and the imposition of work speeds incorporated into machinery, these were far from disappearing with the end of pre-trade union Fordism; if anything, by the late 1990s they become more pressing than ever, precisely in the face of the growth in the productive power of labour and the advent of computer-controlled machinery — but that now takes us a long way from pre-trade union Fordism.

We may or may not choose to see these tendencies as a chapter in a far broader movement of rationalisation which began with the American System of Manufactures and which has not yet fully run its course. In any event, the overall drive to command over worktimes through the "objectivity" of machinery[34] was incubated by other large companies before Ford, explodes with the diffusion of the Fordist assembly line, but is not at all extinguished with its temporary defeat at the end of the 1930s. In fact it seems to impose itself with renewed virulence even in the most remote corners where capitalism has penetrated.

Global post-Fordism and Toyotism

As for the category of post-Fordism, in its obscure formulation by the regulation school, it then opened the way to a number of positions which seemed to be grounded in two unproven axioms: the technological determinism of small-series production which, since the 1960s, is supposed to represent a major break with large series production in the manufacture of consumer durables; and the recent discovery of the productivity of communication between what they choose to call the "producers" in industry.[35]

The first axiom derives from the assertion that material production in general (even in engineering — which is more discontinuous than flow production) today proceeds by small series, because, thanks to the increasing flexibility of machine tools, beginning with the numerical control machinery of the 1950s, it has become easier to diversify products, in particular in the production of consumer durables. This diversification makes it possible to meet the needs of consumers seeking individuality, but also to mould people's tastes and to offer them the little touches and personalising elements that pass for expensive innovations. In short, this tendency is merely a strengthening of the drive to diversification which General Motors had attempted and promoted right from the 1920s, and which enabled it to beat Ford at a time when Henry Ford was saying that his customers could have any colour of car that they wanted as long as it was black. Mass production had only in appearance moulded the mass-worker (a term which is used, but also abused, in identifying changing historical figures in class composition). In some departments of Ford's biggest factory, River Rouge, the Ford silence was broken by the "Ford whisper," or by "discourse by hand signals," one of the elements of working-class resistance up until the decisive confrontation of 1941.[36] Despite the fact that workers had to wear identical blue overalls, and despite the fact that they were not given permission even to think, it was plain that the "producers" had minds which aspired to *individuation, not to a universal levelling*. We were reaching the end of the levelling battle for an equality "which would have the permanence of a fixed popular opinion."[37] Towards the end of the 1920, Henry Ford found himself for the first time in serious financial difficulties, arising out of his insistence on the single-colour Model T. It is worth noting that in the Ford factories, even in the dark years of the 1930s, there were workers willing to risk the sack by buying a General Motors car.[38] Thus, within the auto industry, it was General Motors in the 1920s that invented and brought about a flexible production that matched the needs of the times.[39] Its diversified vehicles were produced by means of a "commonalisation" of machine tools and of the main components of the finished auto. The basis of economies of range was economies of scale. The advent of variety in production did not have to wait for Toyotism, as C. Wright Mills was well aware in the early 1950s, when he denounced the manipulating interplay between mass tastes and "personal touches" in the products of his time.[40]

Furthermore, it is taken as real that Toyotism had already broken with "Fordism" in the 1950s and 1960s, because it needed to be flexible in order for its auto production to cope with a demand that was somewhat diversified. Even the prime advocate of Toyotism[41] makes this clear, and a number of Western researchers, including Coriat, have propagated its myth. The fact was that in the post-War period, Toyota, as was the case with Nissan, was relatively inexperienced as a producer of vehicles; it had begun production only in 1936, and had quickly learned to build itself an oligopolistic position which contributed to the dislodging of Ford and General Motors from Japan a bare three years later. After 1945, with the Toyoda family still at the helm, the company focused on large series production, which was exported, and then also produced abroad. The continuity not with regulationist Fordism but with the US auto sector turns out to be far stronger than the Toyotophile vulgate would be willing to admit.

After a difficult period of post-War reconversion, Toyota tried the path of the cheap run-about (the Toyotapet), and experienced major strikes in 1949 and 1953. It was saved principally by the intransigence of Nissan, when they destroyed the Zenji auto union, but also thanks to United States orders arising out of the Korean War. Subsequently, and for a further twenty years to come, Toyota's range of products, and those of the other Japanese auto companies, was restricted to a very limited number of models. Up until the 1960s the defective quality of these models meant that exports were not a great success. Faced with this lack of success, there began a phase of experimentation based on using multi-jobbing mobile workteams on machine tools with variable programming, and on attention to quality with a view to exports.[42] It was the success of one single model (the Corolla runabout) in the 1970s that laid the basis for a diversification of production, and not vice-versa; and it was a success that Toyota was able to build on abroad as well as at home, where the market was far less buoyant. Up until the 1980s, the variety of Toyota models was prudently limited, and only in the 1980s, when the domestic market experienced a standstill, did the company expand their range of production with a view to winning new markets overseas. *Thus it was not the need for a variety of models, but the mobilisation of the workforce after a historic working-class defeat that explains Mr Ohno's experiments at Toyota.* The principal novelty of his experiments was that whereas General Motors in the 1920s had been content to have several ranges of cars built on separate lines, Toyota created work teams that could be commanded where and when necessary, to multi-jobbed labour on the production of a variety of models along the same assembly line.

As for "just in time" production, this had already been experimented with, in its own way, by the auto industry in the United States in the 1920s, and even after the Depression. The layoffs without pay, which were so frequent in the 1920s, and even more so during the Depression, because of the seasonal nature of demand, was one of the battlefields that was decisive in the creation of the auto union in the United States.[43] In the 1936–37 showdown between the UAW and General Motors, the union was victorious on the planning of stocks and on the elimination of seasonal unemployment. Perhaps those who sing the praises of "just in time" production could take a page or two out of the history of Detroit in the 1930s, or maybe a page from the history of the recent recurring strikes in Europe and the US by the independent car-transporter drivers operating within the cycle of the auto industry, who are actually the extreme appendages of the big companies.

As regards the second thesis, the supporters of the notion of post-Fordism claim that production now requires, and will continue to require, ever-higher levels of communication between productive subjects, and that these levels in turn offer spaces of discretionality to the so-called "producers," spaces which are relatively significant, compared with a past of non-communicating labour, of "the silent compulsion of economic relations"[44] of the modern world. This communication is supposed to create an increasingly intense connectivity between subjects, in contrast with the isolation, the separateness and the silence imposed on the worker by the first and second industrial revolutions. While it is certainly true that processes of learning in production ("learning by doing") have required and still require a substantial degree of interaction, including verbal interaction, between individuals, it remains the case that from Taylorism onwards the saving of worktime is achieved to a large extent through reducing to a minimum contact and informal interaction between planners and doers. Taylorism tried, with scant results, to impose a planning in order to increase productivity, depriving foremen and workers of the time-discretionality which they assumed by negotiating informally and verbally on the shop floor. However, in the era of pre-trade union Fordism it should be remembered that in the periods of restructuring of the factory, of changes of models and of technological innovation, the "whispering" of restructuration was not only productive, but was actually essential to the successful outcome of the operation. Anyway, the silence imposed by authority and the deafening noise of development is what dominates the auto industry through to the mid-1930s.[45] *But the disciplining of silence and of the whisper within the channels of capital's productive communication — is this not perhaps also a constitutive characteristic of the modern factory?* On this point, one might note that industrial sociology, as a discipline, was built on the concealing of the communicative dimension and on the rejection of any analysis of the processes of verbal interaction in the workplace. It is not a mere distraction. Here we have only to remember the words of Harold Garfinkel:

> There exists a locally-produced order of work things; [...] They make up a massive domain of organizational phenomena; [...]

> classic studies of work, without remedy or alternative, depend upon the existence of these phenomena, make use of the domain, and ignore it.[46]

As for the tendency to impose speed-up in totalitarian fashion, this certainly did not disappear with the demise of pre-union Fordism; if anything it is even more in evidence in this tail-end of the twentieth century, precisely in the face of the strengthening of the productive powers of labour. In fact the tendency now assumes some of the characteristics of the pre-union Fordism of the Roaring Twenties: a precariousness of people's jobs; the non-existence of health care schemes and unemployment benefits; cuts not only in the real wage but also in money wages; the shifting of lines of production to areas well away from industrially "mature" regions. Also working hours are becoming longer rather than shorter. In the whole of the West, and in the East too, people are working longer hours than twenty years ago, and in a social dimension from which the regulatory power of the state has been eclipsed. The fact that people are working longer hours, and more intensively, is also thanks to the allegedly obsolete Taylorist chronometer and the "outmoded" Fordist assembly line. Ironically, precisely for France, which is where the regulationist school first emerged, precious data, non-existent elsewhere, show that *work on assembly lines and subject to the constraint of an automated pace of production is on the increase*, in both percentage terms and absolute terms: 13.2 per cent of workers were subjected to it in 1984, and 16.7 per cent in 1991 (out of, respectively, 6,187,000 and 6,239,000 workers).[47]

In the 1950s and 1960s — the "golden years" of Fordism as Lipietz calls them — the international economy under the leadership of the United States pushed the demand for private investment, even more than the consumption of wage goods. *What had appeared to be a stable system began to come apart from the inside*, because at the end of the 1960s the class struggle, in its many different forms, overturned capital's solid certainties as regards the wage, the organisation of the labour process, the relationship between development and underdevelopment, and patriarchy. *If one does not understand the radicality of this challenge, it becomes impossible to grasp the elements of crisis and uncertainty which characterised the prospects for capital's dominion in the twenty years that followed*.[48] The dishomogeneity of the reactions — from the war of manoeuvre against blue collar workers in the industrialised countries, through to capitalism's regionalisation into three large areas (NAFTA, European Union and Japan) and to the Gulf War — denote not the transition to a post-Fordist model, but a continuous recombination of old and new elements of domination in order to decompose labour power politically within a newly flexibilised system of production.

Conclusions

The regulation school looks at the implications of this recombination from capital's side, seeing capital as the centre and motor of the overall movement of society. Hirsch and Roth speak in the name of many when they state that "it is always capital itself and the structures which it imposes 'objectively,' on the backs of the protagonists, that sets in motion the decisive conditions of class struggles and of processes of crisis."[49] Thus it is not surprising that the conclusions that the regulationists draw from their position tend to go in the only direction which is not precluded for them: namely that conflict against the laws of capitalist development has no future, and also that there is no point in drawing attention to the cracks in the edifice of domination. Paraphrasing Mark Twain, one might say that if the regulationists have only a pan-Fordist hammer, they will see only post-Fordist nails to bang.

In taking up this position, not only do the regulationists deny themselves the possibility of analysis of conflictual processes both now and in the future, but they also exclude themselves from the multi-voiced debate which is today focussing on social subjects.[50] This is the only way in which one can explain the regulationists' reduction of the working class in the United States to a mere *Fordised object*,[51] even in its moments of greatest antagonistic projectuality as it was expressed between the Depression and the emergence of the Nazi-Fascist new order in Europe. And given the limits of its position, regulationism is then unable to understand how this working class contributed decisively in the placing of that selfsame United States capitalism onto a collision course with Nazism and fascism. Pre-union Fordism was transient, but not in the banal (but nonetheless significant) sense of Henry Ford financing Hitler on his route to power and decorating himself with Nazi medals right up until 1938, but because what overturned the silent compulsion of the Fordised workforce was the workforce itself, in one of its social movements of self-emancipation — a fact of which the regulationists are not structurally equipped to understand the vast implications at the world level, and for many years to come, well beyond the end of World War II.

As regards today's conditions, what is important is not the examination of the novelties following on the collapse of various certainties in the wake of the fall of the Berlin Wall, but the possibility or otherwise of avoiding the inevitability of the passage to a "post-Fordist" paradigm in which labour power figures once again as a mere object and inert mass. As Peláez and Holloway note, the insistence with which the regulationists invite their audience to look the future in the face arouses a certain perplexity.[52] After all, a belief in the marvels of technology within the organisations of the labour movement has led to epic defeats in the past. What is at stake here is not just the inevitability or otherwise of a system — the capitalist system — which has too many connotations of oppression and death to be acceptable, but even the possibility of any initiative, however tentative, on the part of social subjects. What is at stake here is the possibility of resisting a preconstituted subordination of labour power to the inexorable New Times that are imposed in part, certainly, by the computer chip, but also by powerful intra-imperialist hostilities, which for the moment are disguised behind slogans such as competition and free trade.

What the present leads us to defend is the indetermination of the boundaries of conflictual action. We shall thus have to re-examine a means or two, with a view to clearing the future at least of the more lamentable bleatings.

Up until now the decomposition and anatomisation of labour-power as a "human machine" has been a preparatory process of the various stages of mechanisation; it is a process which capitalist domination has constantly presented as necessary. The point is not whether post-Fordism is in our midst, but whether the sacrifice of "human machines" on the pyramids of accumulation can be halted.

TRANSLATED BY ED EMERY

ENDNOTES

1 For a timely critique of the term "immaterial production," see Sergio Bologna, "Problematiche del lavoro autonomo in Italia" (Part I), *Altreragioni*, no. 1 (1992), pp. 10–27.

2 Michel Aglietta, (1974), *Accumulation et régulation du capitalisme en longue période. L'exemple des Etats Unis (1870–1970)*, Paris, INSEE, 1974; the second French edition has the title *Régulation et crises du capitalisme*, Paris, Calmann-Lévy, 1976; English translation, *A Theory of Capitalist Regulation: the US Experience*, London and New York, Verso, 1979; in 1987 there followed a second English edition from the same publisher. The link between the category of Fordism and that of post-Fordism may be considered the term "neo-Fordism," proposed by Christian Palloix two years after the publication of the first edition of Aglietta's book. Cf. Christian Palloix, "Le procés du travail. Du fordisme au neo-fordisme," *La Pensée* no. 185 (February 1976), pp. 37–60, according to whom neo-Fordism refers to the new capitalist practice of job enrichment and job recomposition as a response to new requirements in the management of workforces.

3 For the regulationist interpretation of Fordism prior to 1991, see the fundamental volume edited by Werner Bonefeld and John Holloway, *Post-Fordism and Social Form: A Marxist Debate on the Post-Fordist State*, London, Macmillan,

1991, which contains the principal bibliographical references for the debate. For the regulation school see, among others, the following works: Robert Boyer, *La théorie de la régulation: une analyse critique*, Paris, La Découverte, 1986; Robert Boyer (ed.), *Capitalismes fin de siécle*, Paris, Presses Universitaires de France, 1986; Alain Lipietz, "Towards Global Fordism?," *New Left Review* no. 132 (March-April 1982), pp. 33–47; Alain Lipietz, "Imperialism as the Beast of the Apocalypse," *Capital and Class*, no. 22 (Spring 1984), pp. 81–109; Alain Lipietz, "Behind the Crisis: the Exhaustion of a Regime of Accumulation. A 'Regulation School Perspective' on Some French Empirical Works," *Review of Radical Political Economy*, vol. 18, no. 1–2 (1986), pp. 13–32; Alain Lipietz, *Mirages and Miracles: the Crisis of Global Fordism*, London, Verso, 1987; Alain Lipietz, "Fordism and post-Fordism" in W. Outhwaite and Tom Bottomore (eds.), *The Blackwell Dictionary of Twentieth-Century Social Thought*, Oxford, Blackwell, 1993, pp. 230–31; Benjamin Coriat, *Penser · l'envers. Travail et organisation dans l'entreprise japonaise*, Paris, Christian Bourgois, 1991; Italian translation, *Ripensare l'organizzazione del lavoro. Concetti e prassi del modello giapponese*, Bari, Dedalo, 1991, with introduction and translation by Mirella Giannini.

4 I say "relatively high productivity" because the assembly line has not always produced results. For example, the Soviet Fordism of the first two five-year plans (1928–32, 1933–37) was the object of some experimentation, particularly on the assembly lines of the Gorki auto factory (thanks in part to the technical support of Ford technicians), but productivity turned out to be about 50 per cent lower than that of Ford's US factory. Cf. John P. Hardt and George D. Holliday, "Technology Transfer and Change in the Soviet Economic System," in Frederic J. Fleron, Jr., *Technology and Communist Culture: the Socio-Cultural Impact of Technology under Socialism*, New York and London, Praeger, 1977, pp. 183–223.

5 In his "Fordism and post-Fordism," op. cit., p. 230, Lipietz maintains incorrectly that the term "Fordism" "was coined in the 1930s by the Italian Marxist Antonio Gramsci and by the Belgian socialist Henrik de Man." Lipietz is obviously referring to "Americanismo e fordismo" (1934) in Antonio Gramsci, *Quaderni del carcere*, vol. 3. ed. Valentino Gerratana, Torino, Einaudi, 1975, pp. 2137–81, a series of notes in which Gramsci takes account, among other things, of a book by de Man which does not directly discuss Fordism. The first edition of de Man's work appeared in Germany in 1926: Hendrik de Man, *Zur Psychologie des Sozialismus*, Jena, E. Diederichs, 1926 and, after a partial French translation which appeared in Brussels in 1927, a complete translation was published under the title of *Au delá du Marxisme*, Paris, Alcan, 1929, based on the second German edition

published by Diederichs (1927). For his prison notes on "Americanism and Fordism," Gramsci had the Italian translation of the French edition published by Alcan: Henri de Man, *Il superamento del marxismo*, Bari, Laterza, 1929. In Europe the term "Fordism" pre-dates de Man and Gramsci, and was already in use in the early 1920s; cf. in particular Friedrich von Gottl-Ottlilienfeld, *Fordismus? Paraphrasen über das Verhältnis von Wirtschaft und technischer Vernunft bei Henry Ford und Frederick W. Taylor*, Jena, Gustav Fischer, 1924; H. Sinzheimer, "L'Europa e l'idea di democrazia economica" (1925), *Quaderni di azione sociale* XXXIX, no. 2 (1994), pp. 71–74, edited and translated by Sandro Mezzadra, whom I thank for this reference. In his article cited above, Lipietz states equally erroneously that "in the 1960s the term was rediscovered by a number of Italian Marxists (R. Panzieri, M. Tronti, A. Negri)." In Italy the discussion of Fordism was addressed, taking a critical distance from Gramsci, in the volume of Romano Alquati's writings, *Sulla FIAT e altri scritti*, Milano, Feltrinelli, 1975, which brought together texts from the period 1961-1967, and in the volume by Sergio Bologna, George P. Rawick, Mauro Gobbini, Antonio Negri, Luciano Ferrari-Bravo and Ferruccio Gambino, *Operai e Stato: Lotte operaie e riforma dello stato capitalistico tra rivoluzione d'Ottobre e New Deal*, Milano, Feltrinelli, 1972, which contained the proceedings of a conference held in Padova in 1967.

6 See in particular, in Werner Bonefeld and John Holloway (eds.) *Post-Fordism and Social Form*, op. cit., the essay by Joachim Hirsch, "Fordism and post-Fordism: The Present Social Crisis and its Consequences," pp. 8–34, and the two essays by Bob Jessop, "Regulation Theory, Post-Fordism and the State: More than a Reply to Werner Bonefeld," pp. 69–91; and" Polar Bears and Class Struggle: Much Less than a Self- Criticism," pp. 145–69, which contain further bibliographical references.

7 Bob Jessop, "Regulation Theory, Post-Fordism and the State," op. cit., pp. 87–88.

8 Joachim Hirsch, "Fordism and Post-Fordism: The Present Social Crisis and its Consequences," op. cit., p. 15.

9 Michel Aglietta (1974), *Accumulation et régulation du capitalisme en longue période. Exemple des Etats Unis (1870–1970)*, Paris, INSEE, 1974.

10 Joachim Hirsch, "Fordism and Post-Fordism: The Present Social Crisis and its Consequences," pp. 25–6.

11 Alain Lipietz, "Towards Global Fordism," *New Left Review*, no. 132 (March–April 1982), pp. 33–47.

12 Ibid., pp. 35–6.

13 On this development, cf. the review by Giuseppe Bonazzi, "La scoperta del modello giapponese nelle società occidentali," *Stato e Mercato*, no. 39 (December 1993), pp. 437–66, which discusses the variously critical recep-

tion of the Japanese model within Western sociology; more briefly and in more general terms, cf. Pierre-François Souyri, "Un nouveau paradigme?," *Annales*, vol. 49, no. 3 (May-June 1994), pp. 503–10.

14 Robert Guillain, *Japon, troisiéme grand*, Paris, Seuil, 1969; Herman Kahn, *The Emerging Japanese Superstate*, Minneapolis, Minn., Hudson Institute, 1970.

15 Robert Brochier, *Le miracle économique japonais*, Paris, Calmann-Lévy, 1970.

16 Jon Halliday and David McCormack, *Japanese Imperialism Today: Co-prosperity in Greater East Asia*, Harmondsworth, Penguin, 1973.

17 Ezra Vogel, *Japan as Number One: Lessons for America*, Cambridge, Mass., Harvard University Press, 1979.

18 Karel Van Wolferen, *The Enigma of Japanese Power*, New York, N.Y., Knopf, 1989.

19 Chie Nakane, *Japanese Society*, London, Weidenfeld & Nicholson, 1970; Italian translation, *La societá giapponese*, Milan, Cortina. Michio Morishima, *Why Has Japan "Succeeded?"*, Cambridge, Cambridge University Press; Italian translation, *Cultura e technologia nel successo giapponese*, Bologna, Il Mulino, 1984.

20 Jean-Loup Lesage, *Les grands sociétés de commerce au Japon, les Shosha*, Paris, PUF; Chalmers Johnson, *MITI and the Japanese Miracle: the growth of industrial policy, 1925–75*, Tokyo, Tuttle, 1986.

21 Masahiko Aoki, *The Economic Analysis of the Japanese Firm*, Amsterdam, Elsevier, 1984; Kazuo Koike, *Understanding Industrial Relations in Modern Japan*, London, Macmillan, 1988.

22 Tai'ichi Ohno, *Toyota Seisan Hoshiki* [The Toyota Production Method], Diamond Sha, 1978; English translation, *The Toyota Production System: Beyond Large-scale Production*, Productivity Press, Cambridge, Mass.; French translation, *L'esprit Toyota*, Paris, Masson, 1989; Italian translation, *Lo spirito toyota*, Torino, Einaudi, 1993.

23 Benjamin Coriat, *Penser · l'envers. Travail et organisation dans l'entreprise japonaise*, Paris, Christian Bourgois, 1991; Italian tranlation, *Ripensare l'organizzazione del lavoro. Concetti e prassi del modello giapponese*, Bari, Dedalo, 1991.

24 Benjamin Coriat, *Ripensare l'organizzazione del lavoro*, op. cit., pp. 32–33.

25 Benjamin Coriat, *Ripensare l'organizzazione del lavoro*, op. cit., p. 85.

26 Satochi Kamata, *Toyota, l'usine du désespoir*, Paris, Editions Ouviriéres, 1976; English translation, *Japan in the Passing Lane: Insider's Account of Life in a Japanese Auto Factory*, New York, N.Y., Unwin Hyman, 1984. By the same author, *L'envers du Miracle*, Paris, Maspéro, 1980.

27 Ray and Cindelyn Eberts, *The Myths of Japanese Quality*, Upper Saddle, N.J., Prentice Hall, 1994.

28 Irving Bernstein, *Turbulent Years: A History of the American Worker 1933–1941*, Boston, Houghton Mifflin, 1969, p. 737.

29 David A. Hounshell, *From the American System to Mass Production (1800–1932)*, Baltimore and London, The Johns Hopkins University Press, 1984.

30 Karl Marx, *Grundrisse: Foundations of the Critique of Political Economy*, Harmondsworth, Penguin, 1973, p. 265: "Society does not consist of individuals, but expresses the sum of interrelations, the relations within which these individuals stand."

31 Stephen Meyer III, *The Five Dollar Day: Labor Management and Social Control in the Ford Motor Company, 1908–1921*, Albany, N.Y., State University of New York Press, 1981, in particular pp. 96–202.

32 Joyce Shaw Peterson, *American Automobile Workers, 1900–1933*, Albany, N.Y., State University of New York, 1987. As Samuel Romer wrote in "The Detroit Strike," *The Nation* (vol. 136, no. 3528), 15 February 1933, pp. 167–68: "The automobile industry is a seasonal one. The factories slow down production during the fall months in order to prepare the new yearly models; and the automobilie worker has to stretch the 'high wages' of eight months to cover the full twelve-month period." Cf. also M.W. La Fever (1929), "Instability of Employment in the Automobile Industry," *Monthly Labor Review*, vol. XXVIII, pp. 214–17.

33 Bernstein, *Turbulent Years*, op. cit., p. 744.

34 David Noble, "Social Choice in Machine Design," in Andrew Zimbalist, *Case Studies on the Labor Process*, New York, Monthly Review Press, 1979, pp. 18–50.

35 An updated synthesis of these positions is to be found in Marco Revelli's essay, "Economia a modello sociale nel passaggio tra fordismo e toyotismo" in Pietro Ingrao and Rossana Rossanda, *Appunti di fine secolo*, Rome, Manifestolibri, 1995, pp. 161–224.

36 Irving Bernstein, *Turbulent Years*, op. cit., p. 740.

37 Karl Marx, *Capital*, vol.1, Harmondsworth, Penguin, 1976, p. 152.

38 Irving Bernstein, *Turbulent Years*, op. cit., p. 740.

39 While not belonging to the regulation school, there are two admirers of the Italian industrial districts who presented flexible production as an innovation typical of the 1970s. Here the reference was not to Japan, but to the eastern part of the Po Valley plain: J. Michael Piore and Charles F. Sabel (1983), *The Second Industrial Divide: Possibilities for Prosperity*, New York, N.Y., Basic Books; Italian translation, *Le due vie dello sviluppo industriale. Produzione di massa e produzione flessibile*, Torino, ISEDI, 1987.

40 Charles Wright Mills, "Commentary on Our Culture and Our Country," *Partisan Review*, vol. 19, no. 4 (July-August 1952), pp. 446–50, and in particular p. 447.

41 Tai'ichi Ohno, *Toyota Seisan Hoshiki* [The Toyota Method of Production], op. cit.

42 Marie-Claude Belis Bourguignan and Yannick Lung (1994), "Le Mythe de la variété originelle. L'internationalisation dans la trajectoire du modéle productif japonais," *Annales*, 49, 2 (May–June), pp. 541–67.

43 M.W. La Fever, "Instability of Employment in the Automobile Industry," op. cit., pp. 214–17. Cf. also note 31 above.

44 Karl Marx, *Capital*, op. cit., p. 899.

45 Joyce Shaw Peterson, *American Automobile Workers, 1900–1933*, op. cit., pp. 54–56; Irving Bernstein, *Turbulent Years*, op. cit., p. 740.

46 Harold Garfinkel (ed.), *Ethnomethodological Studies of Work*, London and New York, Routledge & Kegan Paul, 1986, p. 7.

47 Anon., *Alternatives Economiques*, May 1994, on the DARES data: *Enquétes spécifiques Acemo: Enquétes sur l'activité et les conditions d'emploi de main-d'oeuvre.* My thanks to Alain Bihr for this reference.

48 See the indispensable "Contribution by Riccardo Bellofiore: On Pietro Ingrao and Rossana Rossands, Appunti di Fine Secolo," pub. Associazione dei Lavoratori e delle Lavoratrici Torinesi (ALLT), 24 November 1995. [Editor's Note: A shortened version of Bellofiore's essay appeared in English in *Common Sense*, no. 22, 1977.]

49 Joachim Hirsch and Roland Roth, *Das neue Gesicht des Kapitalismus*, Hamburg, VSA, 1986, p. 37

50 On this theme see Peter Miller and Nikolas Rose, "Production, Identity and Democracy," *Theory and Society*, vol. 24, no. 3 (June 1995), pp. 427–67.

51 During the first two five-year plans under Stalin, the workers on the assembly lines of the Gorky auto factory were referred to as "the Fordised" (*fordirovannye*) by the Soviet authorities.

52 Eloina Peláez and John Holloway, "Learning to Bow: Post-Fordism and Technological Determinism," in Werner Bonefeld and John Holloway (eds.), *Post- Fordism and Social Form*, op. cit., 1991, p. 137.

References

Aglietta, Michel (1974), *Accumulation et régulation du capitalisme en longue période. L'exemple des Etats-Unis (1870-1970)*, Paris, Insee, 1974; *Régulation et crises du Capitalisme*, Paris, Calmann-Lévy, 1976 (2nd edition); English translation, *A Theory of Capitalist Regulation: The US Experience*, London and New York, New Left Books, 1979 (2nd edition, Verso, London and New York, 1987).

Alquati, Romano (1975), *Sulla Fiat e altri scritti*, Milan, Feltrinelli.

Alquati, Romano (1989), *Dispense di sociologia industriale*, vol. III, parts 1 and 2, Torino, Il Segnalibro.

Anonimo (1994), "Taylor n'est pas mort," *Alternatives Economiques*, (May), on DARES data, *Enquetes spécifiques Acemo, Enquetes sur l'activité et les conditions d'emploi de main-d'oeuvre*, Table I.2.1.

Aoki, Masahiko (1984), *The Economic Analysis of the Japanese Firm*, Amsterdam, Elsevier.

Belis-Bourguignan, Marie-Claude and Lung, Yannick (1994), "Le Mythe de la variété originelle. L'internationalisation dans la trajectoire du modéle productif japonais," *Annales*, 49, 2.

Bernstein, Irving (1969), *Turbulent Years: A History of the American Worker 1933-1941*, Boston, Houghton Mifflin.

Bologna, Sergio; Rawick, George P.; Gobbini, Mauro; Negri, Antonio; Ferrari Bravo, Luciano; Gambino, Ferruccio; *Operai e stato: Lotte operaie e riforma dello stato capitalistico tra rivoluzione d'Ottobre e New Deal*, Milan, Feltrinelli, 1972.

Bologna, Sergio, "Problematiche del lavoro autonomo in Italia," *Altreragioni*, 1 (1992).

Bonazzi, Giuseppe (1993), "La scoperta del modello giapponese nella sociologia occidentale," *Stato e mercato*, No. 39.

Bonefeld, Werner and Holloway, John (eds.) (1991), *Post-Fordism and Social Form: A Marxist Debate on the Post-Fordist State*, Houndmills and London, MacMillan.

Boyer, Robert (1986), *La théorie de la régulation: une analyse critique*, Paris, La Découverte.

Boyer, Robert (ed.) (1986), *Capitalismes fin de siécle*, Paris, Presses Universitaires de France.

Brochier, Robert (1970), *Le miracle économique japonais*, Paris, Calmann-Lévy.

Coriat, Benjamin (1991), *Penser · l'envers. Travail et organisation dans l'entreprise japonaise*, Paris, Christan Bourgois, 1991; Italian translation, *Ripensare l'organizzazione del lavoro. Concetti e prassi del modello giapponese*, Bari, Dedalo, 1991, with introduction and translation by Mirella Giannini.

Davis, Mike (1978), "'Fordism' in Crisis: A Review of Michel Aglietta's *Regulation et Crises: L'Expérience des Etats Unis*," *Review*, 2.

Eberts, Ray and Cindelyn (1994), *The Myths of Japanese Quality*, Upper Saddle, N.J., Prentice Hall.

Fox, R. M. (1927), "Fordism: A Critical Examination," The Nineteenth Century and After, CI, no. 2.

Gambino, Ferruccio (1972), *Ford britannica. Formazione di una classe operaia*, in S. Bologna, L. Ferrari Bravo, F. Gambino, M. Gobbini, A. Negri, G.P. Rawick, *Operai e Stato*, Milan, Feltrinelli.

Gambino, Ferruccio (1987), *The Significance of Socialism in the Post-War United States*, in Hefer, Jean and Rovit, Jeanine, *Why Is There No Socialism in the United States*, Paris, Editions de l'Ecole des Hautes Etudes en Sciences Sociales.

Garfinkel, Harold (ed.) (1986), *Ethnomethodological Studies of Work*, Routledge & Kegan Paul, London e New York.

Gottl-Ottlilienfeld, Friedrich von (1924), *Fordismus? Paraphrasen über das Verhältnis von Wirtsckaft und technischer Vernunft bei Henry Ford und Frederick W. Taylor*, Jena, Gustav Fischer.

Gramsci, Antonio (1975), "Americanismo e fordismo" (1934) in *Quaderni del carcere*, vol. 3, ed. V. Gerratana, Torino, Einaudi.

Guillian, Robert (1969), *Japon troisiéme grand*, Paris, Seuil.

Halliday, Jon and McCormack, David (1973), *Japanese Imperialism Today: Co-Prosperity in Greater East Asia*, Harmondsworth, England, Penguin.

Hardt, John P. & Holliday, George D. (1977), *Technology Transfer and Change in the Soviet Economic System*, in Frederic J. Fleron, Jr., *Technology and Communist Culture: The Socio-Cultural Impact of Technology under Socialism*, New York and London, Praeger.

Hirsch, Joachim and Roth, Roland (1986) *Das neue Gesicht des Kapitalismus*, Hamburg, VSA.

Hirsch, Joachim (1991), *Fordism and Postfordism: The Present Social Crisis and its Consequences*, in Bonefeld, Werner and Holloway, John (eds.) 1991.

Holloway, John (1991a), *The Great Bear: Post-Fordism and Class Struggle. A Comment on Bonefeld and Jessop*, in Bonefeld, Werner and Holloway, John (eds.) 1991.

Holloway, John (1991b), *Capital is Class Struggle (and Bears are not Cuddly)*, in Bonefeld, Werner and Holloway, John (eds.) 1991.

Hounshell, David A. (1984), *From the American System to Mass Production (1800-1932)*, Baltimora e London, The Johns Hopkins Univesity Press.

Jessop, Bob (1991a), *Regulation Theory, Post-Fordism and the State: More than a Reply to Werner Bonefeld*, in Bonefeld, Werner and Holloway, John (eds.) 1991.

Jessop, Bob (1991b), *Polar Bears and Class Struggle: Much Less than a Self-Criticism*, in Bonefeld, Werner, and Holloway, John, (eds.), 1991.

Johnson, Chalmers (1986), *MITI and Japanese Miracle: the Growth of Industrial Policy, 1925–1975*, Tokyo, Tuttle.

Kahn, Herman (1970), *The Emerging Japanese Superstate*, Minneapolis, Minn., Hudson Institute.

Kamata, Satochi (1976), *Toyota, l'usine du désespoir*, Paris, Editions Ouvriéres; English translation, *Japan in the Passing Lane: Insider's Account of Life in a Japanese Auto Factory*, New York, N.Y., Unwin Hyman, 1984.

Kamata, Satochi (1980), *L'envers du miracle*, Paris, Maspero.

Koike, Kazuo (1988), *Understanding Industrial Relations in Modern Japan*, London, MacMillan.

La Fever, M.W (1929), "Instability of Employment in the Automobile Industry," *Monthly Labor Review*, vol. XXVIII.

Lesage, Jean-Loup (1983), *Les grandes société de commerce au Japon, les Shosha*, Paris, PUF.

Lipietz, Alain (1982), "Towards Global Fordism?," *New Left Review*, No. 132.

Lipietz, Alain (1984), "Imperialism as the Beast of the Apocalypse," *Capital and Class*, No. 22.

Lipietz, Alain (1986), "Behind the Crisis: the Exhaustion of a Regime of Accumulation. A 'Regulation School Perspective' on Some French Empirical Works," *Review of Radical Political Economy*, vol. 18, No.1–2.

Lipietz, Alain (1987), *Mirages and Miracles: The Crisis of Global Fordism*, London, Verso

Lipietz, Alain (1993), *Fordism and post-Fordism* in Outhwaite, William and Bottomore, Tom, *The Blackwell Dictionary of Twentieth Century Social Thought*, Oxford, Blackwell.

Man, Hendrik de (1926), *Zur Psychologie des Sozialismus*, Jena, E. Diederichs, 1926; 2nd edition, 1927; English translation, *The Psychology of Socialism*, London, Allen & Unwin, 1928.

Marx, Karl (1964), *Il Capitale*, vol. I, Rome, Editori Riuniti.

Marx, Karl (1968), *Lineamenti fondamentali della critica dell'economia politica*, vol. I, tr. di Enzo Grillo, Firenze, La Nuova Italia.

Meyer, Stephen III (1981), *The Five Dollar Day: Labor Management and Social Control in the Ford Motor Company, 1908-1921*, Albany, N.Y., State University of New York Press.

Mezzadra, Sandro (1994), "La costituzione del lavoro. Hugo Sinzheimer e il progetto weimariano di democrazia economica," *Quaderni di azione sociale*, 2.

Miller, Peter and Rose, Nikolas (1995) "Production, Identity, and Democracy," *Theory and Society*, vol. 24, No. 3.

Mills, Charles Wright (1952), "Commentary on Our Culture and Our Country," *Partisan Review*, vol. 19, no. 4.

Morishima, Michio (1982), *Why Has Japan "Succeeded?"*, Cambridge, Cambridge University Press; Italian translation, *Cultura e tecnologia nel successo giapponese*, Bologna, Il Mulino 1984.

Nakane, Chie (1970), *Japanese Society*, London, Weidenfeld & Nicholson; Italian translation, *La societá giapponese*, Milan, Cortina, 1992.

Noble, David (1979), *Social Choice in Machine Design*, in Zimbalist, Andrew, *Case Studies on the Labor Process*, New York, Monthly Review Press.

Ohno, Tai'ichi (1978), *Toyota Seisan Hoshiki* [The Toyota method of production], Tokyo, Diamond; English translation, *The Toyota Production System: Beyond Large Scale Production*, Productivity Press, Cambridge, Mass. 1988; French translation, *L'esprit Toyota*, Paris, Masson, 1989; Italian translation, *Lo spirito toyota*, Torino, Einaudi, 1993.

Palloix, Christian (1976), "Le procés de travail. Du fordisme au néofordisme," *La Pensée*, no. 185.

Peláez, Eloina and Holloway, John (1991), *Learning to Bow: Post-Fordism and Technological Determinism*, in Bonefeld, Werner and Holloway, John (eds.) 1991.

Peterson, Joyce Shaw (1987), *American Automobile Workers, 1900–1933*, Albany, N.Y., State University of New York Press.

Piore, J. Michael, and Sabel, Charles F. (1983), *The Second Industrial Divide: Possibilities for Prosperity*, New York, N.Y., Basic Books; Italian translation, *Le due vie dello sviluppo industriale. Produzione di massa e produzione flessibile*, Torino, Isedi, 1987.

Revelli, Marco (1995), *Economia e modello sociale nel passaggio tra fordismo e toyotismo*, in Ingrao, Pietro and Rossana Rossanda, *Appuntamenti di fine secolo*, Roma, Manifestolibri.

Romer, Samuel (1933), "The Detroit Strike," *The Nation* (vol. 136, no. 3528), 15 February 1933, pp. 167–68.

Sinzheimer, Hugo (1925), *Europa und die Idee der wirtschaftlichen Demokratie*, in *Europas Volkswirtschaft in Wort und Bild. Beiträge zur Wirtschaftserkennis, hrsg. von der "Frankfurter Zeitung," 1925–26*, pp. xvii–xviii, now in Sinzheimer Hugo, *Arbeitsrecht und Arbeitssoziologie. Gesammelte Aufsätze und Reden*, ed. O. Kahn-Freund and Th. Ramm, Frankfurt-Köln, Europäische Verlaganstalt, 1976 ("Schriftenreihe der Otto Brenner Stiftung," 4), 2 Bde., Bd. 1, pp. 221–225; *L'Europa e l'idea di democrazia economica*, trans. Sandro Mezzadra, *Quaderni di azione sociale*, XXXIX, No. 2 (1994), pp.71–74.

Souyri Pierre-Francois (1994), "Un nouveau paradigme?," *Annales*, vol. 49, No. 3.

Van Wolferen, Karel, (1989), *The Enigma of Japanese Power*, New York, N.Y., Knopf.

Vogel, Ezra (1979), *Japan as Number One: Lessons for America*, Cambridge, Mass., Harvard University Press.

6
The End of Work, or The Renaissance of Slavery? A Critique of Rifkin and Negri

George Caffentzis

Introduction

The last few years in the U.S. has seen a return of a discussion of work that is reminiscent of the mid-1970s, but with a number of twists. In the earlier period, books like *Where Have All the Robots Gone?* (Sheppard 1972), *False Promises* (Aronowitz 1972)and *Work in America* (Special Task Force 1973), and phrases like "blue-collar blues," "zerowork" and "the refusal of work" revealed a crisis of the assembly line worker which expressed itself most dramatically in wildcat strikes in U.S. auto factories in 1973 and 1974 (Linebaugh and Ramirez 1992). These strikes were aimed at negating the correlation between wages and productivity that had been the basis of the "deal" auto capital struck with the auto unions in the 1940s. As Linebaugh and Ramirez wrote of the Dodge Truck plant wildcat involving 6000 workers in Warren, Michigan between June 10–14, 1974:

> Demands were not formulated until the third day of the strike. They asked for "everything." One worker said, "I just don't want to work." The separation between income and productivity, enforced by the struggle, could not have been clearer (Linebaugh and Ramirez 1992:160).

This clarity met an even stronger clarity in the auto capitalists' decades-long campaign to reassert control over the work process in their plants and assembly lines. These capitalists did not hesitate to destroy these very plants and assembly lines in order to save themselves. "Rust belt" and "run away plant" became the phrases of the business press when describing auto and other kinds of factory production in the 1980s; these phrases flowed almost seamlessly into "globalization" and "robotization" in the 1990s. The unprecedented result of this campaign was that full time weekly "real" wages in the U.S. manufacturing industry had fallen almost 20% while the work time had actually increased.

But in the mid-1990s books like *The End of Work* (Rifkin 1995), *The Labor of Dionysius* (Negri and Hardt 1994) and *The Jobless Future* (Aronowitz and De Fazio 1994), and phrases like "downsizing" (*New York Times* 1996) and "worker displacement" (Moore 1996) have revived themes associated with the crisis of work at a time when the power relation between workers and capital is the inverse of the 1970s. Whereas in the 1970s workers were refusing work, in the 1990s capitalists presumably are refusing workers!

In this essay I will show that these books and phrases are misleading in claiming that "scientifically based technological change in the midst of sharpened internationalization of production means that there are too many workers for too few jobs, and even fewer of them are well paid" (Aronowitz and De Fazio 1994:xii), or that "technological innovations and market-directed forces...are moving us to the edge of a near workerless world" (Rifkin 1995: xvi), or, even more abstractly, that the "law of labor-value, which tried to make sense of our history in the name of the centrality of proletarian labor and its quantitative reduction in step with capitalist development, is completely bankrupt..." (Hardt and Negri 1994:10).

Jobs and the Manifold of Work

A "jobless future" and a "workerless world" are the key phrases of this literature, but before we can examine the cogency of these phrases for the present and near future it is worthwhile to reflect for a minute on the notions of job and work that they imply.

"Job" is the easier of the two. It has a rather unsavory etymological past. In seventeenth and eighteenth century England (and even today), "job" as a verb suggested deceiving or cheating while as a noun it evoked the scent of the world of petty crime and confidence games. In this context, a "jobless future" would be a boon to humanity. But by the mid-twentieth century "job" had become the primary word used in American English to refer to a unit of formal waged employment with some fixed, contractually agreed upon length of tenure. To have a job on the docks differs significantly from working on the docks; for one can be working somewhere without having a job there. The job, therefore, rose from the nether world of political economy to become its holy grail.

The mystic power of the word "job" does not come from its association with work, however. Indeed, "to do a job" or "to job" were phrases describing a "crooked" way to refuse to work and gain an income. "Jobs, Jobs, Jobs," became the shibboleth of late-twentieth century U.S. politicians because the "job" emphasized the wage and other contractual aspects of work in capitalist society which were crucial to the physical and mental survival of the electorate. Hence a "jobless future" would be hell for a capitalist humanity, since it implies a future without wages and contracts between workers and capitalists.

Although its salience is unmistakable, the job marks off, often quite conventionally and even with dissemblance, a part of the work process; but there is no one-to-one correlation between jobs and work. The same work process can be broken down into one, two or many jobs. Consequently, "work" and its apparent semantic cognate "labor" seem to have a greater claim to reality.

Therefore, the "end of work" denotes a more radical transformation than a "jobless future," because there were many periods in human history when societies were "jobless" — e.g., slave societies and subsistence-producing peasant communities — but there were none, Eden excepted, that were workless. Before one can speak of the end of work, however, one should recognize that here has been a conceptual revolution in the last political generation concerning the meaning of work. For a long period of time, perhaps coincident with the formulation of the collective bargaining regimes in the 1930s and their collapse in the 1970s, "work" was synonymous with "the job," i.e., formal waged work. But since then a vast manifold of work was discovered (Caffentzis 1992; Caffentzis 1996/1998).

This manifold includes informal, "off the books" work which has a wage but could not be officially deemed contractual because it violates the legal or tax codes. This dimension of the manifold tapers into the great region of purely criminal activity which in many nations and neighborhoods rivals in quantity and value the total formal job-related activity. Even more important has been the feminist "discovery" of housework in all its modalities that are crucial for social reproduction (e.g., sexuality, biological reproduction, child care, enculturation, therapeutic energy, subsistence farming, hunting and gathering, and anti-entropic production). Housework is the great Other in capitalist societies, for it stubbornly remains unwaged and even largely unrecognized in national statistics, even though it is increasingly recognized as crucial for capitalist development. Finally, there is a level of capitalist hell which collects all the coerced labor of this so-called "post-slavery" era: prison labor, military labor, "sex slavery," indentured servitude, child labor.

By synthesizing all these forms of work, we are forced to recognize an intersecting and self-reflective manifold of energetic investments that dwarf the "formal world of work" in spatio-temporal and value terms. This vast emerging Presence as well as the inverse manifold of its refusal has transformed the understanding of work profoundly, even though many seem not to have noticed. It certainly puts the jejune distinctions between work and labor (Arendt), between bio-power and capitalism (Foucault), and between labor and communicative action (Habermas) into question while forcing a remarkable expansion of class analysis and an enrichment of revolutionary theory beyond the problematics of planning for factory systems of the future. Most importantly for our discussion, this Manifold of Work problematizes the discussion of work and its supposed end at the hands of technological change.

The End of Work

Unfortunately, the notion of work that is often used in the "end of work" literature is often antediluvian and forgetful of work's capitalistic meaning. This is most clearly seen in Rifkin's central argument in *The End of Work*. He is anxious to refute those who argue that the new technological revolution involving the application of genetic engineering to agriculture, of robotization to manufacturing and of computerization of service industries will lead to new employment opportunities if there is a well-trained workforce available to respond to the challenges of the "information age." His refutation is simple.

In the past, when a technological revolution threatened the wholesale loss of jobs in an economic sector, a new sector emerged to absorb the surplus labor. Earlier in the century, the fledgling manufacturing sector was able to absorb many of the millions of farmhands and farm owners who were displaced by the rapid mechanization of agriculture. Between the mid-1950s and the early 1980s, the fast-growing service sector was able to re-employ many of the blue collar workers displaced by automation. Today, however, as all these sectors fall victim to rapid restructuring and automation, no "significant" new sector has developed to absorb the millions who are being displaced (Rifkin 1995:35).

Consequently, there will be a huge unemployment problem when the last service worker is replaced by the latest ATM, virtual office machine or heretofore unconceived application of computer technology. Where will he/she find a job? There is no going back to agriculture or manufacturing and no going forward to a new sector beyond services. Rifkin applies this scenario to a global context and foresees not millions of unemployed people on the planet in the near future, but billions.

The formal logic of the argument appears impeccable, but are its empirical premises and theoretical presuppositions correct? I argue that they are not, for

Rifkin's technological determinism does not take into account the dynamics of employment and technological change in the capitalist era.

Let us begin with a categorical problem in Rifkin's stage theory of employment. He uncritically uses terms like "agriculture," "manufacturing" and, especially, "services" to differentiate the three developmental stages of a capitalist economy as indicated in the passage quote above and in many other parts of *The End of Work*. One cannot fault Rifkin for making an idiosyncratic choice here, since major statistical agencies like the U.S. Bureau of Labor Statistics also employ these categories to disaggregate employment, production and productivity in the last few decades. The core metaphors that helped shape this trichotomy are rooted in a distinction between material goods (produced on the farm or off) and immaterial services and in the spatial distinction between farm, factory and everywhere else (office, school, store, warehouse, road, etc.) This trichotomy allows for a rough and ready economic typology, with "the service industry" generally functioning as something of a fuzzy default category.

But it is one thing to use a category ex post facto and another is to use a category in a projective way (either into the past or the future). Rifkin's somewhat Hegelian scheme sees technological change as the autonomous moving spirit that transforms one stage to another until it comes to a catastrophic halt in the present "service" stage of history. Yet when we look at capitalistic societies in the past, this neat series is hardly accurate. For example, was seventeenth and eighteenth century England agricultural? The "service industry" in the form of household servants in the larger agricultural estates at that time was quite substantial, but these servants often worked as artisans (manufacturing) and as farm hands (agriculture). Moreover, with the rise of cottage industry agricultural workers or small farmers also doubled or tripled as manufacturing workers on the farm. Finally, throughout the history of capitalism we find a complex shifting of workers among these three categories. Instead of simple the move from agricultural to manufacturing, and manufacturing to service, we find all six possible transitions among these three categories.

The vast literature on the "development of underdevelopment" and on the many periods of capitalist "deindustrialization" abundantly illustrates these transitions which were clearly caused not by some autonomous technological spirit, but by historically concrete and ever varied class struggles and power relations. A machine introduced by capitalists to undermine industrial workers' power can lead to these workers losing their employment and becoming "service workers" or becoming "agricultural workers" according to a complex conjuncture of forces and possibilities. There is no evidence from the total history of capitalism that there is only a linear progression that ends with the last service worker.

Rifkin's schema is further undermined if we examine its future projection. After a look at the wide variety of applications computer technology in the service industry (from voice recognition, to expert systems, to digital synthesizers), Rifkin ominously concludes: "In the future, advanced parallel computing machines, high-tech robotics, and integrated electronic networks spanning the globe are going to subsume more and more of the economic process, leaving less and less room for direct hands-on human participation in making, moving, selling, and servicing" (Rifkin 1995:162). But here the very defaulting function of the category of service makes its future projection problematic for Rifkin, since it will not stay in a single place in logical space in order to be reduced to measure zero by technological change.

Let us consider one of the standard definitions of what constitutes service work: the modification of either a human being (giving a haircut or a massage) or an object (repairing an automobile or a computer). How can we possibly project such a category into the future? Since there are no limitations on the type of modification in question, there is no way one can say that "advanced parallel computing machines, high-tech robotics, and integrated electronic networks spanning the globe" will be able to simulate and replace its possible realizations. Indeed, the service work of the future might very well be perversely defined (at least with respect to the constructors of these machines) as modifications to humans and objects that are not simulateable and replaceable by machines![1] Just as today there is a growth in the sale of "organic," non-genetically engineered agricultural produce, and "handmade," garments made from non-synthetic fibers, so too in the future there might be an interest in having a human to play Bach (even if the synthesized version is technically more correct) or to dance (even though a digitalized hologram might give a better performance according to the critics). I would be surprised if such service industries do not arise. Could they "absorb" many workers displaced from agricultural or manufacturing work? That I do not know, but then again, neither does Rifkin.

Rifkin's inability to project his categorical schema either into the past or into the future reveals an even deeper problem: his inability to adequately explain why technological change takes place in the first place. At the beginning of *The End of Work* Rifkin rejects what he calls "the trickle-down-technology argument" — i.e., the view that technological change in one branch of industry, though causing unemployment there, eventually leads to increased employment throughout the rest of the economy — by appealing to Marx's *Capital* and *Grundrisse*. Rifkin's view of Marx can be surveyed in this extended passage:

> Karl Marx argued that producers continually attempt to reduce labor costs and gain greater control over the means of production by substituting capital equipment for workers wherever and whenever possible...Marx predicted that the increasing automation of production would eventually eliminate the worker altogether. The German philosopher looked ahead to what he euphemistically referred to as the "last...metamorphosis of labor," when "an automatic system of machinery" finally replaced human beings in the economic process...Marx believed that the ongoing effort by producers to continue to replace human labor with machines would prove self-defeating in the end....[as] there would be fewer and fewer consumers with sufficient purchasing power to buy their products (Rifkin 1995:16–17).

This use of Marx is part of a new and widely noted trend among social policy analysts on the US Left, broadly considered. But this revival of Marx's thought is often as selective as is the use of Smith and Ricardo on the Right.[2] In Rifkin's case, he definitely gets the broad sweep of Marx's views on technology right, but with some notable omissions.

The first omission is of workers' struggles for higher wages, for reduced work, for better conditions of work, and for a form of life that absolutely refuses forced labor. These struggles are the prime reasons why capitalists are so interested introducing machinery as weapons in the class war. If workers were docile "factors of production," the urgency for technological change would be much reduced.

The second omission is Marx's Ricardian recognition that every worker permanently replaced by a machine reduces the total surplus value (and hence the total profit) available to the capitalist class as a whole. Since the capitalist class depends upon profits, technological change can be as dangerous to it as to the workers. Hence the capitalist class faces a permanent contradiction it must finesse: (a) the desire to eliminate recalcitrant, demanding workers from production, (b) the desire to exploit the largest mass of workers possible. Marx comments on this eternal tension in *Theories of Surplus Value:*

> The one tendency throws the labourers on to the streets and makes a part of the population redundant, and the absorbs them again and extends wage-slavery absolutely, so that the lot of the worker is always fluctuating but he never escapes from it. The worker, therefore, justifiably regards the development of

> the productive power of his own labour as hostile to himself; the capitalist, on the other hand, always treats him as an element to be eliminated from production. (Marx 1977:409)

Capital's problem with technological change is not the loss of consumers, but the loss of profits.

Marx's most developed discussion of this story is to be found in Part III of *Capital* III: "The Law of the Falling Tendency of the Rate of Profit." There he recognizes that a tendency towards the total replacement of humans by an "automatic system of machinery" must continually be met by "counteracting causes" or else the average rate of profit will actually fall. These counteracting causes either increase the mass of surplus value (e.g., raising the intensity and duration of the working day), or decrease the mass of variable capital (e.g, depress wages below their value, expand foreign trade), or decrease the mass of constant capital (e.g., increasing the productivity of labor in the capital goods industry, expand foreign trade) or some combination or these disjunctive possibilities (Marx 1909: 272–282). Contemporary US capitalism appears to be applying the maximal synthesis of these counteracting causes while the European capitals are being more selective. There is no inevitable capitalist strategy in the drive to overcome workers' struggles and prevent a dramatic decline in the rate of profit. These struggles can lead to many futures — from the reintroduction of slavery, to a dramatic increase in the workday, to the negotiated reduction of the waged workday, to the end of capitalism — depending on the class forces in the field.

But there is one outcome that definitely cannot be included in the menu of possible futures as long as capitalism is viable: Rifkin's vision of "the high-tech revolution lead[ing] to the realization of the ago-old utopian dream of substituting machines for human labor, finally freeing humanity to journey into a post-market era" (Rifkin 1995:56). For capitalism requires the stuff of profit, interest and rent which can only be created by a huge mass of surplus labor, but the total replacement of human work by machines would mean the end of profit, interest and rent. Although Rifkin seems to agree with much of Marx's analysis of the dynamics of capitalism, Marx's fatal conclusion is carefully kept out of the sanguine scenario presented at the last part of his book. Rifkin lays out a future that would combine a drastic reduction in the workday along with a "new social contract" that would provide financial incentives (from "social" or "shadow" wages to tax benefits) for working in "the third sector" — the independent, "non-profit" or volunteer sector between "the public and private" sectors. This sector can become the "service industry" of the 21st century, since it "offers the only viable means for constructively channeling the surplus labor cast off by the global market" (Rifkin 1995:292). That is, it absorbs workers who do not produce surplus value, and provides them with a wage for non-surplus-value creating work.

In other words, Rifkin's vision of the "safe haven" for humanity is a form of capitalism where most workers are not producing profits, interest or rent. He contrasts this vision with a future where "civilization...continue[s] to disintegrate into a state of increasing destitution and lawlessness from which there may be no easy return" (Rifkin 1995:291). But how viable is Rifkin's social Chimera with its techno-capitalist head, its ample, woolly third-sector body, and its tiny surplus-value producing tail? There are proportions that must be respected even when dealing with futuristic Chimeras, and Rifkin's cannot exist simply because the head, however technologically sophisticated, cannot be nourished by such a tiny tail. The capitalism resulting from Rifkin's "new social contract" is impossible, for it is by definition a capitalism without profits, interest and rents. Why would capitalists agree to such a deal after they trumpeted throughout the Cold War that they would rather blow up half the planet than give up a tenth of their income?

This "impossibility proof" is so obvious that one can not help but asking why Rifkin invoked Marx so directly at the beginning of *The End of Work* only to completely exorcise him at the end? Is he avoiding reference to the unpleasantness of world war, revolution and nuclear annihilation that his earlier reflections stirred up? Is he trying to coax, with veiled Marxian threats, the techno-capitalist class into an act of suicide camouflaged as a new lease on life?

Answers to such questions would require a political analysis of the type of rhetoric Rifkin and his circle employ. I forgo this effort. But it is worth pointing out that Rifkin's chimerical strategy is not totally mistaken. After all, he is looking for a new sector for the expansion of capitalist relations. He mistakenly chose the "non-profit," volunteer sector, for if this sector is truly "non-profit" and voluntary, it cannot be a serious basis for a new sector of employment in a capitalist society. (And there is no way to get out of capitalism via a massive fraud, however tempting that might be).

But Rifkin's intuition is correct. For the Manifold of Work extends far beyond the dimension of formal waged work and this non-waged work does produce surplus value in abundance. If it is more directly and efficiently exploited, this work can become the source of an new area of surplus-value creating employment through the expansion of forced labor, the extension of direct capitalist relations into the region of labor reproduction and finally the potentiation of micro- and criminal enterprises. That is why "neoliberalism," "neo-slavery," "Grameenism," and the "drug war" are the more appropriate shibboleths of the Third Industrial Revolution rather than the "non-profit" third sector touted by Rifkin, for they can activate the "counteracting causes" to the precipitous decline in the rate of profit that computerization, robotization and genetic engineering provoke.

Negri and The End of the Law of Value

Rifkin can, perhaps, be indulged in his half-baked use of Marx's thought. After all, he did not come out of the Marxist tradition and his previous references to Marx's work were few and largely in passing. But the themes Rifkin so clearly presented in *The End of Work* can be found in a number of Marxist, Post-Marxist, and Post-modern Marxist writers, often in a much more obscure and sibylline versions. One of the primary figures in this area is Antonio Negri, who developed arguments supporting conclusions very similar to Rifkin's in the 1970s, but without the latter's Marxist naiveté. His *The Labors of Dionysius* (with Michael Hardt), published in 1994, continued a discourse definitively begun in *Marx Beyond Marx* (Negri 1991, originally published in 1979) and continued in *Communists Like Us* (Guattari and Negri 1990, originally published in 1985).[3]

In this section I will show how Negri's more sophisticated and Marxist analysis of contemporary capitalism is as problematic as Rifkin's. It is hard to discern Negri's similarity to Rifkin, simply because Negri's work is rigorously anti-empirical — rarely does a fact or factoid float through his prose — while Rifkin's *The End of Work* is replete with statistics and journalistic set pieces on high-tech. Negri does not deign to write plainly of an era of "the end of work." He expresses an equivalent proposition, however, in his theoretical rejection of the classical Labor Theory or Law of Value with hypostasized verbs. In the late 20th century, according to Negri, the Law is "completely bankrupt" (Hardt and Negri 1994:10) or it "no longer operates" (Guattari and Negri 1990:21) or "the Law of Value dies" (Negri 1991:172).

This is equivalent to Rifkin's more empirical claims, but the equivalence can only be established after a vertiginous theoretical reduction. Negri's version of the classic labor theory of value has as its "principal task...the investigation of the social and economic laws that govern the deployment of labor-power among the different sectors of social production and thus to bring to light the capitalist processes of valorization" (Hardt and Negri 1994:8), or it is "an expression of the relation between concrete labor and amounts of money needed to secure an existence" (Guattari and Negri 1990:21) or it is a measure of "the determinate proportionality between necessary labor and surplus labor" (Negri 1991:172). The Law of Value was alive in the 19th century, but just like Nietzsche's God, it began to die then. It took a bit longer for the Law to be formally issued a death certificate, however.

The bankruptcy, inoperativeness, and death of the Law of Value simply mean that the fundamental variables of capitalist life — profits, interest, rents, wages, and prices — are no longer determined by labor-time. Negri argues, as does Rifkin, that capitalism has entered into a period that Marx, in his most visionary mode, described the "Fragment on Machines" in the *Grundrisse* (Negri 1991:140–141) (Rifkin 1995:16–17). Let me chose just one of the many oft-quoted passages in this vision:

> The development of heavy industry means that the basis upon which it rests — the appropriation of the labour time of others — ceases to constitute or to create wealth; and at the same time direct labour as such ceases to be the basis of production, since it is transformed more and more into a supervisory and regulating activity; and also because the product ceases to be made by individual direct labour, and results more for the combination of social activity....on the one hand, once the productive forces of the means of labour have reached the level of an automatic process, the prerequisite is the subordination of the natural forces to the intelligence of society, while on the other hand individual labour in its direct form is transformed into social labour. In this way the other basis of this mode of production vanishes (Marx 1977:382)

The development of "automatic processes" in genetic engineering, computer programming and robotization since the 1960s have convinced both Negri and Rifkin that the dominant features of contemporary capitalism are matched point-for-point by Marx's vision in 1857–58. The major difference between Negri's work and Rifkin's *The End of Work* is that while Rifkin emphasizes the consequences of these "automatic processes" for the unemployment of masses of workers, Negri emphasizes the new workers that are centrally involved in "the intelligence of society" and "social labor." Whereas Rifkin argues that these new "knowledge workers" (e.g., research scientists, design engineers, software analysts, financial and tax consultants, architects, marketing specialists, film producers and editors, lawyers, investment bankers) can never be a numerically large sector and hence are no solution to the problems created by this phase of capitalist development, Negri takes them as the key to the transformation to communism beyond "real socialism."

It is important to note a terminological difference between Negri and Rifkin, because Negri has over the years termed these Rifkin's "knowledge workers" first in the 1970s to be "social workers," and later in the 1990s he baptized them as "cyborgs" *à la* Donna Haraway (Haraway 1991:149–81). Although singularly infelicitous in its English translation, the term "social worker" directly comes out of the pages of the *Grundrisse.* For when looking for a descriptive phrase that would contrast the new workers in the "information and knowledge sector" to the "mass workers" of assembly line era, many of Marx's sentences — e.g., "In this transformation, what appears as the mainstay of production and wealth is neither the immediate labour performed by the worker, nor the time that he works-but the appropriation of man by his own general productive force, his understanding of nature and the mastery of it; in a word, the development of the social individual" (Marx 1977:380) — deeply influenced him. The social worker is the subject of "techno-scientific labor" and s/he steps out of the pages of the Grundisse as a late 20th century cyborg, i.e., "a hybrid of machine and organism that continually crosses the boundaries between material and immaterial labor" (Hardt and Negri 1994:280–81).[4] The old mass worker's labor-time on the assembly line was roughly correlated to (exchange-value and use-value) productivity and s/he was alienated from the factory system, the social cyborg's labor-time is independent of its productivity but it is thoroughly integrated into the terrain of production.

Rifkin sees the "knowledge class" of "symbolic analysts" as fundamentally identified with capital and explains the new interest in intellectual property rights as a sign that the elite capitalists have recognized the importance of the knowledge class and are willing to share their wealth with it. Knowledge workers are "fast becoming the new aristocracy" (Rifkin 1995:175). Negri has a rather different reading of this class' present and future. The existence of social cyborgs not only is evidence that the dialectic of capitalist development has been "broken," according to Negri, but capital simply cannot "buy it out," because "the social worker has begun to produce a subjectivity that one can no longer grasp in the terms of capitalist development understood as an accomplished dialectical movement" (Hardt and Negri 1994:282) In order words, techno-scientific labor cannot be controlled by capital via its system of wages and work-discipline rounded out with the promise of entrance into the top levels of managerial, financial and political power for the "best." Not only is the social-working cyborg beyond the bounds of capital's time-honored techniques of control, it is also in the vanguard of the communist revolution. Why? Let us first hear and then interpret Negri's words:

> Cooperation, or the association of [cyborg] producers, is posed independently of the organization capacity of capital; the cooperation and subjectivity of labor have found a point of contact outside of the machinations of capital. Capital becomes merely

> an apparatus of capture, a phantasm, an idol. Around it move radically autonomous processes of self-valorization that not only constitute an alternative basis of potential development but also actually represent a new constituent foundation (Hardt and Negri 1994:282)

Negri claims that the cyborg workers have escaped capital's gravitational field into a region where their work and life is actually producing the fundamental social and productive relations appropriate to a communism. These relations are characterized by "self-valorization" — i.e., instead of determining the value of labor power and work on the basis of its exchange value for the capitalist, the workers value their labor power for its capacity to determine their autonomous development — arises from the period when techno-scientific labor becomes paradigmatic (Negri 1991:162–63) (Caffentzis 1987). In effect, Negri's notion of "self-valorization" is similar to the "class for itself" or "class consciousness" of more traditional Marxism; but self-valorization distinguishes the cyborg from the politics of the mass worker and marks the arrival of the true communist revolution ironically percolating in the World Wide Web rather than in the (old and new) haunts of the mass workers, peasants and ghetto dwellers of the planet.

The clash between Negri's picture of the anti-capitalist cyborg and Rifkin's image of the pro-capitalist knowledge worker can make for an inviting theme. But just as Rifkin's knowledge worker (as the last profit-making employee) is built upon a faulty conception of capitalist development, so too is Negri's cyborg. Consequently, it is more useful to consider and critique the common basis of both these views. Negri bases his version of "the social worker" on Marx's *Grundrisse* just as Rifkin does for his knowledge worker, but we should remember that the "Fragment on Machines" was not Marx's last word on machines in a capitalist society. Marx continued work for another decade and filled Volumes I, II, and III of *Capital* with new observations. This is not the place to review these developments in depth. It should be pointed out that in Volume I Marx recognized not only the great powers machinery threw into the production process; he also emphasized machines' lack of value creativity analogous to the thermodynamical limits on availability of work in a given energy field (Caffentzis 1997); but even more crucial for our project is the part of Capital III where Marx revisited the terrain of the "Fragment on Machines." In these passages he recognized that in any era where capitalism approaches the stage of "automatic processes," the system as a whole must face a dramatic acceleration of the tendency for rate of profit to fall. He asked, "How is it that this fall is not greater and more rapid?" His answer was that there are built-in processes in capitalist activity that resist this tendency and therefore the system's technological finale.

These are to be found directly in the Chapter XIV on "counteracting causes" and indirectly in Part II on the formation of the average rate of profit. I mentioned the critical consequences of "counteracting causes" in my discussion of Rifkin, and they apply to Negri as well. Negri imperiously denies "the social and economic laws that govern the deployment of labor-power among the different sectors of social production" and rejects the view that labor-time is crucial to "the capitalist processes of valorization." But capital and capitalists are still devoutly interested in both. That is why there is such a drive to send capital to low waged areas and why there is so much resistance to the reduction of the waged work day. For the computerization and robotization of factories and offices in Western Europe, North America and Japan has been accompanied by a process of "globalization" and "new enclosures."

Capitalists have been fighting as fiercely to have the right to put assembly zones and brothels in the least-mechanized parts of the world as to have the right to patent life forms. Instead of a decline, there has been a great expansion of factory production throughout many regions of the planet. Indeed, much of the profit of global corporations and much of the interest received by international banks has been created out of this low-tech, factory and sexual work (Federici 1998). In order to get workers for these factories and brothels, a vast new enclosure has been taking place throughout Africa, Asia and the Americas. The very capital that owns "the ethereal information machines which supplant industrial production" is also involved in the enclosure of lands throughout the planet, provoking famine, disease, low-intensity war and collective misery in the process (Caffentzis 1990; 1995).

Why is capital worried about communal land tenure in Africa, for example, if the true source of productivity is to be found in the cyborgs of the planet? One answer is simply that these factories, lands, and brothels in the Third World are locales of "the counteracting causes" to the tendency of the falling rate of profit. They increase the total pool of surplus labor, help depress wages, cheapen the elements of constant capital, and tremendously expand the labor market and make possible the development of high-tech industries which directly employ only a few knowledge workers or cyborgs. But another complementary answer can be gleaned from Part II of *Capital* III: "Conversion of Profit into Average Profit," which shows the existence of a sort of capitalist self-valuation. In order for there to be an average rate of profit throughout the capitalist system, branches of industry that employ very little labor but a lot of machinery must be able to have the right to call on the pool of value that high-labor, low-tech branches create. If there were no such branches or no such right, then the average rate of profit would be so low in the high-tech, low-labor industries that all investment would stop and the system would terminate. Consequently, "new enclosures" in the countryside must accompany the rise of "automatic processes" in industry, the computer requires the sweat shop, and the cyborg's existence is premised on the slave.

Negri is correct in connecting the rise of the new workers in the high-tech fields with self-valorization, but it has more to do with capitalist self-valorization — i.e., the right of "dead labor" to demand a proportionate share of "living labor" — rather than workers' self-valorization. Indeed, capital's self-valorization is premised on the planetary proletariat's degradation.

One can easily dismiss Negri's analysis as being profoundly Eurocentric in its neglect of the value-creating labor of billions of people on the planet. Indeed he is Eurocentric in a rather archaic way. He would do well, at least, to look to the new global capitalist multiculturalism and the ideologies it has spawned (Federici 1995), instead of to the rather small circle of postmodern thinkers that constitute his immediate horizon, in order to begin to appreciate the class struggles of today, even from a capitalist perspective.

But the charge of Eurocentricism is a bit too general. What can better account for Negri's methodological oblivion of the planetary proletariat is his adherence to one of the axioms of the Marxist-Leninism: the revolutionary subject in any era is synthesized from the most "productive" elements of the class. It is true that Negri has nothing but scorn for the metaphysics of dialectical materialism and for the history of "real socialism," but on the choice of the revolutionary subject he is Leninist to the core. Negri makes so much of computer programmers and their ilk because of their purported productivity. Since the General Intelligence is productive, then these intellectual workers are its ideal (and hence revolutionary) representatives, even though they have not yet launched a concrete struggle against capitalist accumulation *qua* "social workers" or "cyborgs."

But this methodological identity between revolution and production has proven false time and again in history. Leninists and Leninist parties in the past have often paid for this mistake with their lives. Mao's political development clearly shows that it took the massacre of Communist workers in the cities and many near mortal experiences in the countryside before he recognized that the Taoist principle — the seemingly weakest and least productive can be the most powerful in a struggle — was more accurate than the Leninist. Negri's choice of revolutionary subject in this period — the masters of the ethereal machines — is as questionable as the industrial worker bias of Leninists in the past. Indeed, the failure of *The Labor of Dionysius* (published in the US in 1994) to address the revolutionary struggles of the indigenous peoples of the planet, especially the Zapatistas in Mexico, is a definite sign that Negri's revolutionary geography needs expansion.

Conclusion

Negri and Rifkin are major participants in the "end of work" discourse of the 1990s, although they occupy two ends of the rhetorical spectrum. Rifkin is empirical and pessimistic in his assessment of the "end of work" while Negri is aprioristic and optimistic. However, both seem to invoke technological determinism by claiming that there is only one way for capitalism to develop. They, and most others who operate this discourse, forget that capitalism is constrained (and protected) by proportionalities and contradictory tendencies. The system is not going to go out of business through the simple-minded addition of more high-tech machines, techniques, and workers come what may, for Marx's ironic dictum: "The real barrier of capitalist production is capital itself" (Marx 1909:293), is truer than ever. It might be an old and miserable truth, but still to this day profit, interest, wages and labor in certain proportions are particular, but necessary conditions for the existence of capitalism. Capital cannot will itself into oblivion, but neither can it be tricked or cursed out of existence.

Rifkin tries to trick the system into believing that a viable way out of the unemployment crises he foresees is to abandon profit creating sectors of the economy. He reassuringly says that all will be well if the capitalists are in control of automated agriculture, manufacturing, and service industries and nearly everyone else is working in a non-profit third sector which makes no claim on hegemony. But this scenario can hardly to pass the eagle eyes of the capitalist press much less those of the boardroom without ridicule. So it cannot succeed.

Negri tries philosophical cursing instead. He calls late-20th-century capitalism "merely an apparatus of capture, a phantasm, an idol" ontologically (Hardt and Negri 1994:282). I appreciate Negri's desire to put a curse on this system of decimation, humiliation and misery, but I question his "merely." As the highest organs of capitalist intelligence (like the Ford Foundation) have shown, capital is as impervious to these ontological curses as the conquistadors were to the theological curses of the Aztec priests. Indeed, capital revels in its phantom-like character. Its main concern is with the duration of the phantasm, not its ontological status.

The "end of work" literature of the 1990s, therefore, is not only theoretically and empirically disconfirmed. It also creates a failed politics because it ultimately tries to convince both friend and foe that, behind everyone's back, capitalism has ended. It motto is not the Third International's "Don't worry, capital will collapse by itself sooner or later;" rather it is, "Capitalism has always already ended at the high-tech end of the system, just wake up to it." But such an anti-capitalist version of Nietzsche's motto "God is dead" is hardly inspiring when millions are still being slaughtered in the many names of both God and Capital.

ENDNOTES

1 This "perverse" definition is reminiscent of Cantor's diagonal method that has proven so fruitful in mathematical research in this century. The trick of this method is to assume that there is a list that exhausts all items of a particular class *K* and then to define a member of *K* that is not on the list by using special properties of the list itself.

2 For example, in much of the current discussion of free trade, a low wage level is considered by many to be a Ricardian "comparative advantage." But such a reading is a distortion of Ricardo's views and an invitation to justify repressing workers' struggles. The sources of comparative advantage for Ricardo are quasi-permanent features of the physical and cultural environment of a country, not economic variables like wages, profits or rents.

3 This is not the place to discuss Negri political and juridical life since the 1970s. For more of this see Yann Moulier's "Introduction" to *The Politics of Subversion* (Negri 1989). Negri voluntarily returned to Italy from exile in France in July 1997 and is now in Rebbibia Prison (Rome). There is an international campaign demanding his release.

4 Negri often describes the work of the social worker cyborg as "immaterial." But an analysis of Turing-machine theory shows that there is no fundamental difference between what is standardly called material labor (e.g., weaving or digging) and immaterial labor (e.g., constructing a software program). Consequently, one must look to other aspects of the labor situation to locate its value creating properties (Caffentzis 1997).

REFERENCES

Aronowitz, Stanley 1973. *False Promises: The Shaping of American Working Class Consciousness.* New York: McGraw-Hill.

Aronowitz, Stanley and Di Fazio, William 1994. *The Jobless Future: Sci-Tech and the Dogma of Work.* Minneapolis: University of Minnesota Press.

Caffentzis, George 1987, "A Review of Negri's *Marx beyond Marx*." In *New German Critique,* Spring-Summer.

Caffentzis, George 1990. "On Africa and Self-Reproducing Automata." In *Midnight Notes* 1990.

Caffentzis, George 1992. "The Work/Energy Crisis and the Apocalypse" in *Midnight Notes* 1992.

Caffentzis, George 1995. "On the Fundamental Implications of the Debt Crisis for Social Reproduction in Africa." In Dalla Costa and Dalla Costa 1995.

Caffentzis, George 1997. "Why Machines Cannot Create Value or, Marx's Theory of Machines." In Davis, Hirschl, and Stack 1997.

Caffentzis, George 1998. "On the Notion of a Crisis of Social Reproduction: A Theoretical Review." In Dalla Costa and Dalla Costa 1998.

Dalla Costa, Maria Rosa and Dalla Costa, Giovanna 1998. *Paying the Price: Women and The Politics of International Economic Strategy*. London: Zed Books.

Dalla Costa, Maria Rosa and Dalla Costa, Giovanna 1998. *Women, Development and the Labor of Reproduction: Issues of Struggles and Movements*. Lawrenceville, NJ: Africa World Press.

Davis, Jim, Hirschl, Thomas and Stack, Michael 1997. *Cutting Edge: Technology, Information, Capitalism and Social Revolution*. London: Verso.

Federici, Silvia 1995. "The God that Never Failed: The Origins and Crises of Western Civilization." In Federici 1995.

Federici, Silvia (ed.) 1995. *Enduring Western Civilization: The Construction of the Concept of Western Civilization and Its "Others."* Westport, CT: Praeger.

Federici, Silvia 1998. "Reproduction and Feminist Struggle in the New International Division of Labor." In Dalla Costa and Dalla Costa 1998.

Linebaugh, Peter and Ramirez, Bruno 1992. "Crisis in the Auto Sector." In *Midnight Notes* 1992. Originally published in *Zerowork* I in 1975.

Foucault, Michel 1981. *The History of Sexuality. Volume One: An Introduction*. Harmondsworth: Penguin.

Guattari, Felix and Negri, Antonio 1990. *Communists Like Us*. New York: Semiotext(e).

Hardt, Michael and Negri, Antonio 1994. *The Labor of Dionysius: A Critique of the State Form*. Minneapolis: University of Minnesota Press.

Marx, Karl 1909. *Capital* III. Chicago: Charles Kerr.

Marx, Karl 1977. *Selected Writings*. McLellan, David (ed.). Oxford: Oxford University Press.

Midnight Notes Collective 1992. *Midnight Oil: Work. Energy, War, 1973–1992*. New York: Autonomedia.

Moore, Thomas S. 1996. *The Disposable Work Force: Worker Displacement and Employment Instability in America*. Hawthorne, NY: Aldine de Gruyter.

Negri, Antonio 1989. *The Politics of Subversion*. London: Polity Press.

Negri, Antonio 1991. *Marx Beyond Marx: Lessons on the Grundrisse*. New York: Autonomedia.

New York Times 1996. *The Downsizing of America.* New York: Random House.
Rifkin, Jeremy 1995. *The End of Work: The Decline of the Global Labor Force and the Dawn of the Post-Market Era.* New York: G.P. Putnam's Sons.
Special Task Force to the Secretary of Health, Education, and Welfare 1993. *Work in America.* Cambridge, Mass.: The MIT Press.

7

DEVELOPMENT AND REPRODUCTION

Mariarosa Dalla Costa[1]

I. ZAPATA AND THE WORKERS

Zapata's determined gaze and slightly stooped shoulders in the well-loved photograph paraded by the "cobas" of Alfa Romeo auto workers at Arese in Milan was one of the striking journalistic images of 1994,[2] creating a bridge in real time between the Mexican revolt in January and the struggles of Europe's industrial workers and unemployed. A bridge was thrown through space and historical time to link struggles against continued 'primitive' expropriation of the land to those against the post-Fordist expropriation of labour that brings with it the progressive dismantlement of the public system of social rights and guarantees. The "primitive" expropriation of the land that began five centuries ago with the enclosures in England and which has been continued, and is still continuing,[3] in the more recent forms of colonisation and exploitation in the Third World, is now linked even photographically to the contemporary forms of expropriation and poverty creation in the advanced capitalist countries.

How to build and impose on expropriated men and women the discipline of the wage labour system (with the unwaged labour it presupposes) was the problem posed five centuries ago in initiating the process of capitalist accumulation. It is still the problem today for the continuation of this mode of production and its combined strategies of development and underdevelopment. The creation of mass poverty and scarcity together with the imposition of terror and violence, as well as the large-scale relaunching of slavery, were the basic instruments used to resolve the problem in this system's first phase.

The expropriation of free producers of all the means of production as well as the individual and collective resources and rights that contributed to guaranteeing survival was subjected to a well-known analysis by Marx in his section on primitive accumulation (in *Capital,* Vol. I, Part 8, 1976) to which we refer you for the enclosures and all the other measures that accompanied them, notably the bloody legislation against the expropriated, the forcing down of wages by act of parliament and the ban on workers' associations. Laws for the compulsory extension of the working day, another fundamental aspect of the period, from the middle of the Fourteenth to the end of the Seventeenth century are dealt with in *Capital*, Part Three, Chapter 10, where the subject is the working day.[4]

Concerning the expropriation of the land, Marx observed: "The advance made by the eighteenth century shows itself in this, that the *law itself* now becomes the *instrument by which the people's land is stolen*, although the big farmers made use of their little independent methods as well. The Parliamentary form of the robbery is that of 'Bills for Inclosure of the Commons,' in other words decrees by which the landowners grant themselves the people's land as private property, decrees of expropriation of the people" (Marx, 1976, p. 885). The "little independent methods" are explained in a footnote to the same passage, quoting from a report entitled *A Political Inquiry into the Consequences of Enclosing Waste Lands*: "The farmers forbid cottagers to keep any living creatures besides themselves and children, under the pretence that if they keep any beasts or poultry, they will steal from the farmers' barns for their support; they also say, keep the cottagers poor and you will keep them industrious, etc., but the real fact, I believe, is that the farmers may have the whole right of common to themselves" (Marx, 1976, p. 885, note 15).

This footnote gives a powerful picture of the step-by-step process of expropriation used to produce the misery and poverty essential in establishing the discipline of wage labour. But just as powerful an image is given to us by the isolation of people from all living beings that has characterised and still characterises the human condition in capitalist development. The human being, isolated not only with respect to his/her own species, but also with respect to nature — that "other" treated increasingly as a commodified thing.

Deprivation and isolation: they are in fact the two great accusations, the two great terrains of rebellion symbolised by the poster of Zapata whose watchword was *Tierra y Libertad*. The reappropriation of land was seen by the Zapatistas in 1911 as a fundamental question because it opened up the possibility of reappropriating a collective life free of misery. For even then the reappropriation of the land was pregnant with a multitude of meanings: as the reappropriation of a territory where one could express a different sense of life, of action, of social relations and of work; as a place where one could imagine and build a different future. From this viewpoint, Zapata's nine-year revolutionary epic is one of the great suppressed memories of official Mexican history.

Today's explosion of the *zapatista* rebellion shows how real the problem of the reappropriation of land remains, but also how much it has been magnified by the complex of issues raised by movements in the North and South over the question of land. "Land," here, does not only refer to a means of subsistence — though this would already be an excellent reason for a movement of reappropriation, since many economies based on a non-capitalist relationship with the land have guaranteed the possibility of life for millennia to a large proportion of people for whom capitalist development has offered only hunger and extinction. It refers also to land as the earth, a public space to be enjoyed without frontier; the earth as an ecosystem to be preserved because it is the source of life and, hence, of beauty and continual discovery; the earth as a material reality of which we are part, to be reaffirmed in contrast to the exaltation (especially by male intellectuals) of virtual reality.

But, returning to Marx (*Capital*, Vol.I, 1976, Part 8), the creation of misery starts and proceeds from the *fixing of a price for the land* as well as the land's expropriation. Pricing the land is in fact the solution used for colonies where the aspirant capitalist is unable to find a sufficient number of waged workers. When the settlers arrive at their destination, they find a "free" land where they can settle and work independently. "We have seen that the *expropriation of the mass of the people from the soil forms the basis of the capitalist mode of production*. The essence of a free *colony*, on the contrary, consists in this, that the bulk of the soil is still public property, every settler on it can therefore turn part of it into his private property and his individual means of production, without preventing later settlers from performing the same operation. This is the secret both of the prosperity of the colonies and of their cancerous affliction — their resistance to the *establishment of capital*" (1976, p. 934). In this context, we can leave to one side the obvious criticism that the "public" land freely settled by the settlers belonged, in fact, to the natives. Marx continues: "There (in the colonies) the capitalist regime constantly comes up against the obstacle presented by the producer who, as owner of his own conditions of labour, employs that labour to enrich himself instead of the capitalist. The *contradiction between these two diametrically opposed economic systems has its practical manifestation here in the struggle between them*. Where the capitalist has behind him the power of the mother country, he tries to use force to clear out of the way the *modes of production and appropriation which rest on the personal labour of the independent producer*" (1976, p. 931). Wakefield, the economist Marx quotes in this context, proclaims aloud the *antagonism between the two modes of production*: "To this end he demonstrates that the development of the social productivity of labour, cooperation, division of labour, application of machinery on a large scale, and so on, are impossible without the expropriation of the workers and the corresponding *transformation of their means of production into capital*" (1976, p. 932).

Wakefield's theory of colonisation tries to solve the problem of ensuring an adequate supply of labour for the capitalist's needs by what he calls "systematic colonisation," which as Marx notes England tried to enforce for a time by Act of Parliament. Of Wakefield's theory, Marx adds (1976, p. 938): "If men were willing to turn the whole of the land from public into private property at one blow, this would certainly destroy the root of the evil, but it would also destroy — the *colony*. The trick is to kill two birds with one stone. Let the government set *an artificial price on the virgin soil, a price independent of the law of supply and demand*, a price that compels the immigrant to work for a long time for wages before he can earn enough money to buy land and turn himself into an independent farmer. The *fund* resulting from the sale of land at a price relatively *prohibitory* for the wage-labourers, this *fund of money* extorted from the *wages of labour* by a violation of the sacred law of supply and demand, is to be applied by the government in proportion to its growth, to the importation of paupers from Europe into the colonies, so as to keep the *wage-labour market* full for the capitalists." Marx also pointed out that the *land price laid down by the state* must be "sufficient," which quoting from Wakefield (1833, vol. II, p. 192) he explains means that "it must be high enough 'to prevent the labourers from becoming independent landowners until others had followed to take their place'."

The reference to the setting of a price on the virgin soil is more than just a reminder of a past problem and its analysis in Marx's *Capital*. Today, putting a price to the land and expropriation by illegality, pseudo-legality and violence are issues on the agenda throughout those parts of the Third World where capitalist expansion is currently seeking to break economies and societies based on a different relationship with the land; types of economy which have guaranteed subsistence from time immemorial and which, by the same token, resist wage-labour's discipline and the isolation, hunger and death that usually accompany its imposition. Silvia Federici (1993) and George Caffentzis (1993) underline the cruciality of fixing a price on the land in the policies directed to "develop" the African continent. In their studies of Sub-Saharan Africa and Nigeria in particular, they insist on the importance of this measure from the point of view of the World Bank, the International Monetary Fund and other investors, but they also stress how this procedure became a terrain of struggle and resistance for the population.

Obviously, today, there are many other policies and measures creating hunger and poverty, from the lowering of the export price of agricultural products, which ruins Third World farmers, to those policies that, internationally, have characterised the period of the so-called debt crisis. But this has been dealt with in a recent collection of papers (Dalla Costa M. and Dalla Costa G.F., eds., 1993) and is dealt with extensively by the Midnight Notes Collective (1992).

In this article, the focus is on the two *major operations* of expropriating the land and putting a price on it, since, even though they are usually ignored, they remain as fundamental today for making a profit out of the Third World as they were at the dawn of capitalism in Europe. In fact, the current development strategy of the capitalist mode of production based on the "informatic revolution" continues to imply a strategy of underdevelopment that presupposes these operations which create hunger and poverty in order continually to refound and re-stratify the global working class.

Obviously, the continual imposition of wage-labour discipline at the world level does not imply that all those who are expropriated are destined to become wage-labourers. Today as five centuries ago, this will be the fate of only a small part of the population: those who can will find employment in the sweat shops of the Third World or the countries they emigrate to. The others will be faced solely by the prospect of death by hunger, which may explain the tenacity of resistance and the toughness of the struggles. And, returning to the poster in Milan, it explains the revolt in Chiapas. The *price* of capitalist development understood as a whole, in its facets as development and underdevelopment, is *unsustainable* because it consists of *death*. As I have argued elsewhere (Dalla Costa M., 1995), a central assumption must be that, *from the human viewpoint, capitalist development has always been unsustainable* since it has assumed from the start, and continues to assume, extermination and hunger for an increasingly large part of humanity. The fact that it is founded on a class relationship and must continually refound this relationship at a global level, in conflict with the power that the class of waged and non-waged men and women build through struggle and resistance, only makes its *original unsustainability* more ample and more lethal in time.

The operations that produce hunger, poverty and death, have accompanied the continuous and progressive expropriation of the land, and its rendering as commodity/capital have obviously been redefined in ideological and technological terms over time. "Food policies" brought into effect during the present century, officially in order to solve or mitigate the problem of insufficient nutrition have always been closely linked to "reforms" of the relationship with the land. The outcome has been better nutrition for the few, insufficient nutrition or hunger for the many, and above all a powerful tool for social control by breaking up those organisations that parts of the world's population, in very many areas of the globe, had created in order to achieve better nutrition and a better level of life as a whole.

The "social reforms" characteristic of these policies have always been linked to new divisions and a new hierarchy between the waged and the unwaged as well as within these two groups. Harry Cleaver's essay (1977) remains fundamental for its analysis and the globality of its information as well as for its reports on numerous struggles and the sort of policies adopted to fight them. We agree in full with the assumption that food crises are fundamentally produced by capitalism's political economy. As this author informs us, it is interesting to note how experiments carried out by the Rockefeller Foundation in China in the 1920s and 1930s provided clear evidence of the stabilising effect of better food supplies coupled with some land reform measures on peasant unrest. In the 1950s, politicians were still talking about an Asian rice policy as a tool for halting peasant revolt in many parts of that continent. Later, the issue officially became a humanitarian one.

The Green Revolution, on the other hand, was put into effect in the 1960s in both East and West on the basis of a technological leap in the mechanical, chemical and biological inputs in agricultural policy. The aim was to apply Keynesian principles to agriculture, in other words, achieving wage increases linked to an increase in productivity. But, as Cleaver argues, the whole history of this technological breakthrough in agriculture was linked to the de-composition of the class power of the waged and the unwaged, the continual creation of new divisions and hierarchies, and the progressive expulsion of workers having different forms of relationship with agriculture.

Agricultural technology became more and more subject to criticism and analysis by feminist scholars, being so closely linked to large land holdings, which meant the expropriation and the expulsion from that land of unwaged workers, who were managing to make a living from it, and of waged agricultural workers, displaced by the continual technological change. Important in this connection is the work of Vandana Shiva (1989), whose approach is not Marxist, and who uses the category of the female principle against male reductionist science. An outstanding physicist, Vandana Shiva abandoned India's nuclear programme because she felt that the "reaction of nuclear systems with living systems" was being kept secret from the people. In her well-known work, *Staying Alive: Women, Ecology and Development* (1989), she illustrates the systematic and grave loss of resources for health and subsistence through the reduction in biodiversity imposed in India by the agricultural policies of recent decades; the dependence and poverty created by the imposition of new laboratory hybrids; the drought and human and environmental disasters created by dams and their irrationality by comparison with earlier forms of water management. The history of the enclosure, expropriation and commercialisation not only of the land, but also of its plants, animals, and waters is revived in Shiva's analysis, which is centred on the events of these last decades. There are other important works belonging to the ecofeminist current, first of all the work of Maria Mies

(1986 and, with Shiva, 1993), to mention only the most famous ones. In contrast Mary Mellor's book (1992), while it has many points of contact with the above cited studies, is rather concerned to define a "feminist green socialism."

I share much of the critique advanced in this blossoming of feminist studies on the relationship between human beings and nature and on the North-South relationship. Here, there is not enough space to compare our positions more extensively. But one point I can make is that some ecofeminist scholars look primarily at the forms of struggle and resistance in the Third World, while seeing the First World primarily as an area of excessive consumption whence the assertion of the need for a reduction of production and consumption. For myself and the circuit of scholars I have worked with since the early 1970s, we affirm that besides looking at the Third World struggles, just as much importance should be given to advanced capitalist areas, not only as a source of consumption, but also as a place of labour, hence our stress on the importance of the struggles of waged and unwaged that occur there and their relationship with struggles in other areas. We also see a need to analyse consumption in a more articulated way. By definition, consumption by workers, obviously including housewives, has in fact never been high and, today, is falling dramatically. But these are simply a few hints in a debate that will develop further.

Let us now return to our discourse. Vandana Shiva (1989) says of water and drought:

> The drying up of India, like that of Africa, is a man-made rather than a natural disaster. The issue of water, and water scarcity has been the most dominant one in the 1980s as far as struggles for survival in the subcontinent are concerned. The manufacture of drought and desertification is an outcome of reductionist knowledge and models of development which violate cycles of life in rivers, in the soil, in mountains. Rivers are drying up because their catchments have been mined, de-forested or over-cultivated to generate revenue and profits. Groundwater is drying up because it has been over-exploited to feed cash crops. Village after village is being robbed of its lifeline, its sources of drinking water, and the number of villages facing water famine is in direct proportion to the number of 'schemes' implemented by government agencies to 'develop' water (p. 179).

"Commercial exploitation of forests, over-exploitation of ground water for commercial agriculture and inappropriate afforestation are the major reasons identified for the water crisis" (p. 181).

Time and again, Vandana Shiva points out, famous British engineers who learned water management from indigenous techniques in India, commented on the "sophisticated engineering sense, built on an ecological sense, that provided the foundation for irrigation in India." Major Arthur Cotton, credited as the "founder" of modern irrigation programmes, wrote in 1874:

> There are multitudes of old native works in various parts of India...These are noble works, and show both boldness and engineering talent. They have stood for hundreds of years...When I first arrived in India, the contempt with which the natives justifiably spoke of us on account of this neglect of material improvements was very striking; they used to say we were a kind of civilised savages, wonderfully expert about fighting, but so inferior to their great men that we would not even keep in repair the works they had constructed, much less even imitate them in extending the system (p. 187).

The East India Company, as Vandana Shiva adds, took control of the Kaveri delta in 1799, but was unable to check the rising river bed. Company officials struggled for a quarter century; finally, using indigenous technology, Cotton was able to solve the problem by renovating the Grand Anicut. He wrote later: "It was from them (the native Indians) we learnt how to secure a foundation in loose sand of unmeasured depth...The Madras river irrigations executed by our engineers have been from the first the greatest financial success of any engineering works in the world, solely because we learnt from them...With this lesson about foundations, we built bridges, weirs, aqueducts and every kind of hydraulic work...We are thus deeply indebted to the native engineers."

But the lesson has obviously been overwhelmed by the full flood of the capitalist science of development/profit, what Vandana Shiva calls "maldevelopment."[5] British engineers in the 1700s and 1800s recognised that indigenous technology and knowledge tended to preserve water resources and make them available for the local people. Today, capitalist water-management projects cause drought and deny survival to entire populations. One woman from Maharashtra State in India sings against the dam she has to help build so that crops such as sugar cane can be irrigated while women and children die of thirst (Shiva, 1989):

> As I build this dam
> I bury my life.
> The dawn breaks
> There is no flour in the grinding stone.

I collect yesterday's husk for today's meal
The sun rises
And my spirit sinks.
Hiding my baby under a basket
And hiding my tears
I go to build the dam
The dam is ready
It feeds their sugar cane fields
Making the crop lush and juicy.
But I walk miles through forests
In search of a drop of drinking water
I water the vegetation with drops of my sweat
As dry leaves fall and fill my parched yard.

A response to this mad "enclosure" of water became more and more a problem on the agenda of political networks that monitor and struggle against projects of this kind. The immediate future will show the effects of this effort. An exemplary case is the Bangladesh flood control plan (Del Genio, 1994), presented by the World Bank in London in December 1989. Even though it was claimed to differ from previous projects because of its low environmental impact, other estimates of its effects were so dramatic that an international coalition of organisations, opposed to the World Bank's approach to the canalisation of rivers, was created in Strasbourg in May 1993.

Considering solely the immediate human impact, the building of the Narmada dam in India was expected to require the evacuation of 500,000 inhabitants and aroused strong opposition from the "tribals" and the organisations supporting them. The Bangladesh Flood Action Plan (FAP), coordinated by the World Bank on behalf of the Group of Seven, would require the forced transfer of 5–8 million persons in a territory whose population density is ten times that of India.

Del Genio's article illustrates the reasons cited to justify the plan — on the one hand, mystified assumptions and, on the other, the lethal techniques of the Green Revolution. This plan insists on the need to "propagate modern mechanised agriculture capable of coping with the food crisis" so as to increase the cultivation of modern high-yield varieties of rice which, in its turn, requires a large and regular quantity of water and a system of flood control and irrigation to make it available.

The drawbacks of the high-yield varieties include a dependence on the market and the laboratories, since they are unable to reproduce, and imply the reduction of the genetic diversity of local seeds. Awareness of the drawbacks is growing in the world, and rural workers' grass-roots organisations are putting up increasing resistance to these agricultural improvements that are supposed to be more appropriate for satisfying their nutritional needs. As regards flood control, some of the year's regular flooding bring nutrients which ensures the soil's fertility and top up the water-table as they expand across the plain. Other, purely destructive floods need to be controlled through works different from the planned ones if the aim is to be achieved without destroying the environment, including the humans in it. In this connection, it is worth remembering the level of sophistication achieved in biodiversity by long-term cooperation between humans and nature; among the hundreds of local rice varieties developed in response to the demands of territory and climate, a sub-variety called Aman is capable of growing over 15cm in only 24 hours if the level of the water rises.

As for transferring 5–8 million persons by coercion, this is in itself inconceivable from my point of view, since to uproot a population is like cutting a tree's roots, but in this case a forest's. The first and obvious question that comes to mind is: where and how does one suppose that the peasants are to find the money needed to pay the costs of agricultural modernisation (machinery, fertilisers, etc.)? The answer is identical and repeated thousands of times over in the history of the Green Revolution: only the big proprietors and the big enterprises can sustain the costs. And the others? Work has begun in the meantime...

The peasants and many working with them in international networks are organising resistance and opposition. The Asswan dam and what the consequent loss of the soil nutrients has meant for all the peasants who lived off the soil, plus all the other grave consequences it has precipitated, necessarily comes to mind. For example, the flooding of part of Nubia and, with it, the burial of major relics of that civilisation and the abandonment of the land by those who lived there. But this is only one case in the midst of the many one could cite. When I was in Egypt in 1989, there was talk of a project to turn the Red Sea into a lake. I hope that the growth of the ecological movement, the movements of the native populations and others will have relegated this project to the nightmares of a past era.

Returning to Vandana Shiva, the same observations, made by her and many other scholars today about the dams and other Western water management projects in the Third World, can equally be applied to the technologies that are imposed on Third World agriculture, in livestock raising, and in the destruction of forests to cultivate export crops: the destruction of biodiversity, ecological equilibriums, and the life-cycles that guaranteed subsistence. In short the production of profit for the big companies, the denial of survival for the population.

Even though her cultural and theoretical approach is far from Marxian, when Vandana Shiva interprets the logic of the continual enclosure of segments of nature and the effects it has, she finds no difficulty in concluding that the foundations of capitalist accumulation are the science and practice of the culture of death. Her merit is also to have contributed to bringing to international attention struggles and movements otherwise ignored or neglected. Our argument here is that the Chipko movement in which women organise to stay in the forest even at night, embracing the trees to prevent the logging companies from cutting them down, should be placed on the same level as all the other struggles against various forms of expropriation and attack against individual and collective rights in different parts of the world — not only the right to survival, or better to live, but the right to the self-determination of one's own future.

The economic and life system of the Indian "tribals"[6] who created the Chipko movement which forms the focus of Vandana Shiva's studies and practical activity, is based on a combination of agriculture, livestock raising and the use/conservation of the forest. The forest has a central and many-sided role in the whole system. The forests bear "soil, water and pure air," sing the Chipko women (Shiva, 1989, p. 77), and they play an important nutritional role. Whatever crisis may hit crops or livestock, say the Chipko women, the children will never suffer hunger if there is a forest near. Thus embracing the trees to stop them from being felled is like occupying the land to prevent it being expropriated, or struggling in defence of jobs or a wage or a guaranteed income when survival depends solely on money. This is what we see if we want to spotlight how the different parts of the working social body struggle contemporaneously and in different forms against the same system that exploits and besieges them in different ways.

This is important for getting a real idea of how an opposition to this form of development is growing increasingly at the world level and is refusing to pay its price while seeking other paths for a different future. But I think that the struggles of the Chipko women and all the other movements for the maintenance and defence of an age-old experience and knowledge in humankind's relationship with nature are all the more vital for us. In fact, *the political debate in the "advanced" areas empowering the voice of those who refuse to pay the price of this development must necessarily be an ecological debate, too.*

The other great denunciations advanced by Vandana Shiva, whose work I have considered here, even if briefly, because it is representative of an entire school of feminist studies developed by women in the world's various Souths, concern the genetic manipulation of living species. To the tampering of the nutritional resources of entire communities is added the genetic manipulation of the species. This topic that has attracted extensive attention in recent years from the various circuits of women scholars and activists.

"With engineering entering the life sciences, the renewability of life as a self-reproducing system comes to an end. Life must be engineered now, not reproduced. A new commodity set is created as inputs, and a new commodity is created as output. Life itself is the new commodity..." (Shiva, 1989, p. 91). "The market and the factory define the "improvement" sought through the new bio-technologies... Nature's integrity and diversity and people's needs are thus simultaneously violated" (Shiva, 1989, p. 92).

This biotechnological trend is matched by the determination to patent and "bank" the genetic heritage of the living species. This was denounced by women meeting in Miami in preparation for the Rio conference (*Women's Action Agenda 21*, 1991), but their opposition is widely shared. After patenting cotton, the agro-industrial corporations now want to do the same for rice and soy, two of the fundamental foodstuffs for many parts of the world's population. Increasingly food, already difficult to obtain because of the combination of expropriation of land, technological innovations in farming methods, and the ratio between prices and wages (when there are any), is manipulated, placed beyond access, privatised, monopolised, patented, "banked." A new enclosure. *No Entry: Food!*

In this parabola of technological conquest over nature, expropriation reaches its acme: human beings are expropriated, the living species are expropriated, the earth's own reproductive powers are expropriated to transform them into capital. This mode of production pretends to capitalise the generation and reproduction of life. What a long way capitalism has come since it, indifferent to life, was satisfied with nothing more than appropriating an excessive number of working hours[7] or when it simply pretended to transform all life into work and, to that end, whilst ignoring the contradiction of exploiting free and slave labour at the same time, on the one hand, drained dry the life of the free workers, and on the other, enchained masses of slaves!

But, the amplitude of the various rebellions and struggles in the world in rejection of this type of development is matched by the increasingly massive, lethal and monstrous structures and forms of domination. Considering only the most recent past, from the Gulf War on, the increasingly warlike character of this development has undeniably produced an escalation of war that removes any residual doubts over whether or not it is founded on the science and practice of death. Referring to the wars in the Gulf, ex-Yugoslavia, Somalia, and Rwanda-Burundi finds its limit in the fact that these are simply the wars that have received the most coverage in the media in the last three or four years. We certainly have no intention of underestimating the number of wars that have been pursued in the world without them ever entering the limelight.

If anything, the escalation of war in recent years has confirmed the emptiness of what the major powers said on disarmament. *Rather, war has become increasingly the instrument par excellence for disciplining the working social body at the global level,* through annihilation, terror, division, deportation, and the lowering of living conditions and life expectations. In the end, humans, when they are not *massacred directly, are increasingly "enclosed"* in refugee camps and the more or less concealed concentration camps of war situations.

But, at the same time, the *other face of war* as a *form of development* has been revealed ever more clearly, through the growing monstrosity of the enterprises its macabre laboratory generates. War is recognised as having always been a great laboratory, but since the voracity of capitalist technology has begun to pursue life in the attempt to steal and capitalise its secrets, death has been discovered increasingly as a terrain for profit. In this case, too, the shift is from the "primitive" indifference to the death of masses of individuals expropriated of their means of production and sustenance, to the identification of death, dead bodies or bodies destined in a nonchalant way to die in order to experiment with new technologies or commercialise body parts in trafficking in organs. Besides the traditional markets of arms, post-war reconstructions and techno-industrial experimentation on which our "peace economy" rests, war today offers above all the biggest mass of living/dying guinea-pigs on whom to test, on a mass scale, the new technologies applied to acquire more knowledge of the body and how to operate on it. Here too, it is clear how the part of guinea-pigs has been played above all by the people of the "non-advanced" nations, even if a similar role has recently been emerging for citizens for the most part from the weaker social sectors of the great powers, dispatched to war or used without knowing it in "peace-time."

But war continues to offer new and horrifying terrains on which to reap profits. Trafficking in children,[8] for example. How many for pornography?[9] How many for trafficking in organs?[10] How many for slavery[11] and the traffic in war cripples?[12] How many for prostitution? How many to be sold for adoption by childless couples? Trafficking in adult males and females also goes on, for all the reasons mentioned above, apart from the last.

It is rather strange that, in discussing sustainable development, there is usually no mention of the *unsustainability* for humankind and the environment of the *form* that development has increasingly taken, namely *war.*

The poster with the image of Zapata from which we set out was sent to us from the Chiapas revolt and the war and truce that resulted from it. Carried as a banner by the workers in Milan, it gave voice to the two great expropriations, from the land and from work. At the same time, it poses with all the force expressed in the struggles throughout the world carried on by those who have been expropriated, the question of what is the contemporary relationship between waged and unwaged labour in this development? In the Third World as in the First, what future is there for unwaged labour?

II. Zapata and the Women

It may be a provocation, then, but not excessive to think that, in relaunching the increasingly dramatic question of the relationship between these two great sectors of labour, the poster of Zapata also relaunches the feminist question that emerged and stimulated the women's movement in the early 1970s, i.e., the problem of the unwaged labour of reproducing labour-power. The woman is in fact the unwaged labourer par excellence and experiences in this development a *doubly unsustainable contradiction* (Dalla Costa, M., 1995; Dalla Costa, G.F., 1989). On the one hand, her condition, which has been created by capitalist development, is unsustainable in its typical form in the "advanced areas" as an *unwaged worker*, in that she is responsible for reproducing the labour-power in a *wage economy* (Dalla Costa, M., James S. 1972). On the other, her situation has become increasingly unsustainable as an unwaged worker in an unwaged *subsistence economy* where the expansion of capitalist relations progressively deprives her of the means to fulfil her tasks of reproduction for herself and the community. The contradiction and, with it, the unsustainability of the woman's condition, cannot be solved within capitalism, which forms its basis. To be solved, it requires a totally different conception and organisation of development, but by the same token, women's struggles around their condition amplify the demands of other unwaged social subjects from whose labour this capitalist development continually accumulates value.

Numerous studies of which I mention only some (Michel, Agbessi Dos Santos, Fatoumata Diarra, 1981, Michel 1988; Boserup, 1982; Shiva, 1989) have illustrated how the continual realisation of capitalist projects in the Third World's rural areas, apart from expropriating the land, makes it increasingly difficult for women to gain access to the fundamental means for the production of subsistence: from wood for fuel to water for the home and forage for the animals. Now, hours or days have to be spent in fetching things that were previously fairly close. These resources too have been swallowed up by enclosure/appropriation/commoditisation/capitalisation.

Feminist authors (Mies, 1992) have noted the paradox that precisely for their activities related to acquiring these resources, as well as for having too many children, rural women are blamed for doing harm to the environment. Supposedly, they destroy the forests if they go there in search of wood; they pollute and use up the water sources if they go to fetch water; they use up the earth's resources if they have too many children. It is a typical case of blaming the victims. At the same time, their working and living conditions and, with them, the entire community's life are continually undermined by the debt policies imposed on the Third World countries by the major financial agencies, policies of which the expropriation/privatisation of the land is only one, but fundamental aspect (Dalla Costa M. and Dalla Costa G.F., eds., 1993).

When it is not directly the expropriation and expulsion of the rural communities without anything in exchange, the capitalist proposal which presents itself as an "alternative in the direction of development," not only removes an assured subsistence and replaces it with an uncertain wage, but deepens the gap between the male and the female conditions. Significant once more in this respect is the example (Shiva, 1989) also quoted by Mies (1992) of the Chipko women, who oppose the felling of trees in the Himalayan forests for commercial purposes. As in many cases, the men were less determined in their opposition because they were tempted by the prospect of the jobs they would be given in the saw-mills.

But one of the women's biggest doubts was of how much of that money/wage they would have received — and therefore they opposed the creation of a hierarchy based on having or not having a wage. Above all, they posed the problem of what would happen to all of them when the forest, the basis of their subsistence, had been swallowed up by the saw-mills which, since there would be no more wood to cut, would be closed. The women said clearly that they needed no jobs from the government or private businessmen as long as they kept their land and their forests.

In Shiva (1989), there are many other episodes of this kind. After five centuries in which the scene has been repeated, the lesson has been learned in the most remote corners of the earth. There is a great determination not to put one's life in the hands of the planners of development and underdevelopment,[13] to stop others from plunging whole populations into total uncertainty, which if it does not lead to hunger today will do so tomorrow; a determination to avoid being turned into beggars or refugee camp inmates.

Ecofeminist practices and positions linking nature, women, production and consumption in a single approach are often criticised for "romanticism" by male scholars. One might wonder, if only to raise the most simple question, what value do these scholars attribute to the right to survival of those communities — and there are many of them — whose subsistence and life system are guaranteed precisely by these practices with nature, while the "development proposal" almost always presupposes the sacrifice of the vast majority of the individuals that constitute these communities. Significantly, Mary Mellor (1993) observes in this connection: "I see all this as something that men should prove to be unfounded, rather than as something that the feminists must justify."

As emerges with increasing clarity from the "charters" that the various native peoples have elaborated with the growth in their movement in the last two decades, together with the right to land, i.e., the right to survival/life, there is an increasingly strong demand for the right to identity, dignity, one's own history, the maintenance of the complex of collective and individual rights belonging to one's own culture, and the right to work out one's own future starting from one's own premises. Obviously, there is no intention here of skating over the contradictions within the existing customs and systems of rules, above all those between men and women. If anything, what needs immediate clarification is that capitalist development, far from offering solutions to these problems, most often aggravates them. Politicians promoting development often try to suppress the women's movements which deal with these questions. Nevertheless these movements have grown and are creating an increasing number of new networks, that struggle, denounce and demonstrate great determination in changing a state of affairs clearly causing women harm.

In this connection, the Chiapas revolt is exemplary since it brought to international attention how the Maya women defined their rights with respect to men and society at large. Work and grass-roots debate in the communities produced a code of rights.[14] Some rights concern the economic/social/civil plane such as the right to work, a fair wage, education, basic health care, the necessary food for oneself and one's children, the right to decide autonomously the number of children one wants to have and to rear, to choose one's companion without being required to marry him, to suffer no violence inside or outside the family. Others rights concern the political plane, such as the right to take part in managing the community, to hold office if democratically elected, to hold positions of responsibility in the Zapatista National Liberation Army (ZNLA). The code repeats that women must have all the rights and obligations deriving from revolutionary laws and regulations. As far as one knows, women participate fully in the highest offices in the ZNLA.

I was in Chiapas in the winter of 1992–93, and in San Cristobal I was struck by the numerous posters put up by women's right activists alongside the posters in praise of the guerrilla heroes. A year later, the great work achieved by these women took on new substance and became known throughout the world, disclosing how much progress had also been made within the community as regards the relationship between the sexes. It is significant that an important point in the code of women's rights, corresponding to the centrality this issue has won in the Western world, concerns violence. I would only like to add that, during my visit the year before the revolt, I was told in San Cristobal that the Maya women were no longer willing to go to the hospital to have their children for fear of being raped — evidently not by the natives.

It seems clear that these women's elaboration of their rights was not in a mythical and improbable phase, "after" the movement that was tending towards a radical change in the state of things, but formed an integral part of it. The same thing happened in the elaboration of their rights by the Eritrean women during the Eritrean liberation war, and it is repeated in an increasing number of situations. These facts show how it is invalid to presume a lack of movement in "non-advanced" societies because of a supposed observance of tradition.

I would also like to underscore that the relationship with nature[15] is for all of us a fundamental contribution made by the movements of the native women, yet there is great resistance to it being recognised as such by the more or less historical elaborations of urban male intellectuals that try to find a way to change the world.

As the Chipko movement shows — and numerous other examples are available from various parts of the planet — the leaders are increasingly *women* in *movements that link* the maintenance, recovery and reinterpretation of a relationship with nature with a defence of economic subsistence and the conservation of the identity and historical-cultural dignity of the communities/civilisations to which they belong.

In that their primary task is the reproduction of individuals in wage and non-wage economies, that they are *unwaged subjects par excellence* in both types of economy, and that their possibilities of autonomous subsistence are progressively undermined in the proceeding of capitalist development, women emerge as the *privileged interpreters* for the unwaged of the earth's future. Today, their critique and their theoretical contribution form a necessary moment in the formulation of a different development, or in any case in reasserting the right not to be developed against one's own will and interest.

On the other hand, international networking between women scholars and feminists and women active in various ways and various organisations concerned with the women's condition, development and the native peoples have brought an awareness of these experiences of resistance and struggle, stimulating a closer attention from Italian women researchers as well. Several of them, internationally well known, are cited by Cicolella (1993). One is the *Green Belt Movement* founded in 1977 by the Kenyan woman, Wangari Maathai, who starting from the idea of "afforestation for life," has created green belts around cities in twelve African countries where forests had been replaced by open spaces. Then, the *Gabriela* group in the Philippines began its activities by safeguarding a mountain precious for its natural equilibrium and fragile ecosystem. The *Third World Network* founded by a Chinese jurist Yoke Ling Chee aims at forms of development that truly respond to people's real needs and, above all, are independent of aid from the industrial nations. The *Mapuche movement* in Chile led by Alicia Nahelcheo, who was already active against the Pinochet dictatorship, is today struggling against development projects, the expropriation of land to build power stations, and the cropping for commercial purposes of the *araucaria* tree whose fruit is a basic foodstuff.

But these are only some examples. The forms in which many men and women increasingly try to guarantee their survival and at the same time fight against this type of development can be expected to multiply and emerge further. At the same time, there is a growth of increasingly ample initiatives at the international level[16] designed to contest the legitimacy of, and to halt the directives handed down by, the World Bank and the IMF. At the economic and social level, these are the key points in the management of contemporary development, as well as being the major factors in the poverty and degradation of the "developing" countries.

At the same time, the strong critique and forms of struggle and resistance against this form of development have produced an increasingly vast and articulated debate in which various interpretations of what a different development should be have emerged. Recent summaries (Gisfredi, 1993) of the major positions stress that the centre of it all is the importance of the environment and the cultural context for elaborating an autochthonous project.[17] They also stress the significance of typologies which, in order to identify the fundamental goals of development, list as categories of basic needs, rather than those concerning pure physical survival, those concerning security, welfare, identity and liberty as against violence, material poverty, alienation and repression which typify the way in which governments rule "developing" countries.

Central to approaches such as these remains self-reliance, by mobilising all the human and material resources available locally and by using technologies compatible with the cultural and natural environment. But many other positions could be listed. To the range of approaches of basic needs, self-reliance, and eco-development summarised by the Dag Hammerskjold Foundation (1975), others have been added because, since then, the debate has developed significantly. The most questioned idea is "sustainable development" as it emerged from the famous world commission for the environment and development chaired by Gro Harlem Bruntland. The main criticism is that it confuses development with economic growth and confuses "everyone's future" with the future of the First World.

In any case, it is clear that any definition of a new approach concerning development makes sense only in so far as it grasps the demands of those men and women who have so far paid the heavier price for development while gaining the least from it. And in so far as it recognises the *right to reject development* in all situations where people refuse it, as it often happens in many different parts of the world. In this sense, Gustavo Esteva said as long as ago as 1985, in his comments on a conference of the Society for International Development: "My people are tired of development, they just want to live" (quoted in Shiva, 1989, p. 13).

Granted the perspective described above, a look at the contribution made by movements wanting to approach the question of development from a feminist viewpoint shows, in my view, that the most interesting approaches include eco-feminism, because its starting-point is respect for human life and the life of living beings in general. Since it appreciates rather than devalues the knowledge and experience of the women in the native communities, eco-feminism also relaunches an approach including the relationship with nature as the source of life and subsistence, the right to self-determination, and the rejection of the capitalist model of development.

I think that a cross between this feminism with the more radically anti-capitalist feminism which has analysed the condition and struggles of women and the unwaged in this model of development, posing the question of what perspectives, may make a very interesting contribution. In this context, I would like to recall, if only briefly, Vandana Shiva's conception of nature which forms the foundation of her discourse.

She uses a reading of Indian cosmology in which Nature (*Prakrti*) is an expression of Sakti, the female principle, dynamic primordial energy, the source of abundance. Joining up with the male principle (*Purusa*), Prakrti creates the world. Women, like any other natural being, have in themselves the female principle and, therefore, this capacity for creation and the maintenance of life. According to Vandana Shiva, the reductionist vision typical of Western science continually expels the female principle from the management of life, by the same token interrupting the life cycles and therefore the regeneration of life itself, creating destruction in its place. The reductionist vision with respect to nature and women ensures that they are reduced to means for the production of commodities and labour-power.

> Patriarchal categories which understand destruction as 'production' and regeneration of life as 'passivity' have generated a crisis for survival. Passivity, an assumed category of the 'nature' of nature and women, denies the activity of nature and life. Fragmentation and uniformity as assumed categories of progress and development destroy the living forces which arise from relationships within the 'web of life' and the diversity in the elements and patterns of these relationships (Shiva, 1989, p. 3).

> Feminism as ecology, and ecology as the revival of Prakrti, the source of all life, become the decentred powers of political and economic transformation and restructuring (Shiva, 1989, p. 7).

> Contemporary women's ecological struggles are new attempts to establish that steadiness and stability are not stagnation, and balance with nature's essential ecological processes is not technological backwardness but technological sophistication (Shiva, 1989, p. 36).

Discourse on land, on water, on nature return to us, brought by the native movements and the knowledge of the native women, almost the most precious of the riches that ancient civilisations hid and the secrets that they never revealed.

But with the land, there also returns to us the immense potential of a human diversity that has been able to resist and preserve its heritage of civilisation. And now it gives forceful expression to the will to work its own future autonomously. The need for a relationship with the earth, for liberty, time, and an escape from the modalities of labour and the relations that the capitalist model of development wants to continue imposing also represents a long thirst for expropriated Western humanity. Perhaps, precisely the fact of having being heard so widely in the world, as happened with the Chiapas revolt, gave many their first perception of the real feasibility of a different life project which they had resignedly relegated to a dream of impossible flight — a world in which life would not be all work, nor nature an enclosed park in which relationships are prepackaged, pre-codified and fragmented into atoms. It is evidently because these deep and dolorous chords in expropriated Western humanity were touched that the whole body of working society vibrated together with the Chiapas rebels, beating a thousand keys, transmitting, declaring, sustaining. A thousand arms and a thousand legs were moved, and a thousand voices heard.

A hinterland of communication and liaison has been constructed with the growth of the native movements across the Americas and in the world in the last twenty years. Relations, analyses and information have been more closely and more strongly interwoven, especially recently in opposition to the North America Free Trade Agreement. And all this has become the primary issue for communication between and action by different sectors in the working social body. Workers and non-natives, ecological movement militants, women's groups, and human rights activists have been attracted into a complex support action, helping and monitoring from various parts of the world. But it is clear that, in the last analysis, what has moved all these individuals, groups and associations is the fact of having recognised their own demands in the demands of the native movement; of having seen their own liberation in the native movement's chances of liberation.

The natives have brought the keys, and they are on the table. They can open other doors to enter the Third Millennium. Outside, the full flood has arrived, breaking the concrete banks and drowning the latest high-yield variety of rice...The peasants take out their hundreds of seed varieties, while Aman pushes its stems out above the water.

TRANSLATED BY JULIAN BEES

ENDNOTES

1 This paper was first presented at XIII Conference of Sociology, Bielefeld, Germany, July 18–23, 1994, Section 8: Women, Development and Housework [RC 02: Economy and Society].

2 See *Il Manifesto,* February 8, 1994, but many other newspapers have used the same image. The demonstrating workers were led by the Cobas, the rank-and-file committees created to negotiate on working conditions without passing through the traditional trade-union organisations. The movement now has a national liaison committee.

3 This is the subject of the third part of Midnight Notes Collective (1992).

4 In lectures on *Capital* that I used to give each year, I devoted some comments in 1970 to the fundamental question of the two opposite tendencies characterising the history of the working day. They were published later (Dalla Costa M., 1978). In my university courses, I continue illustrating fundamental parts of *Capital,* especially those concerning primitive accumulation. Social processes in this period which were neglected by Marx in *Capital,* e.g., the great witch-hunt, have been analysed by the feminist scholars I worked with (Fortunati, 1981; Federici and Fortunati, 1984), with the aim of clarifying the capitalist sexual division of labour and the construction of proletarian women's individuality in capitalism. It is no coincidence that this period is considered as crucial by various currents of feminist thought.

5 The term *maledevelopment* and its French equivalent *maledevelopement* were originally coined with a biological meaning in mind, rather than a political one. The reference to the idea that the wrong type of development is male-related is clear.

6 India has about 50 million members of scheduled tribes, recognised as such by the Indian constitution because of their particularly disadvantaged situation. They are found most extensively in the states of Orissa, Andhra Pradesh and Maryana and are at most marginally integrated into the market economy. Their specific social organisation tends to be non-masculinist and generally speaking egalitarian, with a particularly "sustainable" approach to natural

resources. But they are considered as without caste, being despised and exploited as cheap or unpaid labour when they are forced to join agricultural or industrial units. Consequently, "tribals" referring to India, has not only a social-anthropological meaning but a juridical one as well.

7 "Capital asks no questions about the length of life of labour-power"... "What experience generally shows to the capitalist is a constant excess of population"... *"Aprés moi le déluge!* is the watchword of every capitalist and every capitalist nation" (Marx, 1976, Vol. 1, p. 376, 380, 381).

8 In *La Repubblica,* May 17 1994, an article entitled, "Where have the Sarajevo children disappeared to?" Wondering where the children evacuated from the Bosnian war have finished up, the article quoted spine-chilling figures from the humanitarian organisations on trafficking in children and reported the case of one 14-year-old girl who finished with Italian go-betweens and managed to escape. Also mentioned is an article in the weekly, *Focus.*

9 The number of children used in the pornography market was referred to with increasing frequency in the media in 1993–94.

10 International criminal networks and international crime organisations with legal terminals are growing around the clandestine traffic in organs. In this connection, Italian public television has broadcast a series of programs on this issue. One of the most interesting, on March 5, 1994 on the second state channel, provided evidence of a relationship between these organisations and legal terminals in France.

11 It seems worthwhile putting this question given the incredible figures on slavery published recently: 200 million in the world, according to *The Economist* of January 6, 1990. 100 million are reportedly children, according to *Il Manifesto,* 8.06.1994, which quotes a UNICEF report published on the previous day.

12 *Il Mattino di Padova,* 4.06.1994, publishes an article on the discovery and denunciation of an organisation that was exploiting women and war cripples from ex-Yugoslavia. In Mestre, Venice, the former were sent to work as prostitutes, the latter as beggars.

13 An effective description of the creation of underdevelopment through development is provided for the Port Harcourt area in Nigeria by Silvia Federici (1992).

14 Since January 1, 1994, the day on which the revolt broke out, there has been a continual flow of information in the press. In Italy, *Il Manifesto* and other newspapers have reported the major demands of the rebels and with them the women of Chiapas as they were advanced. Two articles with very precise information on the demands as a whole and the details of the mobilisation are Gomez (1994) and Cleaver (1994). A brief synthesis of the

women's rights in the Women's Revolutionary Law is to be found in Coppo and Pisani (eds. 1994). I must add that a book not to be missed for knowing the condition of the Maya women, this time in Guatemala, is Burgos (1991), *My Name is Rigoberta Menchù*.

15 In any case, it needs recognising that, in recent years, even if with different approaches, there has been a growth — internationally — in attempts to link different theoretical elaborations with approaches whose focus is the relationship with nature, particularly Marxism and ecology. The magazine best-known for publishing this type of debate is *Capitalismo. Natura. Socialismo,* which is explicitly located in an eco-Marxist perspective. In this same magazine, a particularly ample discussion has developed around the O'Connor (1992) theses on the "second contradiction of capitalism." On the relationship between the left and ecological issues, see, among others, Ricoveri (1994).

16 Just to mention two initiatives: the Circle of the Peoples coordinated a wide range of associations in a counter-summit against the Naples summit of the Group of Seven on July 8–10, 1994, and, in the first ten days of October of the same year, a large number of associations is taking part in a counter-summit in Madrid for the annual assemblies of the World Bank and the IMF, this year marking the fiftieth anniversary of Bretton Woods and the international financial organisations created there. For the same event, the League for the Rights of the Peoples is working at the Lelio Basso Foundation in Rome to produce a statement on the Bretton Woods institutions to be published when the summit is on in Madrid, just as was done for the IMF general assembly in Berlin in 1988.

17 *Autochthon,* from the Greek [ott pl.] are of the earliest known inhabitants of any country and/or an animal or plant that is native to a region, Greek meaning "from the earth itself" [Editor's Note].

References

Boserup, E. (1982), *Il lavoro delle donne. La divisione sessuale del lavoro nello sviluppo economico,* Torino, Rosenberg & Sellier.

Burgos, E. (1991), *Mi chiamo Rigoberta Menchù,* Giunti, Firenze.

Caffentzis, G. (1993), *La crisi del debito in Africa e sue principali implicazioni per la riproduzione sociale,* in Dalla Costa M. & Dalla Costa G.F.(eds.) 1995.

Cleaver, H. (1977), "Food, Famine and the International Crisis" in *Zerowork, Political Materials* 2, Fall.

Cleaver, H. (1994), "The Chiapas Uprising and the Future of Class Struggle," in *Common Sense,* No. 15.

Coppo, p. & Pisani, L. (eds.) (1994), *Armi indiane. Rivoluzione e profezie maya nel Chiapas messicano*. Edizioni Colibri, Milano.

Cicolella, O. (1993), "Le donne tra crisi ambientale e sviluppo insostenibile," in *Res*, No. 7..

Dalla Costa, G.F. (1989, 1990 2 ed.), *La riproduzione nel sottosviluppo. Lavoro delle donne, famiglia e Stato nel Venezuela degli anni "70*, Angeli, Milano.

Dalla Costa, M. and James S. (1972), *The power of women and the subversion of the community*, Falling Wall Press, Bristol.

Dalla Costa, M. (1978), *Note su La giomata lavorativa in Marx, appunti da un lettorato del Capitale*, Cleup, Padova.

Dalla Costa, M. and Dalla Costa, G.F. (eds.) (1993), *Donne e politiche del debito. Condizione e lavoro femminile nella crisi del debito internazionale*, Angeli, Milano (English translation: *Paying the Price: Women and the Politics of International Economic Strategy*, Zed Books, London, 1995).

Dalla Costa, M. (1995), *Capitalism and Reproduction*, in Bonefeld et al (eds.) (1995), *Open Marxism*, Vol. III, Pluto Press, London.

Dag Hammarskjold Foundation (1975), *What now? Another Development*, Uppsala.

Del Genio, G. (1994), "La Banca inonda il Bangladesh," in *Capitalismo, Natura, Socialismo*, No. 1.

The Economist, 6.01.1990.

Federici, S. Fortunati, L. (1984), *Il Grande Calibano. Storia del corpo sociale ribelle nella prima fase del capitale*, Angeli, Milano.

Federici, S. (1992), *Developing and Underdeveloping in Nigeria*, in Midnight Notes Collective.

Federici, S. (1993), *Crisi economica e politica demografica nell'Africa sub-sahariana. Il caso della Nigeria*, in Dalla Costa M. and Dalla Costa G.F. (eds.) 1993.

Fortunati, L. (1981), *L'arcano della riproduzione. Casalinghe, prostitute, operai e capitale*, Marsilio, Padova (English translation: *The Arcane of Reproduction*, Autonomedia, New York, 1995).

Gisfredi, p. (1993), "Teorie dello sviluppo ed egemonia del Nord," in *Res*, No. 7.

Gomez, Luis E. (1994), "La nuova cavalcata di Emiliano Zapata" in *Riff Raff*, March.

Il Manifesto, 8.02.1994.

Il Manifesto, 8.06.1994.

Il Mattino di Padova, 4.06.1994.

La Repubblica, 17.05.1994.

Marx, K., (1976), *Capital. A Critique of Political Economy*. Volume One, London, Penguin.

Mellor, M. (1992), *Breaking the Boundaries. Towards a Feminist Green Socialism*, Virago Press, London.

Mellor, M. (1993), "Ecofemminismo e ecosocialismo. Dilemmi di essenzialismo e materialismo," in *Capitalismo. Natura. Socialismo*, March.

Michel, A., Fatoumata Diarra A., Agbessi Dos Santos H., (1981), *Femmes et multinationales*, Karthala, Paris.

Michel, A. (1988), "Femmes et development en Amerique Latine et aux Caraibes," in *Recherches feministes*, vol. 1, No. 2.

Michel, A. (1993), *Donne africane, sviluppo e rapporto Nord-Sud*, in Dalla Costa M. and Dalla Costa G.F.(eds.) 1993.

Midnight Notes Collective (1992), *Midnight Oil. Work, Energy, War 1973-1992*, Midnight Notes, Autonomedia, New York, N.Y.

Mies, M. (1986), *Patriarchy and Accumulation on a World Scale. Women in the International Division of Labor*, Zed Books, London.

Mies, M. (1992), *Global is in the Local*, report at the Mount Saint Vincent University, Halifax, Canada, 25.02.

Mies, M. and Shiva V. (1993), *Ecofeminism*, Zed Books, London.

O'Connor J., (1992), "La seconda contraddizione del capitalismo: cause e conseguenze," in *Capitalismo, Natura, Socialismo*, No. 6.

Ricoveri, G. (1994), "La sinistra fa fatica ad ambientarsi," in *Capitalismo, Natura, Socialismo*, No. 1.

Shiva, V. (1989), *Staying Alive: Women, Ecology and Survival in India*, Zed Books, London.

Wakefield, E. Gibbon, (1833), *England and America. A Comparison of the Social and Political State of both Nations*, London.

Women's Action Agenda 21 (1991), in *World Women's Congress for a Healthy Planet*, Official Report, 8–12 November, Miami, Florida, USA, United Nations, New York.

8
Capital Moves
John Holloway

I

Capital moves.

This statement is so obvious that there seems no point in writing it down, much less making it the title of an article. And yet...

In the obvious, commonsense interpretation, the sentence "capital moves" means that capital, normally in one place, gets up and moves. British capital is exported and invested in Africa. Japanese capital moves out of Japan and flows into the United States. Capital is understood as basically fixed, but capable of motion. Capital is attached but capable of detaching itself. Thus: Volkswagen has a car factory in Puebla, but we know that it (a German company) can close its factory and move its capital elsewhere. Capital is capable of movement, but it is defined first in terms of its attachment: attachment to a company (Volkswagen), attachment to a branch of industry (the automobile industry) and attachment to a place (Puebla, Germany). Thus, following the same reasoning, capital invested in the textile industry is often referred to as "textile capital," capital in the banking industry as "banking capital," capital owned by Mexicans as Mexican capital, by US Americans as "US capital," etc. Although the capacity of capital to move, or to detach itself from a particular owner or branch of economic activity, is never put in question, the movement of capital is secondary to its initial definition in terms of attachment or fixity.

In all of these examples, capital is treated as a thing, a thing that can be owned, a thing that is normally attached to a particular place, company, branch of economic activity; a thing that can be moved, from place to place, from company to company, from one branch of activity to another.

All this is obvious; but once we try to deprive capital of its thinghood, it becomes less obvious. Why should we try to deprive capital of its thinghood, why is the obvious analysis of the movement of capital not sufficient? The answer is surely that it depends on what we want to understand. If we want to understand capitalist development as economists, or if we want to understand the way in which capital dominates society, then there is probably no reason to question the thinghood of capital. If, however, we want to understand not the domination and reproduction of capital, but the vulnerability and rupture of capital, if, in other words, we want to understand not how capitalism works, but how it can be destroyed, then we need to open up the thinghood of capital, to break its facticity, to break the illusion/reality of "capital is, capital moves, capital rules, that's the way things are." That is why Marx devoted much of his life to showing that capital is not a thing but a social relation, a social relation which exists in the fetishised form of a thing.

If capital is understood as a social relation rather than a thing, then what does it mean to say that "capital moves"? The answer is now less obvious. How can a social relation move? The movement of capital can only refer to the mobility, or perhaps better, flux or fluidity of the social relations of capitalism, the relations of power under capitalism.

What the mobility of capitalist social relations means can best be seen by contrasting capitalism and feudalism. Under feudalism, the relation of domination/exploitation was a direct and personal one. A serf was bound to a particular lord, a lord was limited to exploiting the serf that he had inherited or could otherwise subjugate. Both sides of the class divide were bound: the serf was tied to a particular lord, the lord was tied to a particular group of serfs. If the lord was cruel, the serf could not decide to go and work for another lord. If the serfs were lazy, unskilled or otherwise insubordinate, the lord could discipline them but could not simply fire them. The relationship between serf and lord had a fixed, immobile character. The resulting discontent was expressed in revolt by the serfs on the one hand, and the pursuit by the lords of other ways of expanding power and wealth on the other. The personal, immobilised relationship of feudal bondage proved inadequate as a form of containing and exploiting the power of labour. Serfs fled to the towns, the feudal lords accepted the monetisation of the relation of domination.

The transition from feudalism to capitalism was thus a movement of liberation on both sides of the class divide. Both sides fled from the other: the serfs from the lords (as stressed by liberal theory), but also the lords from the serfs, through the movement of their monetised wealth. Both sides fled from a relation of domination which had proved inadequate (as a form of domination). Both sides fled to freedom.

Flight to freedom is thus central to the transition from feudalism to capitalism. But there are, of course, two different and opposing senses of freedom here (a dualism which is the central contradiction of liberal theory). The flight of the serfs was a flight from subordination to the lord, the flight of those who, for one reason or another, no longer accepted the old subordination, the flight of the insubordinate. The flight of the lords was just the opposite: when they converted their wealth into money, it was a flight away from the inadequacy of subordination, a flight from insubordination. On the one side, the flight of insubordination, on the other side the flight from insubordination: viewed from either side, it was the insubordination of labour that was the driving force of the new mobility of the class relation, the mutual flight of serf and lord.

The flight of-and-from the insubordination of labour, the mutual repulsion of the two classes did not, of course, dissolve the class relation. For both serf and lord, the flight to freedom came up against the reassertion of the bond of mutual dependence. The freed serfs found that they were not free to stop work: since they did not control the means of production, they were forced to work for a master, someone who did control the means of production. To survive, they had to subordinate themselves again. However, this was not a return to the old relation: they were no longer tied to one particular master, but were free to move, to leave one master and go and work for another. The transition from feudalism to capitalism involved the de-personalisation, dis-articulation or liquefaction of the relations of domination. The relation of exploitation was not abolished by the dissolution of the ties of personal bondage, but it underwent a fundamental change in form. The particular bond that tied the serf to one particular master was dissolved and replaced by a mobile, fluid, disarticulated relation of subordination to the capitalist class. The flight of insubordination entered into the very definition of the new class relation.

On the other side of society, the erstwhile lords who converted their wealth into money[1] found too that freedom was not all they had imagined, for they were still dependent on exploitation, and therefore on the subordination of the exploited, the workers, their former serfs. Flight from insubordination is no solution for the lords turned capitalists, for the expansion of their wealth depends on the subordination of labour. They are free to abandon the exploitation of any particular group of workers (for whatever reason — laziness, inappropriate skills, whatever) and either establish direct links of exploitation with another group of workers or simply participate through non-productive investment in the global exploitation of labour. Whatever form their particular relation to the exploitation of labour takes, the expansion of their wealth can be no more than a part of the total expansion of wealth produced by the workers. Whatever the form of class domination, labour remains the sole constitutive power. Just as in the case of their former serfs, flight to freedom turns out to be flight to a new form of dependence. Just as the serfs' flight from subordination leads them back to a new form of subordination, the lords' flight from insubordination leads them back to the need to confront that insubordination. The relation, however, has changed, for capital's flight from insubordination is central to its struggle to impose subordination (as, for example, in the ever-present threat of factory closure or bankruptcy). The flight from insubordination has become a defining feature of the new class relation.

The insubordination of labour is thus the axis on which the definition of capital as capital turns. It is the mutual repulsion of the two classes, the flight of and from subordination, that distinguishes capitalism from previous class societies, that gives a peculiar form to the exploitation on which capitalism, like any class society, is based. The restlessness of insubordination enters into the class relation as the movement of labour and capital.

From the start, the new class relation, the relation between capitalists and workers (or, more accurately, since it is a depersonalised relation, between capital and labour) is a relation of mutual flight and dependence: flight of-and-from insubordination, dependence on re-subordination. Capital, by its very definition, flees from insubordinate labour in pursuit of more and more wealth, but can never escape from its dependence upon the subordination of labour. Labour, from the start, flees from capital in pursuit of autonomy, ease, humanity, but can escape from its dependence upon and subordination to capital only by destroying it, by destroying the private appropriation of the products of labour. The relation between capital and labour is thus one of mutual flight and dependence, but it is not symmetrical: labour can escape, capital can not. Capital is dependent on labour in a way in which labour is not dependent upon capital. Capital, without labour, ceases to exist: labour, without capital, becomes practical creativity, creative practice, humanity.

Both serf (now worker) and lord (now capitalist) remain as antagonistic poles of a relation of exploitation-and-struggle, but that relation is no longer the same. The insubordination of labour has entered into the definition of the relation as restlessness, mobility, liquidity, flux, fluidity, constant flight.[2] The class relation has become a constantly shifting, inherently mobile relation, in which all capitalists participate in the exploitation of all workers and all workers contribute to the reproduction of capital, and in which the patterns of exploitation are constantly changing, kaleidoscopically.

With the transition to capitalism, the dialectic of insubordination/subordination of labour which is the core of any class relation acquires a distinctive form — the antagonistic movement of the flight of-and-from the insubordination of labour to its renewed subordination. This peculiar historical form is expressed in the familiar categories of political economy: in the existence of labour power and of the products of labour as commodities, in the existence of value, money, capital. All of these categories express the indirect or disarticulated character of capitalist domination. All express the fact that, in capitalism, the subordination of labour is mediated through "freedom," the "freedom" of the worker and the "freedom" of the capitalist, or, in other words, the flight of-and-from insubordination. These categories therefore, often taken to embody the law-bound character of capitalist development, are in reality expressions of the defining presence of the insubordination of labour within the capitalist relation of subordination, that is to say, of the chaos at the heart of capitalist domination.

This seems upside-down. We are not accustomed to thinking of value, for example, in these terms. It is more common to think of value as establishing order (the "law" of value), as being the social bond in a society of autonomous producers. This is correct, but only if the emphasis is on the critique of liberal theory. The notion of the "law of value" says in effect: "despite appearances, the apparently autonomous producers of capitalist society are bound together by a social connection which operates behind their backs — the law of value." If, on the other hand, we start not from the appearance of fragmented individualism, but from the historical irruption of the insubordination of labour into the very definition of subordination, then value expresses the fragmentation wreaked by this irruption upon the more cohesive domination of feudalism. The law of value is simultaneously the lawlessness of value, the loss of any social control over society's development, the presence of insubordination within subordination. Value is the political-economic expression of the presence of the contradictory flight of-and-from insubordination within subordination itself, just as freedom is its categorial expression in liberal political theory.

Value, in the form of money, is the new liquidity of the class relation. It is the fact that social relations come to be mediated through money that makes it possible for the worker to shift from one master to another, in each case selling his or her labour power in return for a certain amount of money. It is the fact that the lord-turned-capitalist can convert his wealth into money that makes it possible for him to abandon one group of workers and move to another, and to participate in the global exploitation of labour.

Money not only liquefies the class relation, it also transforms or fetishises it. It gives its own colouring to the class relation, making the relation of subordination/insubordination appear as a relation between rich and poor, a relation of inequality between those with money and those without money rather than one of antagonism. It transforms the antagonistic relation of subordination/insubordination into a relation of money, transforms the flight of-and-from insubordination which defines the capital-labour relation into the movement of money, the movement of capital (understood as an economic phenomenon).

The banal sentence with which the article began, "capital moves" has now acquired a new meaning. It is a tautology. "Capital moves" does not mean that capital is normally still and now moves, but that capital is inherently mobile.

II

Capital, then, is a social relation. But it is not simply a social relation of exploitation/subordination/domination. It is a social relation of subordination (etc) in which the defining presence of insubordination is expressed as unceasing restlessness, mobility. This mobility is both functional (as capital is metamorphosed from productive to commodity to money capital, and back) and spatial (as capital flows/flees through the world in search of a means of self-expansion). The peculiar unity of subordination/insubordination which is the differentia specifica of capital is expressed in the unity of production and circulation, or in the unity of the different functional forms of the circuit of capital (discussed by Marx in Volume II of *Capital*), or in the unity of the world as the locus of class struggle (the relation between insubordination and subordination). Conversely, the dislocations of production and circulation, or of the different functional forms of the circuit of capital, or of the spatial flow/flight of capital can only be understood as the disunity-in-unity of insubordination and subordination, the constant inability of capital to contain labour, the constant overflowing of insubordination from subordination, the existence of labour against-and-in (and not just in-and-against) capital.

All this is just a rephrasing and development of what has been a central theme of the Conference of Socialist Economists (CSE) debate over the last twenty years and more — the critique of structuralism, of the separation of structure and struggle. The separation of structure and struggle is, crucially, the separation of subordination and insubordination. It has been common in the mainstream (and overwhelmingly structuralist-functionalist) Marxist tradition to think of capitalism as a basically self-reproducing system of domination/subordination ocasionally disrupted by class struggle (the open manifestation of insubordination), as a self-reproducing economic system, in which the exploited workers are victims, except on the rare occasions on which they engage in open struggle. In this tradition, the labour theory of value is understood as the mechanism which explains the self-reproduction of capitalism: there is a peculiar blindness to the most obvious feature of the labour theory of value — namely, that it is a theory of capital's dependence upon labour, a theory therefore of class struggle. It is in the face of this stultifying, and above all disempowering tradition of mainstream Marxism that it is important to reassert the unity of insubordination and subordination, the corrosive, destructive, chaotic presence of insubordination within the definition of subordination itself.

The way in which the notion of the mobility of capital is used in many current discussions of the "internationalisation" or "globalisation" of capital is one example of the separation of subordination and insubordination, structure and struggle. In such discussions, labour, if it features at all, appears only as a victim of the latest developments in capitalist domination. The actors in such discussions bear such names as US capital, Japanese capital, European capital, finance capital. Debate centres on the extension of the power of "finance capital," on the "inter-imperialist" rivalry between "US capital," "Japanese capital" etc. All of these categories rest on the notion of capital as a thing, a notion that excludes the attempt to understand the restlessness of capital in terms of the power of insubordination. If current changes in capitalism are understood in terms of the conflict between different national capitals,[3] then class struggle, if it appears at all, can only appear as a reaction to the changing form of domination, not as the substance of the change. Everything is turned upside down: the "globalisation" of capital (which I take to refer to the enormous increase in the speed and scale of the flow/flight of capital in money form) is seen as an increase in the power of capital, rather than as a manifestation of capital's incapacity to subordinate labour.[4] The violence of money is a measure of capital's flight from the insubordination of labour, and of the desperation of its need to re-subordinate.[5]

Marxism is a theory, not of the power of capital, but of the power of insubordinate labour.

Acknowledgements

My thanks, for their critical comments on the original draft of this paper, to Ana Esther Ceceña, Andrés Barreda and their seminar group in the UNAM, to Chris Arthur, Werner Bonefeld and to Paul Stewart as co-ordinating editor for *Capital and Class*.

Endnotes

1 In a helpful comment on the first draft of this paper, Chris Arthur remarks that "the paper virtually asserts that the capitalist is the lord with a new hat on. This is historical revisionism on a grand scale with no evidence given. He should at least concede to the usual story that a new mode of produc-

tion meant, at a minimum, the decline of the lord and the rise of the capitalist, at a maximum a sharp class struggle between the two, punctuated by episodes like the French Revolution." Chris is quite right: the argument of the paper is indeed that the capitalist is the lord transformed. What matters is not the question of personal continuity (present in some cases, absent in others), but the understanding of the transition from feudalism to capitalism as a change in the form of the relation of domination and struggle or, better, of the inbsubordination/ subordination of labour. If class is understood not as a group of people ("capitalists," "lords"), but as the pole of an antagonistic relation of domination (cf. Marx; Gunn 1987), then it is clearly wrong to see the struggle between capitalists and lords as a struggle between two classes. It was, rather, a struggle over the form of class domination, the form of subordinating insubordinate labour. For "historical revisionism" on a genuinely grand scale, see Gerstenberger (1990), who supports a similar argument against the orthodoxy of Marxist historians with an impressive wealth of evidence (in English see Gerstenberger 1992; Holloway 1993; Gerstenberger 1993).

2 It follows that class antagonism cannot be understood simply in terms of production, but in terms of the unity of circulation and production. The view of production as primary and circulation as secondary tends to lead to a view of the working class as the class of people subordinated in production, that is, the industrial proletariat. If capital is understood in terms of the unity of production and circulation (or the unity of the flight of-and-from insubordination and the imposition of subordination), then a different picture emerges. Capital lives by subordinating and then fleeing from the insubordination which is inseparable from subordination: it sucks in labour to exploit and then spits it out as unpalatable. The antagonism which defines the working class is not one of subordination, but of subordination/insubordination: the working class are not subordinate victims but the insubordinate from whom capital flees and whom it must subordinate. If capital lives by sucking and spitting, the working class can accurately be defined as the unpalatable sucked and spat of the earth.

3 The only possible justification for the notion of a "national capital" would be in terms of the understanding of the national state as an obstacle to the equalisation of the global rate of profit (cf. *Capital,* Vol III, ch. 10), but I have not seen such an argument made, and in any case it would have to be made in class terms. I see absolutely no reason for granting a priori validity to such questionable categories as "Britain," the "United States," "Mexico," "Ireland," "Japan," etc. Like any other category of social theory, these must be criticised.

4 For a development of some of the arguments in this paper, see Bonefeld (1993), Bonefeld and Holloway (1995).

5 This paper seems to float in the air, but it does not. Behind it lies the question of the relation between the zapatista uprising in Chiapas and the devaluation of the Mexican peso, together with the upheavals on the world financial markets (the "systemic risk" to world capitalism) which the uprising has provoked. The understanding of the flight of capital from Mexico as an economic phenomenon quite distinct from the revolt in Chiapas (the separation of structure from struggle) makes it more difficult to establish the unity between the two forms of discontent, in the countryside of Chiapas and in the world's biggest city. The connecting fuse, once lit, could change the world. [Editor's Note: The issues raised here have been developed further in Holloway, John and Peláez, Eloina (eds.) *Zapatista,* Pluto, London, 1998; and Holloway, John "Zapata in Wallstreet," in Bonefeld, Werner and Psychopedis, Kosmas (eds.) *The Politics of Change,* Palgrave, London/New York.

REFERENCES

Bonefeld W. (1993), *The Recomposition of the British State,* Dartmouth, Aldershot.

Bonefeld W. and Holloway J. (1995), *Global Capital, the National State and the Politics of Money,* Macmillan, London.

Gerstenberger H. (1990), *Die subjektlose Gewalt: Theorie der Entstehung bürgerlicher Staatsgewalt,* Verlag Westfälisches Dampfboot, Münster.

Gerstenberger H. (1992), "The Bourgeois State Form Revisited," in W. Bonefeld, R.Gunn, K. Psychopedis (eds), *Open Marxism,* Vol. 1, Pluto Press, London.

Gerstenberger H. (1993), "History and 'Open Marxism': A reply to John Holloway," *Common Sense* no. 14.

Gunn R. (1987), "Notes on Class," *Common Sense* no. 2.

Holloway J. (1993), "History and Open Marxism," *Common Sense* no. 12.

Marx K., *Capital.*

9

The Politics of Change: Ideology and Critique[1]

Werner Bonefeld

Introduction

"Globalisation" has been established as one of the organising terms of contemporary political economic inquiry. The term indicates that the idea of a cohesive and sequestrated national economy and domestic society no longer holds and that everyday life has become dependent on global forces. It is claimed that "globalisation" represents a qualitative transformation of capitalism in that there has developed a new relationship of interdependence beyond the national states. Marx's view of the world market and his notion that the need for a constantly expanding market for its products, chases the bourgeosie over the whole surface of the globe, appears to be emphasised by the "theory" of globalisation. Yet, it is not. For the globalisationists, there is no such thing as the bourgeoisie; instead "capitalism" is viewed as some sort of economic mechanisms that imposes itself "objectively" upon the social individual, rendering both the working class and the bourgeoisie helpless. Both are seen to be subjected to the risk that globalisation appears to present (Beck, 1992).

The defining elements of "globalisation" can be briefly summarised as follows:

1) The increasing importance and significance of the financial structure and the global creation of credit, leading to the dominance of finance over production: Harvey (1989) has argued that finance capital has become an independent force in the world and Strange (1988; 1991) has emphasised the increased structural power exercised by the financial superstructure;

2) The growing importance of the "knowledge structure" (Strange 1988; Giddens 1990): Knowledge is said to have become an important factor of production;

3) The increase in the rapidity of redundancy of given technologies and the increase in the transnationalisation of technology: Here the emphasise is on knowledge-based industries, inreasing reliance on technological innovation, and increased risk of technological backwardness (Giddens, 1991);

4) The rise of global oligopolies in the form of multinational corporations: Corporations are said to have no choice but to go global and multinational corporations, together with, and importantly, transnational banks have become most influencial powers beyond the national states and their national economies (Strange, 1991);

5) The globalisation of production, knowledge, and finance is said to have led, on the one hand, to the retreat of the national state as a regulative power (Strange, 1996), and the globalisation of political power in the form of a plural authority structure associated with the UN, G7 (now G8), on the other (Held, 1995). The erosion of the national state is seen to lead to (a) greater global institutional and regulatory uncertainty and (b) to the hollowing out of national liberal-democratic systems of government. The national state is seen to have transformed into a "competition state" (Cerny, 1990, 1997).

The so-called new freedom of capital form national regulative control and democratic accontability is said to lead to increased ecological destruction, social fragmentation, and poverty. For Hirsch (1995), globalisation is based on a class society without classes. Globalisation is thus seen to render workers powerless to withstand economic dictates (Anderson, 1992, p. 366). In short, globalisation is viewed as the realisation of capital's impossible dream: to accumulate uncontested.

The above has summarised the main planks of globalisation orthodoxy.[2] The next two sections supply a critical commentary on "globalisation': Where does the global begin, where does it end?

What is Globalisation?

Over the last decade there has been an increase in the trafficking of women and children, prostitution and slavery. New markets have emerged in human organs and babies, reducing the proprietors of labour power not only to an exploitable resource but, also, to a resource to be operated on and sold, with babies being produced for export (see Federici, 1997). Some have suggested that we witness the re-emergence of conditions of primitive accumulation.[3] These works show clearly that Marx's insight according to which "a great deal of capital, which appears today in the United States without any certificate of birth, was yesterday, in England, the capitalised blood of children" (Marx, 1983, p. 707), still remains a powerful judgement of contemporary conditions.

Looking at the above summary of globalisation orthodoxy, this human suffering is neither acknowledged nor of any concern for the theory of "globalisation." For its proponents globalisation has somewhat "solved" the crisis of capitalist accumulation, has left behind "social relations between people" and thereby undermined resistance to capitalist exploitation. All that can be done is to recoup the loss of liberal-democratic values by transnationalising democratic government. Only in this way, it is suggested, will the rights of the citizens of the world be secured.

What is to be understood by the notion of the liberal democracy and its state? Liberals, since Adam Smith, have argued that the state is indispensable for the provision of the exact administration of justice to resolve clashes of interest, the protection of property; the military defence of its territory; for the povision of public goods that are essential for, but cannot be provided by, the market; and for facilitating relations of equality and freedom, including the "encouragment" of competition and therewith of conditions of so-called market self-regulation.[4] Have these liberal "notions" of the proper role of the state been undermined by globalisation? This does not seem to be the case and, indeed, the globalisationists argue that globalisation emphasises the bourgeois state as a liberal state. What, then, do we make of the notion that the state is in "retreat"? Commentators offer the notion of the competition state as an adequate definition of the state under conditions of globalisation. What are the states competing about? Are they competing to extend, safeguard and exploit their comparative advantages? Is the competition state something like this: The state should not and cannot try to protect jobs by interfering with investments because, "if a capital is not allowed to get the greatest net revenue that the use of machinery will afford here, it will be carried abroad" leading to "serious discouragement to the demand for labour" (Ricardo, [1821] 1995, p. 39). Does the competition state vindicate Ricardo's insight? For the globalisationists, liberal democracy has been undermined at the same time as which the "national state" has been transformed into a neo-liberal state.[5] The so-called retreat of the state, then, stands for its reasseration as a liberal state! As Cerny (1996) sees it, only "residual functions" are left to it, particularly in those areas geared to ensuring capital competitiveness. Before globalisation, then, the state is seen to have behaved in a socially responsible way, regulating the economy in terms of a comprehensive social democratic project where everyone is supposed to have been a member of the "one-national boat" (see Hirsch, 1997). Against the background of the struggles of the 1950s and 1960s, this globalisationist retrospective of the past is not only absurd. It is also dishonest (see Bonefeld, 1999).

With Marx, we might wish to argue that "theoretical mysteries ... find their rational solution in human practice and in the comprehension of this practice" (Marx, 1975, p. 5). For globalisation orthodoxy, however, such a view is deeply problematic, if not "anachronistic" (Hirsch, 1995). For them, it is not human social practice but the developmental logic of the economy that is decisive — social practice is merely conceived as a derivative, that is something that can be derived from the "objective" logic of economic mechanisms. The notion of the globalisation of capital not only assumes that "capital" has suddenly left its domestic skin by globalising its existence but also that "capital" has globalised "itself," has suddenly become more based on scientific expertise, has discovered monetary accumulation beyond and dissociated from productive accumulation, has expanded into a borderless world. In short, for the globalisationists, capital appears to have suddenly, since the late 1980s, discovered the world market! Where was "capital" before? What does it mean to say that "capital" has "de-nationalised" itself? Was capital constituted nationally, was it a national capital, in the past?

Globalisation orthodoxy posits the capital relation as a relation of capital to itself rather than as a social relation of production. In other words, the conceptualisation of capitalist development is based on the competitive relationship between capital and capital — a self-relation. The social constitution of this relation cannot be determined: The answer to the question what is "capital" is already presupposed: capital is capital and vice versa. As shown by Gunn (1991), this refinement amounts to an infinite regress of meta-theories, seeking to discover the practical meaning of invisible principles. The eternal quest of political economy (and of those seeking to supply a blue-print of a new faced capitalism) to discover the practical meaning of invisible (as well as inevitable) principles ends up as an irrational exercise because what needs to be understood is presupposed as something beyond reason.

The attempt to find "truth" in the "invisible" has always been the character of traditional theory, that is, of a theory which resists an understanding of our social world as a world made by humans and dependent upon human social practice — however perverted or enlightened this practice might be (see Horkheimer, 1992).

In short, analytical approaches to "globalisation" fail to conceptualise the fundamental relationship between labour and capital. This relationship remains untheorised and is replaced by a tautological understanding of capital as a self-relation. In this view, labour is merely seen in terms of the wage relation, that is as a labouring commodity (on this: Bonefeld, 1995a). As a consequence, labour as the substance of value is excluded theoretically and class struggle obtains merely in terms of a domestic working class which is controlled by capital through the threat of moving production to areas more favourable to exploitation. The notion that capital is a thing, and not a social relation, belongs, of course, very much to the tradition of political economy. However, it is disturbing that globalisation orthodoxy appears to have forgotten its own theoretical heritage. Adam Smith at least sought to provide a scientific understanding of the constitution of the bourgeois world — however flawed his theory of value. For the globalisationists the world is accepted as a given, as a thing in-itself. In this way, globalisation orthodoxy represents a vulgarised version of classical political economy: it does not raise the question of the social constitution of value and accepts, as a consequence, that the world of capital is regulated by the invisible principle of an effective, efficient, and fair power of an almighty hand.

The proposal, then, to re-democratise the political regulation of capitalist accumulation is based on the acceptance of the invisible.[6] How might it be possible to make the invisible accountable to democratic principles? For the proponents of transnational democracy, neo-liberal market freedom is structurally unable to generate social acquiesence and they recommend "democratisation" on a transnational level as a means of faciliating relations of freedom and equality. The debate, then, on transnational democracy goes beyond the vulgar liberalism associated with Hayek in that it seeks an arrangement whereby the global relations of liberty would be institutionally embedded. It seeks, in other words, to safeguard market freedom through institutional safeguards and guarantees. Might there not be a good case to argue that the proposals for a transnational democracy seek to guarantee the rights of citizenship at the global level so that the liberating potential of hard labour can be cherished on the basis of equality, freedom and Bentham? In sum, the proponents of globalisation, on the whole, do not "like" what "capital" is doing when left unattended by regulative institutions of a liberal-democratic sort. Yet, while they might not "like" the invisible's hard hitting "hand," they are forced to accept it because the acceptance of the "market" entails that the cunning of reason amounts to no more than the invisible's own project.

State and Society

The concepts "state" and "society" are usually understood in a "domestic" sense. The "state" is perceived in terms of national sovereignty — a sovereignty which is exercised over a definite territory and in relation to a people or peoples.

The relationship between "state and society" is perceived as one of the administration of political space, including especially the people living in this space. This understanding of the relationship between state and society is "domestic" insofar as the inquiry into the constitution of the "state" is based on an understanding of the relationship between a given society and its state. As a consequence, the study of the inter-relation between states is conceived in terms of diplomacy, trade, as well as inter-national cooperation, conflict and competition.[7] In this view, the politics of national states are conceived in terms of Ricardo's notion of comparative advantage. The "globalisationists" emphasise this by arguing that the national state has transformed into a competition state and dismiss it by stressing that the national state is in retreat. Does globalisation merely mean that capital has left its national society behind, that capital has de-nationalised itself, and that, as a consequence, has "hollowed out" the national state? Is the state in retreat because its has lost its "basis," that is, its national economy and therewith its national society? What is a national society?

The notion that "society" connotes a national entity seems, at first sight, uncontroversial. We are used to speak about British society and so on. Though, what is society? In classic political economy, society was understood in terms of its economic constitution. On this, the classic statement is provided by William Robertson (1890, p. 104) who argued that "in every inquiry concerning the operation of men when united together in society, the first object of attention should be their mode of subsistence." The relationships of subsistence, of social production and reproduction, are one of capital. Would this mean that society amounts to capital? Is capital society? We know about the attempts of political economy to define "capital." Usually it is seen as a "thing" with invisible but hard-hitting qualities, which supplies structure and dynamic to "society." Here, society and capital are seen as interrelated but nevertheless as different things and the relationship between them remains obscure in so far as something "invisible" determines the constitution and dynamic of social relations. Marx's critique of political economy supplied a — negative — solution. His conception of social relations overcame the dichotomy between society and capital by arguing that "capital" is not a thing but rather a definite and contradictory social relationship of production. There is no need here to review his critique of fetishism and theory of exploitation. For our purposes, the understanding of society as a capitalist society, as a society of class antagonism subsisting through exploitation and constituted by class struggle is sufficient because it raises two interconnected issues:

1) the critique of the domestic character of capital and therewith the domestically defined antagonism of labour to capital;

2) the critique of the state as an impartial administrator of political space.

The capital relation is, by its very form, a global relation. Indeed, Marx argued that the world market constitutes the presupposistion of capitalist social reproduction "as well as its substratum" (Marx, 1973, p. 228). This would imply that the relationship between the state and society is not a relationship between the national state and its national society. Rather, the state subsists as the political form of the social relations of production only in relation to the world market. Thus, as von Braunmühl (1976, p. 276; my translation) puts it, "each national economy can only be conceptualised adequately as a specific international and, at the same tame, integral part of the world market. The nation state can only be seen in this dimension." The national state relation to "society" is fundamentally a relationship between the national state and the global existence of the social relations of production, that is, of the class antagonism between capital and labour. It is this global dimension "in which production is posited as a totality together with all its moments, but within which, at the same time, all contradictions come into play" (Marx, 1973, p. 227).

The New World Order

The term New World Order has become a catch-phrase employed to describe developments post-1989. It refers to a new, as yet undefined, rearranging of political space since the end of the Cold War. Within the framework of this paper, new world order has a slightly different and distinct meaning. Sudden movements of vast amounts of money have, over the past years, triggered three big crises of political stability. The first was the European currency crises in 1992 and 1993, the second the plunge of the Mexican peso in December 1994 which rocked financial markets around the world, and the third the so-called Asian crisis since 1997. Currency instability and speculative runs on currencies have been described as a new form of foreign policy crisis (see Cockburn and Silverstein, 1995; also: Benson, 1995). This does not mean that old-style foreign policy crises with aggression between states, movements of troops, the threat of nuclear war, and bombing of populations, have been replaced by potential national bankruptcy and the threat of global financial collapse. The former continuous to exist in deadly form; and the potential of global financial collapse has been part of the history of capitalism since its inception. Nevertheless, there have been significant changes in the relationship between the national state and the global economy. These changes have been working themselves through the capitalist world since the breakdown of the Bretton Woods system in the early 1970s.

The consequences of the breakdown of the system of Bretton Woods can be summarised as follows:

1) The crisis of the post-war attempt of integrating labour politically, economically, and socially through commitments to full employment, politics of inclusion and prospects of higher living standards — or, as Agnoli (1967/1990) saw it, a politics of pacification effected through institutionalisation;

2) The construction of regional systems of co-operation (NAFTA; EU; APEC) around the most powerful capitalist states: the USA, Germany, Japan.

3) The emergence of new currencies as international standards of "quality," i.e. financial security, certainty and measure of other currencies (DM/Euro, Yen and Dollar), replacing the dollar as the sole quality currency. The emergence of these currencies hints at a new territorialisation around blocs of regional co-operation and a new inter-bloc imperialist rivalry.

The breakdown of the Bretton Woods system of fixed exchange rates occurred shortly after the tremendous wave of struggle associated with 1968.[8] The revolt of those years, as in the early part of the century following on from the Bolshevik revolution of 1917, was contained in part through violent suppression, but to a much greater extent through the expansion of credit. The consequences of "1968" (the accumulated wave of struggle that showed its crest in 1968) were less dramatic but nevertheless equally profound as the upheavals of the earlier part of the century. The precarious relation between the monetary system and the rate of productivity was ruptured fundamentally, as reflected in the breakdown of the Bretton Woods system in 1971 (on this: Marazzi, 1995).

The struggles of the late 1960s manifested a new intensity of discontent that had been unknown since the late 1920s. Furthermore, the exploitation of labour's productive power was confronted with depressed rates of profits.[9] The exploitation of labour's productive power had become much too expensive. In other words, the post-war attempt at integrating labour's productive and disruptive power through institutionalisation was failing. Capital responded by financialising profits and by moving labour-intensive production to so-called developing countries where cheap labour costs were seen to provide competitive advantages. Yet, despite this expansion of productive capital to new centres of cheap labour, the dissociation between montary accumulation and productive accumulation continued unabated and on an increasing scale. From the late 1960s, especially since the oil hike in 1974, the dramatic increase in global money capital has not been matched by the reduction of necessary labour, the constitutive side of surplus labour. Wealth started to be accumulated in the money form without a corresponding increase in the exploitation of labour power in the factory. Capital's attempt to "liberate" itself from the contested terrain of production and to go beyond itself by asserting itself in its most "rational" form of money capital (M...M′) indicates the fictitious character of capitalist reproduction. Since the early 1970s, the rate of monetary accumulation has by far outstripped that of productive accumulation. In fact, the creation of a credit-superstructure amounts to an accumulation of "unemployed" capital (cf. Marx, 1966), of capital which is suspended from the direct exploitation of labour. At the same time, however, the creation of a global "credit-superstructure" represents an accumulation of claims on the future exploitation of labour. In short, the guarantee of M—M′ depends on M—P—M′, that is, the exploitation of labour.[10]

Growing investment into the fantastic world of monetary self-expansion recomposed the global relations of exploitation and struggle. The world market became a market in money (on this: Walter, 1993). The attempt to make money out of money created a much more fragile capitalism on a world scale. Without the global search for profit in money it would have been unthinkable for the Mexican crisis of 1982 to have had such an immediate knock-on effect on "western" banks and through them on the global circuit of capital. Mexico 1982 indicated that the formidable attempt at containing social relations through a policy of tight money associated with monetarism had reached an impasse. The "crisis of 1982" indicated a tremendous recomposition of the class relation. Seemingly "marginal" pockets of resistance to the politics of austerity, a politics that was introduced from the mid 1970s, threatened to transform the attempt to make money out of poverty into a severe global financial crisis. The dissociation of monetary accumulation from productive accumulation — the so-called dominance of the financial structure — rather than heralding a new phase of — globalised — capitalism, is intensely crisis-ridden. Besides, it amplifies and transmits labour unrest across the globe through its impact on the global relations of money.

In the wake of Mexico 1982, monetarist policies of austerity were hastily abandoned, leading to a politics variously described as "delinquent Keynesianism" or "military Keynesianism" and permitting the USA to emerge, during the 1980s, as the biggest debtor country. On a global scale, the rapid shift from a policy of tight credit to a policy of credit expansion acted like a neutralising "agent" as it helped to co-opt parts of the working class to the project of prosperity. The credit-sustained boom of the 1980s acknowledged that sustained accumulation is the best guarantee for the containment of class conflict. Poverty, unemployment and marginalisation of superfluous labour power coincided with prosperity. The decomposition of resistance to austerity was based on poverty, a poverty which was the mirror image of a credit-driven prosperity.

The significance of credit expansion as a central principle of capitalist rule reasserted itself. The policy of deregulation, flexibilisation, privatisation and the fragmentation of social relations went hand-in-hand. In the face of poverty, prosperity fragmented and undermined opposition to austerity. Thus, credit-expansion not only sustained the boom of the 1980s in an increasingly fictitious dimension. It also helped to promote the notion of the market, unleashing a pre-emtive counter-revolution through the imposition of abstract equality, i.e., the equality of money. The policy of market freedom associated with neo-liberalism equated citizenship with the power of money. Everybody is equal before money. Money knows no special privileges. It treats poor and rich as equals. The imposition of the abstract equality of money involved the imposition of inequality because "the power which each individual exercises over the activity of others or over social wealth exists in him as the owner of exchange values, of money. The individual carries his social power, as well as his bond with society, in his pocket" (Marx, 1973, p. 157).

Neo-Liberalism's policy of market freedom rested on a systematic exercise of state power that defined social activity on the basis of the market — "poverty is not unfreedom" (Joseph/Sumption, 1979, p. 47). Resistance to a control through debt was thus decomposed on the basis of what Hirsch (1991) refers to as the "southafricanisation" of social relations. This view is shared by Negri (1989, p. 97) who argues that the "ideal of modern-day capitalism is apartheid." However, and as Negri insists, unlike Hirsch, apartheid is the ideal but not the reality. The reality is capitalist crisis and its containment through a policy of credit expansion within a framework of "deregulation" whose purpose was the reduction of deficits through the intensification of exploitation in exchange for deteriorating conditions and wage restraint.

Neo-liberalism's aim of adjusting working class consumption to productivity growth was never successful however painful the results of its attempt. In spite of all the hardship, all the misery, all the cost-cutting, all the poverty, all the intensification of work and the restructuring of the labour-process, the fact that "investment is not lifting off...is perhaps testimony to the radicality of the challenge to capitalist power, and of the fear that followed from it that every upturn in the economy would reactivate conflict. A testimony, in short, that the dismantling and restructuring of all parts of the capitalist valorization process is still in full motion" (Bellofiore, 1997, p. 49). Although, as Dalla Costa (1995, p. 7) puts it, "social misery" or "unhappiness" which Marx considered to be the "goal of the political economy" has largely been realised everywhere, capital has failed to redeem the promise of future exploitation by subordinating labour in the present. In other words, the inflation of money capital in relation to productive activity confirms negatively the difficulty in securing the subordination of social relations to the abstract equality of exchange relations and, through them, exploitation. Far from stimulating investment, employment and output, the result of credit expansion in a tight monetary framework was the deterioration of conditions and mass unemployment. There was no breakthrough in productive investment relative to the accumulated claims on surplus value still to be pumped out of labour.

The reconstitution of the circuit of social capital does not just require, as during the 1980s, a divisive and fragmenting decomposition of class relations. Rather, it involves the imposition of valorization upon social labour power. Such an imposition implies not just the intensification of work and the repressive exclusion from production of those disregarded as being inessential. It entails the transformation of money into truly productive capital, i.e. capital employed to create value through the exploitation of labour (M—P—M'). Without this transformation, capital faces its ultimate contradiction: The most rational form of capital (M—M') becomes meaningless (*begriffslos*) because it loses its grip on labour, the substance of value.[11] In other words, money, rather than betting on future exploitation, has to be transformed into an effective command over labour in the present. This means that the exploitation of labour has to deliver rates of profit adequate to redeem debt and to allow for expanded capitalist accumulation. This exploitation of labour presupposes the recomposition of the relation between necessary and surplus labour. There is no surer indication than the ballooning of bad debt that capital has not succeeded in imposing a recomposition of the relations of exploitation adequate to the accumulated claims upon surplus value (see Holloway, 2000).

The experience of the last twenty-five years suggests that the transformation of money into truly productive capital is both essential and impossible. When a repeat performance of the crash of 1929 threatened in October 1987, even the most fierce monetarists advocated expansion — anything to avoid the catastrophe, and confrontation, that a slump would bring. As Samuel Brittan of the *Financial Times* put it in 1987, "when a slump is threatening, we need helicopters dropping currency notes from the sky" (quoted in Harman, 1993, p. 15). This response to the 1987 crash, specific though it was, has always been at the forefront of bad debt management. As Susan George (1992, p. 106) has argued, "during the 1980s, the only thing that was socialised rather than privatised was debt itself." The current attempt at preventing a world-wide collapse of bad debt, and through it at guaranteeing the capitalist property rights on the future exploitation of labour, shows the same politics of socialisation: banks are refinanced and kept afloat by the state in its role as lender of last resort and that is, by taking money out of the hands of workers. While the social wage of the working class has been attacked and labour intensified, and while conditions have deteriorated and while the working class is told that it is free to look after herself, banks, it appears, can not be asked to be regulated on the basis of market freedom: swim or drown. Their losses are socialised while their profits are protected by the law of private property. The strutural adjustment politics advocated by the IMF entails the imposition of poverty upon those whose labour secures the validity of credit as a claim on surplus value still to be pumped out of the worker. The IMF response to the crisis in Asia represents, as during the so-called debt crisis of the 1980s, an imposition of poverty: work harder for less reward to secure the banking system and with it the capitalist property rights of exploitation.

Yet, the recession of the 1990s, the Mexican crisis of 1994–95, the European currency crises of 1992–93, and the Asian crisis of 1997–98, the Russian crisis of 1998 and the Brazilian crisis of 1999, indicate that there seems to be no way forward, for capital or for labour. Yet this is not the first time. Writing in 1934, that is after the first global imperialist war and in the face of fascist/fordist attempts of discipling labour,[12] Paul Mattick suggested that capitalism had entered an age of permanent crisis: The periodicity of crisis is in practice nothing other than the recurrent reorganisation of the process of accumulation on a new level of value and price which again secures the accumulation of capital. If that is not possible, then neither is it possible to confirm accumulation; the same crisis that up to now had presented itself chaotically and could be overcome becomes permanent crisis. In contrast to previous crises of capitalism, which had always led to a restructuring of capital and to a renewed period of accumulation, the crisis of the 1930s appeared to be so profound and prolonged as to be incapable of solution. Crisis, Mattick suggested, had ceased to be a periodically recurring phenomenon and had become an endemic feature of capitalism.

Mattick's suggestion, pessimistic though it was, turned out to be far too optimistic. The crisis was resolved, in blood. Capital was restructured and the basis for a new period of accumulation created. The "golden age" of post-war capitalism is now a memory, as is the blood-letting through war and gas. Once again it would seem that we are in a situation of permanent crisis. It is possible that the crisis will be permanent, with a progressive "south-africanisation" of the world. It is possible too that the crisis will not be permanent, that it will in fact be resolved: what the resolution of "permanent crisis" can mean stands behind us as a warning of a possibly nightmarish future.

The prospect of a world constituted by human dignity and sincerity has to go forward through a critique of political economy, including, of course, revamped versions of Keynesianism. The summoning of a new world order should be taken seriously. The old "new world order," the world order post-1945, was brought about by a nightmare. While I share Lipietz's (1985) nightmare about a capitalism walking on the thin air of credit, I do not share his call to keep capitalism away from the abyss. This is, despite its good intensions, a dangerous view to take. It is dangerous because it accepts suffering without dignity and thus endorses the rescue of capital through the continued treatment of humanity as a resource for the accumulation of abstract wealth. This treatment resolved the crisis of the 1920s and 1930s.

Conclusion

Globalisation orthodoxy fails to see "globalisation" as a major "capitalist offensive" and, from within this view, fails to address the very contradiction that lies at its heart. This paper has argued that this contradictions is constituted by the presence of labour's productive and disruptive power, a power in and through which capital "exists." Globalisation orthodoxy fails to see the misery of our time and projects, instead, capitalist global reorganisation as an inevitable development. This view ignores that the globalisation of capital is at the same time the globalisation of labour's presence in and against capital, and is ill-equipped to comprehend the vast implications of current developments. These I summarised in terms of Mattick's notion of a permanent crisis. Lastly, methodologically, globalisation orthodoxy is founded on an analytical theoretical persepctive. At best, this perspective confers on capitalist development an objectivity that merely serves to generalise empirical data in abstract theoretical terms. In this way, the ideological projections of "capital" are confused with reality. This perspective fails to supply enlightenment as to the crisis-ridden nature of globalisation. Instead, it offers abstract generalisations which already presuppose that the market reigns supreme. As was mentioned earlier, the uncritical acceptance of the market entails that the cunning of reason amounts to no more than the invisible's own project. Globalisation is thus rendered practical as the project of the invisible itself. Against this view the paper argued that "in the misery of our time, we find the 'positive' only in negation" (Agnoli, 1992, p. 50). And the national state? Surely, the gobalisationists are quite right to argue that globalisation has rendered obvious the myth of the national state as a framework for the achievement of conditions where the free development of each is the condition for the free development of all. According to the advocates of bourgeois society, the spectre of communism has been replaced by the spectre of democracy at the same time as spectre of globalisation has undermined the conditions of liberal-democratic government. History when it was declared to be dead, appears full of surprises: is this the irony of history or the making of history?

ENDNOTES

1 This is an updated and corrected version of the essay that first appeared in English in *Common Sense* no. 24.

2 For alternative views on globalisation see, for example, Boyer and Drache (1996); Hirst and Thompson (1999); Ruigrok and van Tulder (1995) and Weiss (1998). These authors provide rich empirical evidence that questions the "abstract generalisation" of the globalisations orthodoxy. Their argument is, however, firmly fixed within the globalisation agenda which presupposes the state and the economy as distinct structures; the proponents of globalisation argue that the economic has gained autonomy over the state and the critics argue that the state still holds regulative power over the economy, rendering it capable of reasserting itself over economic relations, allowing a socially just regulation of capital. Neither provides a class analysis of globalisation. On this see, Bonefeld (2000), Burnham (2000) and Holloway (2000).

3 See, amongst others, the contributions to Dalla Costa and Dalla Costa (1995, 1997), Dalla Costa (1995), Midnight Notes (1992) and Dalla Costa's contribution to this volume.

4 This list of "state functions" draws on Skinner's introduction to Adam Smith's *The Wealth of Nations*, Penguin, Harmondsworth.

5 As Agnoli (1997) and Clarke (1992) have shown, the capitalist state is fundamentally a liberal state whatever its specific historical form. For a critique of liberal-democarcy and its current transformation, see Agnoli (2000).

6 The idea of the "economy" as a force in its own right depends on the understanding of capital as the subject. Backhaus (1997) has shown, that this conception amounts to no more than the theoretical hypothesis of political economy and Türcke (1986) has argued that the endeavour to conceive capital as the subject amounts to an attempt to posit the invisible and that is to conceptualise God. For the academic left, the conception of capital as the subject supplies reassurance about its own involvement in the class struggle. Intransigence towards the existence of humanity as a resource is replaced by a "critical" rationalisation of, and reconciliation with, capital as a self-constituted subject. Traditionally, the upshot is the demand for the rational planning of economic resources, including the resource labour.

7 For a critique of this view see, Bonefeld (2000); Burnham (1994, 1995); Holloway (1995); and Picciotto (1991).

8 Parts of the following section draw on a paper written jointly with John Holloway, "Money and Class Struggle," published in Bonefeld and Holloway (eds) (1995).

9 See Armstrong etal (1984) and Mandel (1975) for documentation.

10 For an interpretation of Marx's work on money and credit, see Bologna (1993); Bonefeld (1995b); Neary and Taylor (1998); Negri (1984); and Ricciardi (1987).

11 On this, see Marx (1966) and, for commentary, Bonefeld (1995b).

12 On this see Gambino's contribution to this volume.

REFERENCES

Agnoli, J. (1967/1990), *Die Transformation der Demokratie,* Ça ira, Freiburg.

Agnoli, J. (1992) "Destruction as Determination of the Scholar in Miserable Times," *Common Sense,* no. 12, reprinted in this volume.

Agnoli, J. (1997), *Faschismus ohne Revision,* Ça ira, Freiburg.

Angoli, J. (2000), "The Market, the State and the End of History," in Bonefeld, W. and K. Psychopedis (eds.) 2000.

Anderson, P. (1992), *Zones of Engagement,* Verso, London.

Armonstrong. P. etal. (1984), *Capitalism Since World War II,* Fontana, London.

Backhaus, HG. (1997), *Die Dialektik der Warenform,* Ça ira, Freiburg.

Beck, U. (1992), *Risk Society,* Sage, London.

Bellofiore, R. (1997), "Lavori in Corso," *Common Sense,* no. 22.

Benson, G. (1995), "Safety Nets and Moral Hazard in Banking," in K. Sawamoto etal. (eds.) *Financial Stability in a Changing Environment,* Macmillan, London.

Bologna, S. (1993), "Money and Crisis," *Common Sense* no. 13 and 14.

Bonefeld, W. (1995a) "Capital as Subject and the Existence of Labour," in W. Bonefeld et al. (eds.) 1995.

Bonefeld, W. (1995b) "Money, Equality and Exploitation," in Bonefeld/ Holloway (eds.) 1995.

Bonefeld, W. (1999), "Globalization and the State," *Studies in Political Economy,* no. 58.

Bonefeld, W. (2000), "The Spectre of Globalization," in Bonefeld, W. and K. Psychopedis (eds.) 2000.

Bonefeld, W. and J. Holloway (eds.) (1995), *Global Capital, National State and the Politics of Money,* Macmillan, London.

Bonefeld, W. and K. Psychopedis (eds.) (2000), *The Politics of Change,* Palgrave, London.

Bonefeld, W., Gunn, R., Holloway, J. and K. Psychopedis (eds.) (1995), *Open Marxism* Vol. III, Pluto, London.

Boyer, R. and D. Drache (eds.) (1996), *State Against Markets*, Routledge, London.
Burnham, P. (1994) "Open Marxism and Vulgar International Political Economy," *Review of International Political Economy*, vol. 1, no. 2.
Burnham, P. (1995) "Capital, Crisis and the International State System," in Bonefeld/Holloway (eds.) 1995.
Burnham, P. (2000), "Globalization, Depoliticization and Modern Economic Management," in Bonefeld, W. and K. Psychopedis (eds.) 2000.
Cerny, P. (1990), *The Changing Architecture of Politics: Structure, Agency, and the Future of the State*, Sage, London.
Cerny, P. (1996), "International Finance and the Erosion of State Policy Capacity," *International Organization* vol. 49, no. 4.
Cerny, P. (1997), "The Dynamics of Political Globalisation," *Government & Opposition*, vol. 32, no. 2.
Clarke, S. (1992), "The Global Accumulation of Capital and the Periodisation of the Capitalist State Form," in Bonefeld, W. et al (eds.) *Open Marxism*, vol. I, Pluto, London.
Cockburn, A. and K. Silverstein (1995) "War and Peso," *New Statesmen and Society*, February 24, 1995.
Dalla Costa, M. (1995) "Capitalism and Reproduction," in Bonefeld et al. (eds.) 1995.
Dalla Costa, M. and G. F. Dalla Costa (eds.) (1995) *Paying the Price*, Zed Books, London.
Dalla Costa, M. and G.F. Dalla Costa (eds.) (1997), *Women, Development and Labour Reproduction*, African World Press, Lawrenceville.
Federici, S. (1997), "Reproduction and Feminist Struggle in the New International Division of Labour," in Dalla Costa, M. and G.F. Dalla Costa (eds.) 1997.
George, S. (1992), *The Debt Boomerang*, Pluto, London.
Giddens, A. (1990), *The Consequences of Modernity*, Polity, Cambrigde.
Giddens, A. (1991), *Modernity and Self-Identity*, Polity, London.
Gunn, R. (1991), "Marxism, Metatheory, and Critique," in Bonefeld and Holloway (eds.) *Post-Fordism and Social Form*, Macmillan, London.
Harman, C. (1993) "Where is Capitalism Going?," *International Socialism*, no. 58.
Harvey, D. (1989) *The Conditions of Postmodernity*, Blackwell, Oxford.
Held, D. (1995), *Democracy and Global Order*, Polity, Cambridge.
Hirsch, J. (1991), "Fordism and Post-Fordism," in Bonefeld/Holloway (eds.) *Post-Fordism and Social Form*, Macmillan, London.
Hirsch, J. (1995), *Der nationale Wettbewerbsstaat*, id-edition, Berlin.

Hirsch, J. (1997), "Globalization and the Nation State," *Studies in Political Economy*, no. 58.

Hirst, P. and G. Thompson (1999), *Globalisation in Question*, Polity, Cambridge.

Holloway, J. (1995), "Global Capital and National State," in Bonefeld and Holloway (eds.) 1995.

Holloway, J. (2000), "Zapata in Wallstreet," in Bonefeld, W. and K. Psychopedis (eds.) 2000.

Horkheimer, M. (1992), *Kritische und traditionelle Theorie*, Fischer, Frankfurt.

Joseph, K. and J. Sumption (1979), *Equality*, John Murray, London.

Lipietz, A. (1985), *The Enchanted World*, Verso, London.

Mandel, E. (1975), *Late Capitalism*, New Left Books, London.

Marazzi, C. (1995) "Money in the World Crisis," in Bonefeld and Holloway (eds.) 1995.

Marx, K. (1966) *Capital* vol. III, Lawrence & Wishart, London.

Marx, K. (1973) *Grundrisse*, Penguin, Harmondsworth.

Marx, K. (1975), "Theses on Feuerbach," *Collected Works*, vol. 5, Lawrence & Wishart, London.

Marx, K. (1983), *Capital* vol. I, Lawrence & Wishart, London.

Mattick, P. (1934), "Zur Marxschen Akkumulations- und Zusammenbruchs-theorie," *Rätekorrespondenz*, no. 4.

Midnight Notes (1992) *Midnight Oil: Work, Energy, War 1973–1992*, Autonomedia, New York.

Neary, M. and G. Taylor (1998), *Money and the Human Condition*, Macmillan, London.

Negri, A. (1984), *Marx Beyond Marx*, Bergin & Garvey, Massachusetts.

Negri, A. (1989) *The Politics of Subversion*, Polity Press, Cambridge.

Picciotto, S. (1991) "The Internationalisation of Capital and the International State System," in S. Clarke (ed.) (1991), *The State Debate*, Macmillan, London.

Ricardo, D. (1995), *On the Principles of Political Economy and Taxation*, Cambridge UP, Cambridge.

Ricciardi, J. (1987), "Rereading Marx on the Role of Money and Finance," *Research in Political Economy*, vol. 10.

Robertson, W. (1890) *Works* vol. II, Thomas Nelson, Edinburgh.

Ruigrok, W. and R. van Tulder (1995), *The Logic of International Restructuring*, Routledge, London.

Strange, S. (1988), *States and Markets*, Pinter, London.

Strange, S. (1991) "An eclectic approach," in C.N. Murphy and R. Tooze (eds.) *The New International Political Economy*, Macmillan, London.

Strange, S. (1996), *The Retreat of the State,* Cambridge University Press, Cambridge.

Türcke, Ch. (1986), *Vermittlung als Gott,* von Klempen, Lüneburg.

von Braunmühl, C. (1976), "Die nationalstaatliche Organisiertheit der bürgerlichen Gesellschaft," *Gesellschaft* no. 8/9, Suhrkamp, Frankfurt.

Walter, A. (1993), *World Power and World Money,* Harvester Wheatsheaf, London.

Weiss, L. (1998), *The Myth of the Powerless State,* Polity, Cambridge.

10

THE CRISIS OF POLITICAL SPACE

Antonio Negri

When people use the notion of a "New World Order," they are bringing into a single frame three powerful concepts: order, world-scale globalisation and the newness of the relations established between them.

This new connectedness of "world" and "order" seems to constitute a *new paradigm*, in other words a new way of arranging political power and the physical space of the world. In order to understand this new coming-together, we therefore need first to think about these concepts — to establish what they used to mean, and what is the crisis of the former ways in which they were connected; and then we will need to penetrate to the originality of the new connection, and its dynamics. At that moment we will perhaps be in a position to understand the depth of the change that has taken place.

Let us begin with the concept of *order*. In the modern era, the concept of social and political order is very close to the concept of *sovereignty* — a territorial sovereignty which only with the passage of time becomes "national sovereignty." Thus we need to examine the concept of sovereignty and that of national sovereignty separately.

The concept of sovereignty is a concept of a power that has nothing above it. It is a secular conception of power, opposed to any notion of a power based outside its own dynamic. It is thus an absolute *quoad titulum* in reference to its source. However, when one considers it in its exercise *quoad exercitium* the concept of sovereignty is rather a singular concept. This in no sense diminishes its character of absoluteness, but it is precisely in singularity that sovereignty is exercised. Modern sovereignty is singularised by virtue of the fact that it is exercised over a territory, and in relation to a people or peoples. International law is founded on this singularity *jus gentium*, or, better, the right of sovereigns, which originally consisted in resolving conflicts between sovereign singularities by means of pacts. "By means of pacts," and thus a right that is absolutely weakened, an exchange rather than a juridical contract or administration. But the concept of sovereignty is not singularised only in relation to the exterior: it is also singularised domestically, where it presents itself as a concept of *legitimation*, or as a relation between power and its subjects. Or, better, as an inter-relation with subjects. Modern sovereignty may be a power which has nothing above it, but it has a lot of things below it. In particular it has below it a space (a territory) and a multitude (the citizenry). The legitimation, to put it in Weberian terms, may take various forms (traditional, charismatic, legal/rational); in all cases it is a relationship between sovereign and subjects — a relationship within which there exists jointly both the expression of authority and the obedience (and/or disobedience) of the subjects.

Thus a living and inhabited space is found at the basis of modern citizenship. Order is the result of an activity of government which meets acceptance and/or passivity among a given group of citizens over the extent of a territory. In this perspective, sovereignty as order becomes *administration*; in other words, sovereignty organises itself as a machinery of authority which extends through and structures territory. Through the activity of administration, territory is organised, and structures of authority are extended through it. Increasingly within the dynamics of modern sovereignty, the connection between administration and territory becomes intimate and full. The nature of the economic regime (mercantilist or liberalist) matters little; the nature of the political regime (absolutist, aristocratic or popular) also matters little. Space finds itself absorbed into the scenarios of sovereignty in ways that are increasingly coherent, and each particularity is structured by the whole in a progressively irresistible manner.

It takes the concept of nation a while before it combines with that of sovereignty. National sovereignty, at the start of the nineteenth century, was not in opposition to sovereignty; rather it perfected the modern concept of sovereignty. It is a powerful specification of sovereignty, which exalts the connection between sovereign and subjects, and at the same time the potency of the whole. This double operation is possible because the nation state presents itself as a self-sufficient cultural, ethnic and economic entity within which the spiritual element overdetermines the sum of its determinations. The process of legitimation is hypostasized in nature and/or in the spirit. Between Sieyes and Novalis, between Fichte and Mazzini, between Hegel and Hertzel, the concept of nation spiritualises that of sovereignty, and makes the space of sovereignty an absolute entity. In the concept of national sovereignty, territory and people are like two attributes of one same substance, and government is the relation which consecrates this unity. The modern concept of sovereignty, in its close relationship to territory, is carried to extreme consequences.

Modern politics — or again the sovereign — is thus a figure which assembles into an absolute different aspects of social life: a people, a territory, an authority. The concept of sovereign power becomes all the stronger as its aspects are unified and overdetermined within the continuous historical development of modern sovereignty. This process of absolutisation and intensification of relations is also at the root of the concept of *democratic sovereignty*. Democratic sovereignty integrates territory *qua* space of the life of a people. Legitimation, in this case, seeks to be dialectical. Administration becomes bio-politics. The Welfare State, the *état-providence* and the *Sozialstaat*, are figures of perfected sovereignty, in a progressive and uninterrupted continuity which seems to complete the anthropological process of the sedentarisation of hordes, to the point where it configures within a given space the global time of social life.

So, from an external point of view, sovereignty is characterised by a monopoly of legitimate physical force; by the exclusive ability to mint the social norms of exchange for reproduction (money); by the singular structuring of the forms of communication (national language, education system, etc); by the democratic (biopolitical) definition of legitimation. It is an absolute process of *territorialisation*.

Modern sovereign states have, in the course of the centuries of their hegemony, exported their absolute power outside of the territories they had originally integrated and moulded within the rules of domination. *Imperialism* (as also colonialism) consisted of occupying zones of the world, and exploiting peoples to whom was denied, by this means, the possibility of acceding to territorial or national sovereignty. In the territories of imperialism, order, legitimation and administration are not auto-centred, but are functional to and dependent on the imperialist state.

Thus far we have posed a number of premises enabling us to get the measure of the *earthquake* which is today shaking the old paradigm of sovereign order. An earthquake which touches all the elements of the old order, and which has created *open conjunctures* wherein many hypotheses exist side by side, and in which one can identify a number of tendencies at work. The changes under way are so profound and extensive that we are not yet in a position to identify directions of development with certainty; they do, however, permit — in fact they demand — new parameters of analysis.

Today the first element that is obvious is that this earthquake is *deterritorialising*. It shakes the old paradigm of order in its most intimate aspect: the relation to space, the progression towards a space that is increasingly organised. The paradigm of order is forced to come to terms with a space which lacks traditional determinations — or worse, a space that is limitless. There are three elements which should permit us to define this breakdown and provide an approach to a new power scenario. These are: *the bomb*, *money*, and *the ether*.

The Bomb

The development of nuclear technologies is one of the elements that has laid the basis for the present earthquake. It is to this development that we owe the reign of terror which has maintained stability over the "thirty glorious years" of Keynesian development; but more particularly we owe to the bomb the extension of the notion of *limited sovereignty* to the great majority of countries of the world. A monopoly of legitimate physical force — this was one of the original qualifications of sovereignty. Today this qualification, which once included the ability to declare war, no longer belongs to the great majority of states. Major wars begin to become unthinkable; not, however, small wars, limited conflicts, international policing operations, civil wars, dirty wars, guerrilla wars, etc, etc. It was within this perspective that the bomb first appeared, as Günther Anders was already pointing out in the 1950s: it was the operation of a violence that was absolute, a new metaphysical horizon which deprived sovereignty of its own territory and denied resistance the possibility of action.

And yet this dialectic of deterritorialisation finds — or rather could find — a limit in *imperial hegemony*, or in the necessity of imposing a new order, of imposing a new territorialisation on growing processes of deterritorialisation.

Is this new hegemonic pole really in the process of formation? The conditions for it are there: however this does not mean that this new hegemonic pole necessarily has to emerge as a sovereign continuity of the old order (the USA, for example); it might instead be made up of an ensemble of international powers and organisations. The game is on, and bets — and hypotheses — are being placed on which tendency will eventually win.

In any event — and this is the element that I want to stress — the sovereign monopoly of legitimate physical force (which is one of the key characteristics of the modern concept of sovereignty), is here completely sidelined. Even in a scenario where world hegemony was conquered by an old power (the USA, for example), the content of *its* sovereignty would have to be completely and radically requalified: the worldwide extension of domination modifies the form of that domination. Imperial sovereignty presents itself as a *nuclear territorialisation of a universal deterritorialisation*: here we have a useful initial definition of imperial hegemony.

Money

The construction of the *world market* is a second element of the earthquake which we are experiencing. This has involved, in the first place, a monetary deconstruction of national markets, and of national and/or regional contexts of monetary regulation. All this began between 1971 and 1973, when the USA detached gold from the dollar and ended convertibility, thus putting an end to a long period of fixed exchange rates. The end of Bretton Woods. The consequence of this was very soon revealed in the highly aleatory nature of the markets, in which monetary relations found themselves subordinated to movements of *financial powers*. In this situation national *money* tends to lose all characteristics of sovereignty. Even the dollar, which seemed to have taken on a role as a measure or "standard" of the other moneys, becomes increasingly subordinated to the financial markets. And this, paradoxically, becomes obvious with the fall of the Berlin Wall, in other words from the moment in which — the Cold War having been won — the USA finds itself deprived of *command rent* by its allies. A national money, with the characteristics which it had during the period of modernity, is inconceivable today. At this level too, the process of globalisation becomes a very powerful agent of radical transformation. With a series of dramatic consequences:

1. The impossibility of monetary regulation at the national level — whether in Keynesian, or simply monetarist, terms;

2. The definitive undermining of all processes of welfarist intervention at the national level, and the crisis of democratic sovereignty which derives from that fact;

3. The push towards the construction of regional and multinational organisations/groupings, with the aim of building a relative resistance to the powers of finance and speculation, and thus to create new possibilities (illusions) for planning their own future;

4. The erratic emergence, in the chiaroscuro of the crisis, of certain currencies (dollar, Deutschmark, yen...) as *imperial moneys*. Here too, while modern sovereignty is becoming increasingly *residual*, and the process of global deterritorialisation progresses with the construction of the world market, there is a hint of a new possibility of *territorialisation*, which is *unilateral* — not constructed on monetary values, obviously, but solely on political values. Is this possible? What are the real alternatives (and in what forms, and within what time-scale) to the affirmation of the dollar (or of other currencies) as imperial money?

The Ether

The fixing of language and defence of that language, the construction of an educational system, and the protection of culture now more than ever are the substance of sovereign prerogatives. However from now on all this is dissolved in the airwaves. Modern systems of communication are not subordinated to sovereignty: quite the contrary, sovereignty is subordinated to communication.

In the field of communication, the paradoxes implied in the dissolution of territorial and/or national sovereignty, and by the breakdown in the singularised relationship between order and space, are taken to extremes. In fact communication's capacity for deterritorialisation is wholly original; it no longer merely limits or weakens modern sovereignty; it removes even the possibility of a link between a given order and a given space. Except... within the complete *circularity* of signs and the indefatigable continuity of that circularity. From this there derives a conception of territory as "*circulatory territory*" and therefore the impossibility of singularising the relationship of order to territory. Deterritorialisation is the *primum*; circulation is the form in which it unstoppably manifests itself; and thus in the ether languages become functional to circulation and dissolve all relations of sovereignty. As for education and culture, they have no choice but to subject themselves to the "society of the spectacle."

In this experience we reach an outer limit in the dissolution of the relationship between order and space: henceforth we can only view this relationship within *an other place* — an "elsewhere" which is original in being uncontainable within the articulation of the sovereign act.

The space of communication is completely deterritorialised. It is absolutely other, in relation to the residual spaces that we have identified in analysing the crisis of the the monopoly of legitimate physical force, and that of the definition of monetary measure. What we have here is not a residue, but a *metamorphosis*: a metamorphosis of all the elements of political economy and theory of the State, which derives from the fact that we have entered a phase of *real subsumption* of society within capital. In other words, communication is the form of the capitalist process of production at the point where capital has conquered and subjected to itself the whole of society, in real terms, globally, by suppressing any margins of alternative: if ever an alternative is to be proposed, this will have to be done through the intermediary of the society of real subsumption, and it will have to be constructed within it, playing up new contradictions. The alternative will be posed within the "new," in fact within the "very new."

The imperial tendency is also operational within the ether. Once again this tendency is seen at first sight in the continued existence of *American power* and in its expansion. The space which is being created with this breakdown of relations of sovereignty is very often American. However in none of the situations which we have examined is the reference to the function of imperial reterritorialisation more unstable than here. Unlike what is happening on the terrains of force and money, communication is actually a relation of production, involving the development of capital and, at the same time, a transformation of the forces of production. This dynamic produces a powerfully open situation in which American power comes into confrontation with the power of social subjects — of all those who are increasingly actively involved in the interactive production of communication. In this place more than any other, which is a place of circulation, imperial domination over the new forms of production/communication has proved to be uncertain.

The earthquake which has destroyed territorial and/or national sovereignty is thus deep and thorough-going. The space of politics becomes undefinable, and within it we can no longer count on the functioning of dialectical connections, or even simply of functional connections. In the formal subsumption of world space to capital there still existed intermediations which offered points of reference to given biopolitical processes. Today we can consider the Fordist period as having been a phase of transition (from formal subsumption to real subsumption) within which, little by little, all determinations tend to be erased. We find ourselves looking at a space which is smooth, with occasionally a few variously striated zones, a space that is unified, and periodically identifiable by the hierarchies which run through it; a space that is invested by a continuous circulatory movement, within which one can occasionally perceive resistances. Or, again, to put it in another way, we are living in a universal suburb, characterised by variations of speed — sometimes one can identify centres, on this desolate horizon, maybe one, maybe many, but at any event what we have here is a power which invests a new space, a *new power*.

Obviously, our problem is to decide whether this new space is in the process of being organised, and if it is, then we must describe how. How is this new deterritorialisation expressing itself in terms of administration. I do not necessarily think that it is possible to advance more broadly in this direction. But it would nevertheless be useful to pose a number of premises, or, rather, to anticipate an ideal type which might enable clarification of the road to be followed. The *ideal type of empire* could be useful to us. It is radically different from the concept of imperialism (which consisted, as we have seen, in a specification of sovereignty) because the space of empire is without preconstituted determinations; it is a centre which is dislocated over numbers of terrains, and which circulates without finding obstacles. Within a unified world-space, individual states combine within fluxes and networks that are always in movement; countries exist in a context in which *peace* is guaranteed by a permanent and effective policy of international policing. When this breaks down, conflicts are isolated. In all cases, the sovereign characteristics of single states are weakened and recomposed within collective functions of the market and the organisation of communication and policing.

Post-modern ideologies have made much of the weakening of the characteristics of sovereignty. They have also, and by the same token, made much of the new dimensions of the fragmentary, the local, and the particular, and the emergences of new identities (which here and there break the flat surface of postmodernity). In my view these descriptions are not sufficient for providing an understanding of the fundamental nature of the empire: this consists of moving beyond mere manifestation of the fragmentary and the complex, into organising in a unitary manner within the fragmentary, within the complex, within the intermingling and control of identities. Postmodern ideologies have made great play with a given situation of which, up until now, they have not perceived the new structuring dynamic.

It was Foucault and Deleuze who best grasped the figure of empire (considered here solely from the point of view of the construction of an ideal type). The threefold model which they propose for the evolution of the political regimes of modernity (from "*ancien regime* society" to "disciplinary society," to "control society") identifies the dynamic of weakening sovereignty within the transition from disciplinary society to the control society — not as something evanescent, but quite the contrary, as modernisation and optimisation. "Control society" is the framework within which imperial power is deployed. In raising the summit of command to an enormously high level, the possibility of mediations in the resolution of conflicts and therefore the dynamic requalification of all particularities within the process of power, becomes very much greater. Force and discipline are thus included within politics of control.

But let us now take a look at the model of empire which Polybius constructed. The Roman empire, we are told by this Greek intellectual who lived in Rome, was a synthesis of the three forms of government defined by classical antiquity: the empire was monarchic with the emperor, aristocratic in the Senate, and democratic-republican in its tribune functions. And what about today? Is what we are seeing in the organisation of a new imperial power once again Polybius's threefold model? Perhaps. A definitive monarchic centre, the exclusive holder of force, has not yet emerged, although one can say that it is increasingly identifiable in tendency. But the two other aspects of the model required by the imperial synthesis are there: on the one hand the financial aristocracy and the discipline which it imposes on substantial fractions of overall labour power at the worldwide level; and also the republican power of control, or that disciplinary reflex which is embodied in what is left of the single national states, and which is increasingly represented in a contractual role in relation to the imperial authority.

The empire is thus there, just around the corner, waiting for us inexorably, as something which is already in place. As a political philosophy, post-modernity has been a warning sign telling of empire — sad and inadequate, but effective.

Far stronger and more real are the warning signs that are etched in the crises and the temporary pauses of the constitutive process of empire. Where are they to be seen? Essentially in conflicts between orders of values and in contradictions between procedures. *Increasingly strong hybridisations* become apparent when we consider the space of the proper and the improper, of the economic and the political, of the legal and the illegal, and when the traditional considerations of law and the social (not forgetting the moral) comes up against the spatial opening-up of empire. In the lives of states and communities a large part of public activity is henceforth devoted to the resolution of these conflicts, to the recomposition of the procedures which govern them, and thus to the "management" of these hybrid spaces.

We clearly have to ask whether the life of empire — in this, which would be its first real form — rather than being invoked for the solution of major international conflicts, should not here be invoked to deal with the individual conflicts affecting the material aspects of the existence of peoples and nations.

This now brings me to my final formulation. For me it is so fundamental that I would be very happy if it found an equal footing in everything that I have said so far, even in reductive fashion — because it is no less essential. My conclusion is the following: the breakdown of the modern relation between order and space is a radical rupture, the sign of a mutation of paradigm. What this rupture presents to critical thought and action is *a new transcendental of the political*. When politics is looked at within the dimension of empire, one can no longer conceive it in the dimension of single national spaces. From now on, concepts of politics, sovereignty, legitimation, administration etc are completely thrown into question — they certainly go into crisis, they may be subject to re-arrangement, but in the long term they are also open to overthrow and subversion, because they no longer have any relation to the old paradigm of national, international, territorial and cosmopolitical order. Today the multinational level is played out within a space that is quasi-national. There are no alternatives to the verticality of the new imperial power — the only alternatives are in who will actually own imperial power (will it be the USA or a conglomerate of different sovereign states that will take power over the empire?), or in the games that might be played in terms of transversality. In any event we are already right in there. We are citizens of this world which is preparing to make public its new international organisation — in other words *the imperial nature of the relations of domination*. Whether or not one agrees with this development, we must necessarily view it as inevitable, and we will have to recognise that many of the contradictions which democratic action has experienced hitherto are going to reproduce themselves on terrains that are infinitely more complex. From now on power can only be looked at from within the framework of this new political transcendental.

TRANSLATED BY ED EMERY

Part Three

The Critique of the Political

11
The Capitalist State: Illusion and Critique

Werner Bonefeld

I

Johannes Agnoli has reminded us of the need to complement Marx's critique of political economy with the critique of the political, of the state. Marx never wrote his projected book on the state. This has let generations of Marxists to argue over "the" Marxist theory of the state.[1]

Would Marx's book on the state really have been a theory of the state — and not a critique of the state? Yet, it was a theory of the state that was sought. Whereas Marx, if he taught us anything at all, taught us to think independently and that is critically, his work was, in the guise of Marxism-Leninism, now appearing merely as a school of thought under the name of analytical Marxism, canonised and jealously guarded against heterodox deviations. Fearful of heresy and blinded by faith, Marx's business of destructive critique was abandoned in favour of a rhetorically radicalised bourgeois research project. Instead of "Marx the destructive critic," Marx was endorsed as a theoretician "of" this and that.[2] Furthermore, since there was not much to find in Marx in terms of a ready theory of the state, Marx's work was seen to amount merely to an economic theory — Marxian economics. The subtitle of *Kapital,* "A Critique of Political Economy," was put aside, transforming Marx's critique of political economy into a mere critique of bourgeois economics.[3] This made Marx a much-less-destructive figure and moderated his revolutionary cunning and reasoning. In fact, Marxian economics rejects Marx's understanding of labour as the constitutive power of social existence, and reduces human relations to something that is merely attendant upon economic laws. Economics is what Marx called the relationship of the things between themselves.[4]

The assumption that Marx's work amounted to a "Marxist" economic-science leads naturally to the demand for a Marxist theory of the state. This can either be done in terms of the so-called state derivation debate of the 1970s, or in terms of a Marxist political theory associated with the work of Poulantzas. The derivation debate sought to "derive" the category state from Marx's *Kapital*. The economy was seen as the base from which to "derive" the categories of the political "superstructure." This was not a "derivation" of categories from human social relations — but a derivation of the political from the economic; the economic was presupposed and the political appeared as a mere derivative of economic categories.[5] The Poulantzerian offer of a Marxist political theory amounted to a highly complex theoretical maze which externalised structure and struggle, separated the economic from the political, leading to the characterisation of living labour as a structural agent capable of reproducing those same structures that rendered the agent an exploitable resource. Poulantzas (1973) saw his work as a contribution to Marxist political theory that corresponds to so-called Marxist economics.[6] In short, "Marxist" political theory accepted the bourgeois separation between the political and economic; rendering Marx's enunciation of "critique" harmless and without bite.

The net result of a "Marxist" political theory was a division between abstract theory and a descriptive — or higher journalistic — account of "social reality." Political theory — whether Marxist or not — deals with constitution in terms of state-building and political emancipation. There is no need here to review at length Marx's critique of political emancipation. He equated political emancipation with the integration of labour into the capital relation as a labouring commodity, as wage labour. This integration entails the suppression of human emancipation. This is the classic quotation:

> All emancipation is a return of the human world and human relationships to humans themselves. Political emancipation is the reduction of man, on the one hand, to a member of bourgeois society, an egoistic and independent individual, on the other hand, to a citizen of the state, a moral person. Not until the real individual man has taken the abstract citizen back into himself and, as an individual man, has become a species-being in his empirical life, in his individual work and individual relationships, not until man recognises and organises his *'forces propres'* as social forces and thus no longer separates social forces from himself in the form of political forces, not until then will human emancipation be completed. (Marx, 1964, p. 370).

The notion, then, of a Marxist political theory amounts to the renewal of the apoprias of bourgeois political thought and, because of its espousal of the state as a subject in its own right, the suppression of human emancipation. Marx's destructive critique is thus replaced by a constructive critique[7] which aims, in its reformist guise, at a fairer integration of labour into the capital relation and, in its revolutionary guise, the central planning of economic resources, including the "resource" of human labour. Whereas Marx (1983, p. 447) argued that "to be a productive labourer is...not a piece of luck, but a misfortune," the proclamation of the socialist republic of labour presented this misfortune as history's inner most aim.

II

There is no doubt that a critique of the political is needed. There is no doubt also that this critique cannot be enunciated as a theory of the state. Marx did not have an economic theory nor a theory of crisis as opposed to a "theory of accumulation" or a "theory of something." Marx supplied a critique of political economy, including a conceptualisation of the category "state." His project was not to offer analytical tools for the fine-tuning of a perverted world but, rather, to negate capital, including its state. This negation does not amount to a "closed" dialectical analysis that culminates in the negation of the negation, and therewith the reconciliation with bourgeois relations of power (*Herrschaftsverhältnisse*). His critique is negative and destructive. As Agnoli (1992, p. 45) puts it, "Marx wanted neither to construct nor affirm. He wanted primarily to negate." This critique is of course not a critique for critique's sake. It criticises the perverted forms of capital in order to bring to the fore their social foundation, that is the human basis of their existence. Marx's critique, then, is subversive: the critique of the perverted forms entails their conceptualisation as forms of human existence and thus as forms through which human dignity subsists in the mode of being denied. In short, it seeks to make visible what is hidden behind the so-called structures and their apparent incestuous relations with themselves, their self-relations, and to reveal the human being which stands condemned as a mere resource or as a factor of production, as the basis of human existence. The foundation of human existence can only be the human being herself.[8]

In contrast to Marx's radical conception of Man (*Mensch*), economic theory, and with it all theory that announces a project of analytical derivation, is forced to accept the world of capital as a world where the human being obtains as a factor of production that requires more fine tuning to improve its effective, efficient, and economic usage. The analytical derivation of human existence from the presupposed world of hypothesised structures not only accepts without question the deadly slogan that work is liberating. It also accepts the commodified existence of human social practice as history's finest achievement. The circumstance that these structures presuppose the bloody grimace of exploitation, is either quietly overlooked or prudently forgotten. In short, the derivation of the human being from presupposed structures is not only traditional in its theoretical approach and perspective but, also, politically reactionary. The derivation of the human being from hypothesised structures does not inquire about the foundation of the human world and instead presupposes that this foundation is beyond comprehension — it is said to reside in the invisible whose hand makes the world go round. The acceptance of the invisible hand as the administrator of exact justice does not really lead to a vicious circle of metatheories. It leads, in fact, to the return of traditional theory's most pressing concern, that is to legitimate existing relations of power. The "original position" of political theory is that of an *ancilla constitutionis* [servant to existing powers].

The weapon of critique shows that the world we inhabit is our world, rather than the world of capital, a world created by human practice, dependent upon human social practice and open to the constitutive power of human practice. Thus the Marxian notion that the emancipation of the working class can only be the work of the working class itself. This emancipation can not rely on the wage relation. The category of wage labour is already a perversion; it is premised on human social practice as a commodified practice. However "real" this perversion, it only supplies an understanding of the movement of fetishised forms. It does not provide an understanding of the constitution of these forms. Marx's critique of fetishism shows the absurdity of a world in which humans exist, and exist so with necessity, in the form of personified conditions of production, i.e., the personification of things. The standpoint of critique shows the other side — i.e., the social constitution — of this strange, and murderous, personification. It shows human sensuous activity, an activity which exists against itself in the commodified form of wage labour. Thus the critique of capital amounts to a critique of "labour," of individualised, alienated labour, a labour whose social existence confronts the individual producers as an external and independent thing. Capitalist social relations rest on the divorce of the mass of the population from the means of production. This divorce was the result of primitive accumulation and it is the presupposition on which the capitalist exploitation of labour rests. Capital, as Marx (1972, p. 492) argues, is "the form assumed by the conditions of labour" and that is, of labour that is free from her means: "object-less *free labour*" (Marx, 1973, p. 507) "under the command of capital" (ibid., p. 508). Marx's critique of political economy reveals the human basis of capitalist forms. This content exists in a mode of being denied and that is, it obtains in the form of a labouring commodity. Thus "the absurdity of a mode of production on which bourgeois purposive-rationality, profitability, and respectability feed, was exposed. It stood naked" (Agnoli, 1992, pp. 45-6). Marx's critique vindicated the negative role of philosophy according to which humanity is not a resource but a purpose.

In sum, Marx's call for revolution stands in sharp contrast to "Marxian" attempts of supplying a theory of the state. Political theory — whether couched in Marxist language or not — amounts to an attempt of making labour's presence in the capital relation more agreeable. Any desire for communism is rendered redundant in favour of a more favourable regulation of the labour question. Favourable to whom? The risk run by Marxism as a theory of society, or as a theory of the state, is that of becoming complicit in the alienation and domination to which it is officially opposed.

III

The human being is inseparable, that is, it can not be separated, unless through force and violence, into an economic factor of production and, separated from it, a political being endowed with the rights of citizenship. In bourgeois society however this separation is real in practice: the separation of the human being from the means of production and the constituted existence of these as capital, underlies the separation between the political and the economic. The "logic of separation" is the "real generation process of capital" (Marx, 1972, p. 422) and "the whole system of capitalist production is based on the fact that the workman sells his labour-power as a commodity" (1983, pp. 405-6). It is this separation of labour from her means that supports the conventional view of the state as a structure which is separate from the "economic." In other words, while the economist treats human purposeful activity as a factor of production, the focus of the political scientist falls on the democratic and legal constitution of the social and political rights and duties of the citizen. However, the so-called human factor of production is no less a citizen as a person endowed with equal rights and conversely the citizen is no less a factor of production as a wage-labouring commodity. Political theory, the theory of the state, is fundamentally an affirmative theory of separation, and that is a theory of power as constituted power. It presupposes the existence of labour as object-less labour, as a labouring commodity and, because of this presupposition, contributes to the containment of labour as a human factor of production.

The separation of labour from her means is constitutive of the apparent relative autonomy of the political from the economic and, conversely, the relative autonomy of the economic from the political. In bourgeois society, the emancipation of the political from society amounts to the creation of a political system that administers the common concerns of bourgeois society and supervises the proper conduct of bourgeois exchange relations. The political emancipation of the state entails its role to guarantee the relations of abstract equality. The emancipation of the state from society rests on these relations and that is, it is based on the separation of living labour from her means and secures the continuous reproduction of this separation through law and order. Hence, the attempts of political theory to construe the state as a distinct form of political organisation that resides outside social relations and that merely intervenes, from the "outside," into society to secure and guarantee the foundations upon which the society of burghers rest: the rights of private property. Everybody is equal before the law and as equals, all are treated identical as abstract citizens endowed with standardised rights. The state, in sum, guarantees the equality of rights in the inequality of property. The state then supervises the commensurability of the relations of inequality with the relations of equality — the reduction of difference to equality in law and money. The specific character of human beings is thus denied and their existence as mere character-masks of exchange relations is affirmed as if these were a person apart. Auschwitz, as Adorno reminds us, not only confirmed the violence of the bourgeois relations of abstract equality and abstract identity. It also confirmed the bourgeois exchange relations of pure identity as death.

In sum, the critique of political economy amounts to the critique of the form of the state: the form of the state does not stand outside history but it is rather the organisational form of a capitalistically producing and bourgeois (*bürgerlich*) constituted society. The form of the state, as Marx put it in the *Grundrisse,* is the concentration of bourgeois society. The state, then, is the political form of bourgeois society; it is the form in which the safeguarding of the equality of rights is focused politically. The law of the (labour-) market presupposes, as its conditions, the capitalist state that protects the inequality in property through the safeguarding of the equality of rights, of abstract equality.

Every social crisis which upsets the political sounds the death warning of this separation of the human being into, on the one hand, an economic factor of production, and citizen on the other. The constitutive basis of bourgeois society is the inseparable essence of human existence: living labour. While, in other words, "the subdivision of labour is the assassination of a people" (Urquhart, quoted in Marx, 1983, p. 343), it consolidates the "original" separation of labour from its conditions through further and further fragmentations of the social labour process. Yet, however much social labour is fragmented, divided and subdivided, human cooperation remains "the fundamental form of the capitalist mode of production" (Marx, 1983, p. 317). Without human cooperation, their would be neither production nor exchange. This cooperation exists against itself in the commodity-form that integrates the "assassination of a people" with the respectful forms equal and free exchange relations that are protected and safeguarded by the state.

IV

The capitalist state is the first in human history with no direct access to the material product of labour. The subordination of social relations to the capitalist state is characterised by impersonal or abstract forms of dependency in terms of law and money. Within the framework of bourgeois freedom, "individual" freedom is the freedom of contract between equals regardless of their inequality in property. The law in its abstract majestic form treats poor and rich as equals. It treats the owners of the means of production and the free labourer as identical subjects, as legal subjects. The law is blind to privileges. It is a law of equality. Contractual relations represent the form in which, according to law, freedom obtains in the form of a legally bound recognition of private individuals in their relation to one another. The contract is the juridical form of freedom — the master of the contract is the state. Neither does the law "announce" itself as if it were a force in its own right. Nor does the law "enforce" itself. The law requires the maker of the law to fill it with material force, that is to implement it indiscriminately, imposing upon social relations the abstract quality of their existence as personifications of formal equality. The capitalist state rests on the social constitution of these rights and protects them through the regulation of law and money. This, then, is the subordination of social relations to the law of private property, that is equality, freedom and Bentham. The treatment of all as equals before the law characterises the form of the state as an "illusory community" (cf. Marx and Engels, 1962). It treats the real existing individual as constituted "character-masks" or "personifications" (on this: Marx, 1983), and espouses the interest that is common to all character-masks: their universal existence for each other as a resource, as a utility.

The capitalist state posits the political form of the separation of human social practice from her means. The abstract citizen endowed with human rights and the wage-labourer endowed with the freedom of contract are two sides of the same separation. Each individual is treated as an equal in law. Instead of despotism, the state imposes order through law; instead of relations of conflict, the state administers contractual relations of social interaction; instead of privileges, the state imposes upon social relations the free and equal market relations, that is, the political organisation of the working class in the form of the wage relation. The form of the state entails — or, rather, it just is — the coercive suppression of social emancipation in favour of the legal standardisation of abstract equality. This guarantee of the rights of private property entails the coercive character of the state; it forbids poor and rich equally to steal bread.

The political relations do not primarily correspond to, or reproduce, economic relations, as if both relations merely followed their own separate laws of development. Rather, the political complements the economic as, together, different forms of the same fundamental class antagonism. The political guarantee of contract amounts to the containment of labour in the perverted form of wage labour, that is the commodity form through which human productive power subsists. The capitalist state is a capitalist state not because the bourgeoisie has occupied the good offices of the state. It is a capitalist state because of its form: the separation of the political from society. This separation rests on the original separation of the mass of the population from the means of subsistence and production. The separation of the state from society entails the violence of the original accumulation of capital: as the master of the law, the state monopolises the violence of the original separation in terms of law and order, that is it imposes the condition of separation, of expropriation, upon social labour power through the enforcement of the law of abstract equality. The content of the state is thus expressed in its form, that is the emancipation of the political from the economic. This emancipation is a mode of existence of the separation of labour from her means and their existence as capital. The form of the capitalist state entails its function to guarantee the separation of labour from her means through the protection of the rights of private property. The existence of the capitalist state rests on this separation. The other side of this separation is labour's existence as a labouring commodity whose rights are protected through law and order. The law does not discriminate. It treats all owners of commodities as equals. The separation of the political from the economic entails the state as an apparently "impartial" regulator of the rule of abstract equality, protecting the owner of labour power and the owner of the means of protection equally against theft: the state guarantees the rights of contract between capital and labour and thereby safeguards the property rights of capital as rights of exploitation and appropriation. This, then, is what Marazzzi (1995) refers to as the imposition of work through the commodity form, an imposition that is politically focused in the form of the state as the master of the law of abstract equality.

The law of capital consist of the expanded reproduction of the divorce of the mass of humanity from the means of production. This can be achieved only through the progressive exploitation of living labour, the substance of value and therewith surplus value. The individual capitalist has constantly to expand "his capital, in order to preserve it, but extend it he cannot, except by means of progressive accumulation" (Marx, 1983, p. 555). The risk is bankruptcy. Thus, mediated through competition, personified capital is spurred into action. "Fanatically bent on making value expand itself, [the personified capitalist] ruthlessly forces the human race to produce for production's sake," increasing "the mass of human beings exploited by him" (ibid.). Capital depends on "object-less labour." Each individual capital has not only to produce, but to increase relative surplus value in order to avoid bankruptcy. Thus living labour has to be expelled form production so as to reduce necessary labour, the constitutive site of surplus labour, to its utmost. The relationship between necessary labour and surplus labour is that of the constituent parts of the working day and the class relation which constitutes it. Capital exists only in anti-thesis to living labour as the substance of value. Yet, this anti-thesis is asymmetrical in that capital can not liberate itself from labour. This is only possible on labour's side. Capital has to reduce necessary labour to increase surplus labour and at the same time impose necessary labour upon the world's working class so as to assert itself as a "perennial pumping-machine of surplus labour" (Marx, 1966, p. 822). Labour, in short, does not stand external to capital. Rather, it is a presence — a constitutive presence — in capital. Labour is the substance of value.

Let us recap. The state enforces the norms of private property and therewith safeguards the social recognition of these norms. This relation of the state to society implies that private individuals exist as abstract individuals endowed with standardised rights and, as such, treated as abstract citizens. The political regulation of law and order denies the existence of class. At the same time, behind the sanction of the right of property there lies the doubly free labourer and the concentration of the means of existence in the hands of capital. Behind formal equality and formal freedom lies social reproduction in the form of capital. The formal safeguarding of rights entails the substantive guarantee of exploitation, rendering the state inseparable from the economic and vice versa. The guarantee of exploitation through law and order obtains through the guarantee of contract, that is the legal form through which the exploitation of labour subsists. The form of the state inverts hence from its exalted transcendental position as the incarnation of political emancipation, to the political master of the law of abstract equality, safeguarding exploitation through the guarantee and protection of the commodity form, including the commodity form of labour's productive power, that is her wage-labouring existence. The form of the state entails its content as the political organiser of the "republic of the market."

In short, the political guarantee of contract, the provision of law and its enforcement, involves the state in the containment of labour's constitutive presence in the capital relation not only through the legalisation of the social relations of production but, also, their stratification. The legalisation of social relations presupposes their stratification, and vice versa. The state, then, does not "intervene" into bourgeois society. Rather, it is the organised force of bourgeois society and as such seeks to secure the reproduction of the social relations of production in politically supervised, legally controlled, non-conflictual forms; in short: in civilised forms of violence.

The bourgeois separation, then, between the political and the economic, the so-called relative autonomy of the political, is real — it has a real existence. It is real in terms of the formal mode of existence of the political. It is, in other words, as real as the fetishism of the value form which reports a human world that obtains merely as a derivative of the relations between the things themselves. The critique of fetishism shows a different world, a disenchanted world that rests on human social practice however perverted or enlightened this practice might be. The acceptance of the constituted fetishism of the state as an independent power, as a power in its own right, merely espouses the bourgeois identification of the state as an indispensable protector of private property. The form of the state thus indicates formal freedom and formal equality as "community," the content of which is the "perpetuation of the labourer" — the "sine qua non of the existence of capital" (Marx, 1983, p. 536). The "autonomised power of the state" (cf. Marx, 1974, p. 882) entails its content of upholding the rights of contract. This puts the state right back into the society of burghers. The state and economy, then, do not exist as two different form of social organisation. Rather, the state is a bourgeois state. It is inseparable form bourgeois society. It is, as Marx (1973, p. 108) put it the "concentration of bourgeois society." In conclusion, in contrast to Poulantzas' attempt at a political theory of the state, Marx's critique of the state as the "concentrated and organised force of society" (Marx, 1983, p. 703) entails the critique of the fetishism of the state form as something that guarantees the universal rights of Man and whose power is such that, given the right conditions, it can be used to implement and secure these rights against the special interests of capital. The state no doubt appears as an impartial administrator of political space and impartial upholder of the right of property independently from each commodity owner. However, the circumstance that labour is "object-less" and because of this is condemned to perform as a commodity under the command of capital, gives the game away. The "concentration of the coercive character of bourgeois society in the form of the state" (Agnoli, 1990) posits the state, in regard to labour, as an instance of oppression (containing labour as wage labour) and, at the same time, an instance of her wage-labouring existence in capitalism. The political guarantee of private property includes the guarantee of the wage relation, that is, it guarantees the property rights of the worker: labour power and its reproduction. In short, the "purpose of the state is the perpetuation the slavery of the worker" (cf. Marx, 1969, p. 33) In conclusion, the treatment of the state through political theory and political philosophy lenses — whether couched in Marxist language or not — amounts to an unquestionably useful, and that is consensus creating and therewith pacifying, or peace-making, deceitful publicity.

V

Marx argued in the 18th Brumaire, that all political upheavals have perfected the state instead of smashing it. There is no doubt that "political upheavals" are quite incapable of realising Marx's ideal of "the society of the free and equal" (cf. Agnoli, 2000). The existence of the "political" as an apparently distinct form of social organisation presupposes the notion of bourgeois revolution. Bourgeois revolutions allow merely for the political emancipation of the individualised individual as a bearer of the universal rights of abstract equality. Capital's perpetual requirement for new beginnings connotes a no-less perpetual new beginning for labour, for labour's productive and destructive power upon whose containment capital depends. Within the established relations of the class antagonism between capital of labour, bourgeois revolutions merely allow for a history with a bloody and grotesque grimace — a grimace whose violence is as elementary as it is meaningless (*begriffslos*). In short, they manifest the delusions of bourgeois freedom — better: the freedom to accumulate abstract wealth for accumulation's sake. In these revolution, the promise of a better world, a human world, where human dignity obtains as the condition of the society of the free and equal, where humanity is a purpose, is endorsed as the freedom of private property, a freedom where humanity obtains as an exploitable resource.

The political guarantee of abstract equality, freedom and Bentham imposes upon social relations the conditions of their existence as mere personifications of the accumulation of abstract wealth. The guarantee, then, of the property rights of capital involves the attempt to bind the present to the future, safeguarding the validation of monetary claims on the future exploitation of labour in the present through force. In this process, the self-contradictory form of the state is the "harmonies' last refuge" (Marx, 1973, p. 886), — harmonies of formal equality and formal freedom upon which exploitation rests. The state as the harmonies' last refuge represents thus "communal interest" (cf. Marx and

Engels, 1962), imposing formal exchange equality through the sacrificing of social relations to the meaningless (*begriffslose*) form of money.[9] The imposition of money involves the political safeguarding of economic freedom as the abstract average of equality, the incarnation of which is money. The state attains existence as the collective representative of "money" as the most elementary form of private property, involving law and order control as its precondition, premise and result. The imposition of the value form involves not only the subordination of social relations to money capital's impossible, but no less and necessarily violent, quest of making money out of money but, more fundamentally, the monetary decomposition of class relations on the basis of the wage relation.[10] Capital has to contain labour as the condition of its own existence. The antagonism between capital and labour involves, as already reported, the contradiction that capital has to impose necessary labour upon the world's working class and at the same time reduce necessary labour to the utmost so as to increase surplus labour. The other side of the exploitation of labour's productive power is the crisis of capitalist overaccumulation — better: overaccumulation is the false name that is given to overexploitation. From labour's perspective, then, the exploitation of her productive power leads not only to the overaccumulation of capital. The development of her productive power is also limited by capital. Full employment is intelligible as the ideal state of affairs only in a society where humanity does not exist as an exploitable resource but as a purpose. For labour, then, her freedom, the free development of her productive power, entails the transformation of the means of production into means of human emancipation. Such emancipation stand in direct contrast to the surrogate community that the state presents.

The perpetual increase in labour's productive power is based on the capitalist requirement to produce exchange value, ie. money, at the same time as abstract labour, in the form of money, transcends its capitalist form. The other side, then, of labour's productive power is the potentially irredeemable accumulation of unemployed capital, of debt. Marx (1966, p. 438) characterised this situation as "the abolition of the capitalist mode of production within the capitalist mode of production itself." Within capitalist society, this contradiction can only be contained through force (*Gewalt*) including not only the destruction of productive capacities, unemployment, worsening conditions, and widespread poverty, but also the destruction of human life through war and starvation. "Force" is as meaningless and elementary as money. Labour's antagonism to, its constitutive social power against capital is the other side of money's "transcendental power." "Money is now pregnant" (ibid., p. 393) with a future which threatens to push it into the museum of history. The politics of money is intrinsically oppressive. Everybody is equal before money. Money knows no special privileges. It treats poor and rich as equals. The imposition of the abstract equality of money involves the imposition of inequality because "the power which each individual exercises over the activity of others or over social wealth exists in him as the owner of exchange values, of money. The individual carries his social power, as well as his bond with society, in his pocket" (Marx, 1973, p. 157). The subterranean use of force that the reproduction of the inequality in property through the imposition of abstract equality entails, is not the exception but, rather, lies at the heart of the politics of money. In other words, the normality of the seemingly equal character of the form of money reveals itself as coercion. The form of the state is charged with upholding the law of abstract equality; it is the social foundation upon which the state rests. The violence of capital's original beginning is not abandoned in the imposition of abstract equality upon social relations. Rather, it subsists through the "civilised" forms of law and order, of equality and freedom. These forms are the constituted forms of violence — violence as civilised normality.[11] The state of money is the state of law and order.

With Marx, we might wish to argue that "theoretical mysteries ... find their rational solution in human practice and in the comprehension of this practice" (Marx, 1975, p. 5). The productive and destructive power of labour needs, then, to be made manifest theoretically and practically. Without such a manifestation of labour's power, history will remain a history of bourgeois revolutions, revolutions that deny human dignity in the name of freedom — the freedom of capital. For social practice to be free and equal, another revolution is required — a revolution where humanity leaves behind its self-imposed immaturity and becomes a subject in possession of her own affairs. Such a future rests on the abolition of the conditions that render human existence a resource, exchanged and accumulated in the form of money and guaranteed by the state.

VI

The core "problematic" of Marx's critique is this: how is it possible to understand the circumstance that human social practice is constitutive at the same time as human beings appear to be ruled by already existing abstractions.[12] From within political philosophy, this question is posed, at best, in terms a critical gap between a less than perfect political reality and the pleasant norms of equality and freedom.[13] This project allows merely for a moralising criticism which does not comprehend that the pleasant norms are adequate to their content, the bad reality of exploitation. The "attitude of the bourgeois to the forms of his existence expresses itself through universal forms of morality" (Marx and

Engels, 1962, p. 164). In this section of *The German Ideology,* Marx sketches the character of the bourgeois relations of reproduction as follows: everyone is dependent on everyone else, and each person can only reproduce himself inasmuch as all others become means for him. Furthermore, each individual can only pursue and realise his own particular interests when his conditions of reproduction, which are identical to those of everyone else, are accepted, respected, and recognised by everyone else. The particular will of the individual obtains thus through a will in which all individuals are united, which is common to all that is, is universal. This universal "interest" denotes the bourgeois condition of existence through which particular interests are realised.

> The individuals who rule in these conditions — leaving aside the fact that their power must assume the form of the state — have to endow their will, which is determined by these definite conditions, with a universal expression as the will of the state, as law, an expression whose content is always determined by the relations of this class, as the civil and criminal law demonstrates in the clearest possible way. Just as the weight of their bodies does not depend on their idealistic will or on their arbitrary decision, so also the fact that they enforce their own will in the form of law, and at the same time make it independent of the personal arbitrariness of each individual among them, does not depend on their idealistic will. Their personal rule must at the same time assume the form of average rule. Their personal power is based on living conditions which in their development are shared by many individuals, and the continuation of which they, as ruling individuals, must preserve in opposition to others while at the same time maintaining that they hold these conditions to be for the good of all. The expression of this will, which is determined by their common interests, is the law. It is precisely because individuals who are independent of one another assert themselves and their own will, and because on this basis their attitude to one another is bound to be egotistical, that self-denial is made necessary in law and right (ibid., p. 311)

and assumes the form of the state — the master of the law.

Marx's work focuses on forms, at first on forms of consciousness (i.e., religion and law), then later on the forms of capital. The focus on forms was identical with the critique of the inverted forms of social existence, an existence constituted by human social practice. All these forms obtain as inverted forms of a "community" that is external to the individuals, and from which they must emancipate themselves in order ever to be able to interact with one another "as individuals" (ibid., p. 70f). This central idea is presented most emphatically in *The German Ideology*: "The reality [*das Bestehende*], that communism creates, is precisely the real [*wirkliche*] basis for rendering it impossible that any reality should exist independently of individuals, in so far as this reality is only a product of the preceding intercourse of the individuals themselves" (ibid., p. 70). It is thus a matter of deciphering the appearance [*Schein*] of independence that this "surrogate of community" posits (ibid., p. 74) in order to reveal its "human basis" (cf. Marx, 1983, p. 94) and then of abolishing it practically from the world, allowing human beings to enter into relationship with one another, not as character-masks, but as social individuals.

Marx sees this new figure of society anticipated in the

> community of revolutionary proletarians, who extend their own control over the conditions of their own existence and those of all members of society. It is as individuals that the individuals participate in it. It is exactly this combination of individuals (assuming the advanced stage of modern productive forces, of course) which puts the conditions of the free development and movement of individuals under their control — conditions which were previously abandoned to chance and had won an independent existence over and against the separate individuals precisely because of their separation as individuals" (Marx and Engels, 1962, p. 74).

In sum, the critique of the state is not satisfied with a "critical" comparison between a less than perfect political reality, on the one hand, and the pleasant norms of equality and liberty, on the other. Instead, it scrutinises these normative rights and reveals them as rights which presuppose exploitation and expropriation. There is no place for the form of the state in a communist society or in a revolutionary movement. The state is a capitalist state. Its role is to secure the rights of private property through law and its enforcement.

In conclusion, the form of the state presupposes the separation of the mass of the population from the means of production. This separation is the social basis on which the form of the state rests. A society where the free development of each is the condition for the free development of all, can not rest on this separation. It is this separation that renders human productive power a commodity. The determination of the state as the "concentrated and organised force of society" is based on the insight that the idea of "equal rights" is in principle a bourgeois right. In its content, it is a right of inequality (see Marx, 1968). Hence Marx's judgement that all who live from their labour and the sale of their labour power "find themselves directly opposed to the form in which, hitherto, the individuals, of which society consists, have given themselves collective expression, that is, the State; in order, therefore, to assert themselves as individuals, they must overthrow the State" (Marx and Engels, 1962, p. 77).

ENDNOTES

1 Many friends supplied comments. I would like to acknowledge in particular Ana Dinerstein's useful advice. The usual disclaimers apply.

2 On this see Gunn (1992).

3 On this see Bonefeld (2001).

4 See Backhaus (1997) for a succinct account on Marx's work as a critique of economic categories *sans phrase*.

5 It would be wrong, however, to view the state derivation debate in this wholesale way. While some contributors derived the state from the anatomy of bourgeois society and its so-called objective laws of capitalist development (Altvater, 1978), others rejected this economic reductionism and analysed the state as a form of class struggle (Holloway and Picciotto, 1978). The argument of this chapter builds on this critical contribution (see also Bonefeld, 1992). On the state derivation debate, see Clarke (1991); Holloway and Picciotto (eds) (1978).

6 The state derivation debate and Poulantzas theory of the state overlap in Hirsch's (1978) contribution.

7 Political theory, Marxist or not, views conflict in essentially constructive terms. The characterisation of conflict as a constructive conflict is intrinsic to the notion of a pluralist society and has been influential in the study of a variety of fields such as industrial relations and theories of parliamentary democracy. The understanding that conflict is endemic in a pluralist society does not mean that conflict should be provoked. It means that rules, procedures, and laws are invoked which regulate conflict and through which conflict can express itself in constructive forms. A theory of the functionality of conflict is presented, for example, by Coser (1956) and has been developed within the Marxist framework by Poulantzas (1973). See also Agnoli's contribution to this volume.

8 On this see especially his "Contribution to Critique of Hegel's Philosophy of Law. Introduction," esp. p. 182, in *Collected Works*, vol. 3, Lawrence & Wishart, London.

9 On this see Bonefeld (1995a); and Neary and Taylor (1998).
10 On this see Marazzi (1995) and Bonefeld and Holloway (1995).
11 On this see Benjamin (1965).
12 Space forbids a lengthy discussion of this point. For accounts see especially Bonefeld (1995); Holloway (1995) and Negri (1991, 1999). This part draws on Reichelt (2000).
13 For a recent endorsement of this see, Callinicos (2000).

References

Agnoli, J. (1990) Die Transformation der Demokratie und andere Schriften zur Kritik der Politik, Ça ira, Freiburg.

Agnoli, J. (1992) "Destruction as the Determination of the Scholar in Miserable Times," *Common Sense*, no. 12, reprinted in this volume.

Agnoli, J. (2000) "The State, the Market, and the End of History, in Bonefeld, W. and K. Psychopedis (eds.) *The Politics of Change*, Macmillan, London.

Altvater, E. (1978) "Some Problems of State Intervention," in Holloway, J. and S. Picciotto (eds) 1978.

Backhaus, H.G. (1997) *Dialektik der Wertform*, Ça ira, Freiburg.

Benjamin, W. (1965) *Zur Kritik der Gewalt und andere Aufsätze*, Suhrkamp, Frankfurt.

Bonefeld, W. (1992) "Social Constitution and the Form of the Capitalist State," in Bonefeld, W. etal. (eds) *Open Marxism*, vol. I, Pluto, London.

Bonefeld, W. (1995) "Capital as Subject and the Existence of Labour," in Bonefeld etal. (eds.) *Open Marxism*, vol. III, Pluto, London.

Bonefeld, W. (1995a) "Money, Equality and Exploitaton," in Bonefeld, W. and J. Holloway (eds.) *Global Capital, National State and the Politics of Money*, Macmillan, London.

Bonefeld, W. (2001) "Kapital and its Subtitle: A Note on the Meaning of Critique," *Capital & Class*, no. 75.

Bonefeld, W. and J. Hollway (1995) "Conclusion: Money and Class Struggle," in Bonefeld, W. and J. Holloway (eds.) *Global Capital, National State and the Politics of Money*, Macmillan, London.

Callinicos, A. (2000) *Equality*, Polity, Cambridge.

Clarke, S. (1991) *The State Debate*, Macmillan, London.

Coser, L.A. (1956) *The Functions of Social Conflict*, The Free Press, Glencoe.

Gunn. R. (1992) "Against Historical Materialism," in Bonefeld, W. etal. (eds.) *Open Maxism* vol. II, Pluto, London.

Hirsch, J. (1978) "The State Apparatus and Social Reproduction" Holloway, J. and S. Picciotto (eds.) 1978.

Holloway, J. (1995) "From Scream of Refusal to Scream of Power, in Bonefeld, W. etal. (eds.) *Open Marxism* vol. III, Pluto, London.
Holloway, J. and S. Picciotto (1978) "Introduction: Towards a Materialist Theory of the State," in Holloway, J. and S. Picciotto (eds) 1978.
Holloway, J. and S. Picciotto (eds) (1978) *State and Capital*, Arnold, London.
Marrazi, C. (1995) "Money in the World Crisis," in Bonefeld, W. and J. Holloway (eds.) *Global Capital, National State and the Politics of Money*, Macmillan, London.
Marx, K. (1964) *Zur Judenfrage*, in MEW 1, Dietz, Berlin.
Marx, K. (1966) *Capital* vol. III, Lawrence & Wishart, London.
Marx, K. (1968) *Kritik des Gothaer Programms*, in *MEW* 19, Dietz, Berlin.
Marx, K. (1969) *Die Klassenkämpfe in Frankreich 1848 bis 1950*, in MEW 7, Dietz, Berlin.
Marx, K. (1972) *Theories of Surplus Value* Part III Lawrence & Wishart, London.
Marx, K. (1973) *Grundrisse*, Penguin, Harmondsworth.
Marx, K. (1974) *Grundrisse* Dietz Berlin.
Marx, K. (1975) "Theses on Feuerbach," *Collected Works*, vol. 5, London, Lawrence & Wishart.
Marx, K. (1983) *Capital* vol. I, Lawrence & Wishart, London.
Marx, K and F. Engels (1962) *Die deutsche Ideology*, MEW 3, Dietz, Berlin.
Neary, M. and G. Taylor (1998) *Money and the Human Condition*, Macmillan, London.
Negri, A. (1991) *The Savage Anamoly* University of Minnesota Press, Minnesota.
Negri, A. (1999) *Insurgencies*, University of Minnesota Press, Minnesota.
Poulantzas, N. (1973) *Political Power and Social Classes*, New Left Books, London.
Reichelt, H. (2000) "Jürgen Habermas' Reconstruction of Historical Materialism," in Bonefeld, W. and Psychopedis, K. (eds.) *The Politics of Change*, Macmillan, London.

12

From the Revolution Against Philosophy To the Revolution Against Capital

Mike Rooke

"The chief defect of all hitherto existing materialism — that of Feuerbach included — is that the thing (*Gegenstand*), reality, sensuousness, is conceived only in the form of the object (*Objekt*) or of contemplation (*Anschauung*), but not as human sensuous activity, practice, not subjectively."

The conclusion to Marx's critique of bourgeois philosophy, was summed up with characteristic simplicity in his first thesis on Feuerbach, written in 1845. The materialism Marx refers to represented the most advanced form of bourgeois philosophy at that time, conducive to the rising bourgeois class in its struggle against feudal power. Science was its inspiration and its guide, and for Marx it had assumed its most radical form in the work of Feuerbach. The importance of Marx's recognition of this "chief defect" is that he had grasped the limitations of, and therefore transcended the epistemological dualism at the heart of, this materialism. This was a breakthrough of immense importance for Marx's thought.

The theory of knowledge which ran as a continuous thread through the work of the British empiricists and the French materialists of the 17th and 18th centuries rested on a view of the human subject as the passive receptor of stimuli from the external world. Its progressive aspect lay in the implication that human subjects were the product of the environment and nature, not divine providence. This materialist epistemology depended on a dualist conception of the world — one divided into subject and object. According to Marx it was in turn, contemplative and mechanistic.

Contemplative in the sense that the subject relates to the external world through a process of passive cognition, thus determining the primary question for this materialism: the truth or otherwise of our knowledge of the external world. But the question of the objectivity of knowledge was according to Marx, a scholastic one insofar as "practical, human-sensuous activity" is left out of account. And this is what materialism had ignored, leaving it to idealism to mark out the active contribution that the subject makes in the process of knowledge, albeit in an abstract fashion (as "sensuous contemplation").

Mechanistic in the sense that cognition is conceived as a one-way causal process, connecting two discreet and independently existing abstractions — subject and object. For Marx, to the extent that we can talk about a knowable world, it must be understood as the relational result of human sensuous activity. Conceiving the external world as it exists independently of human knowledge of it has no importance for Marx — it is a non-question. For him there is no pre-human, objective world, or even Kantian "things-in-themselves." The knowable world is at once the product of human selection, classification and transformation. This is what Marx means when he talks of world objectification, a concept derived from Hegel that denotes the creation of the world through the social labour of human beings. The world, nature, is man's creation — hence Marx's phrase: nature is man's inorganic body.

So whereas for materialism the starting and end point of inquiry is how the external world, nature, can be known, and known objectively, for Marx the starting point is an inquiry into the social labour of human beings, for it is by virtue of this practical activity that the world is produced. It follows that this inquiry implies the construction of a natural science of man. Furthermore, insofar as man's productive activity has evolved over time such a science must be historical. While in a philosophical sense Marx may be seen to have shifted the theoretical focus from the plane of epistemology (theory of knowledge) to that of ontology (theory of being), there has in fact been a supersession of philosophy as such.[1] Marx had arrived at the point of constructing a materialist natural science that was both historical and dialectical. Historical in that its raw material was the productive activity of human beings (labour) conducted under definite and changing social relations, and dialectical in that Marx has dissolved the separation of subject and object into the notion of labour as world objectification. For Marx as for Hegel dialectic concerned the relation of subject and object.[2]

By the mid 19th century the consolidation of bourgeois economic and social power was reflected in the emergence of positivism as a dominant ideology. Expressed most clearly in the social sciences, it developed to a further degree (under the impact of the natural sciences) the dualism systematised first by Cartesian rationalism. In its reliance on the empirically given, raw sense data of the external world (the "facts"), positivist modes of thought dispensed with any constituting subject (Kant), or totality (Hegel). The separation of the individual subject from the external world was expressed at the level of knowledge, which is why the dominant interpretive framework for bourgeois social theory was that of epistemology.[3] This fundamental dualism gave rise to a host of familiar antinomies: between thought and action; theory and practice, judgements of fact and value ("is" and "ought"), ends and means, etc.

Having transcended this epistemological dualism, Marx proceeded to fashion an intellectual framework that would bring into unity his working categories. The starting point and the pivotal category was labour. But it was labour apprehended in a unique way. Marx was alone in asking the all important question: what kind of labour is it that produces value? His answer lay in the concept of abstract labour, that is labour rendered abstract by virtue of its exchangeability in the market as a commodity (ie., labour power bought and sold in advance of its consumption). Thus, value, abstract labour, and therefore alienated labour, are aspects of the same social relation. Arising from this wage labour-capital relation are the economic categories of capitalism, systematised in bourgeois political economy and expressing the phenomenon of commodity fetishism. Lukacs extended and generalised the effect of commodity fetishism in his notion of reification — the reflection in thought of the perceived autonomy of a fragmented and objectified world beyond human control. At root this is only the human contemplation of labour's alienated activity. Thus the category of labour, which for Marx is the necessary mediation between subject and object (and the means to dissolve this separation), is developed to the point of uncovering the secret of capitalism: the extraction of surplus value from the direct producers. But for Marx the exploitation of labour and the alienation of labour cannot be separated. Paying labour its full reward would not end alienated labour, for these both reside in a mode of production where labour is rendered abstract for the purpose of producing value — labour becomes a commodity. The negativity of labour, which drives the class struggle, derives not only from the mechanism of exploitation but from the character of capitalist work. In this sense class struggle at the point of production is a revolt not just against inadequate payment but against the inhuman character of work under capitalism, and therefore prefigures the abolition of the wage-capital relation and the reification of consciousness that goes with it. This is the real and full import of the overcoming of the subject-object dualism which Lukacs attempted in his 1923 book *History and Class Consciousness*. In it he talks of the proletariat (subject) as inseparable from the capitalist system (object) which constitutes it, and the impossibility of changing the former without changing the latter. The proletariat becomes the identical subject-object of history in its struggle against wage labour. Whereas Classical German philosophy (principally in the persons of Fichte and Hegel) had only conceived of overcoming the dualism of subject and object on the plane of philosophy, Marx's great achievement was to ground it in the proletarian revolution against capital.[4]

The first movement for proletarian emancipation after Marx was the Second International, its principal institutional force German Social Democracy. The major theoreticians of this movement were Engels, Kautsky, Plekhanov and Labriola. In its fundamental philosophy the Marxism of the Second International has been described as "naturalist," signifying a conception of dialectics as the science of the same general laws governing both nature and humanity. History was conceived as a succession of modes of production, emerging and declining with a necessary inevitability, and it was the task of Marxists to identify these objective laws in order to work with the grain of historical progress. It followed that given the immutability and inevitability of the working of such laws, intervention to create history was seen to be less important than gaining knowledge of it: given the inevitability of the decline of capitalism, it was also inevitable that the working class would eventually win power. Its methodological leaning was epistemology: correct knowledge was the mark of scientificity, a view reflecting the enormous prestige held by natural science by the end of the 19th century. Second International Marxism thus reproduced the fundamentals of the contemplative and mechanical materialism that Marx had earlier rejected, and an approach to history that was rigidly deterministic.

This was in fact an enormous retreat from the theoretical vantage point reached by Marx. Most of Marx's insights into alienated labour and commodity fetishism, and the implications of these for the nature of the socialist revolution were never absorbed by the theoreticians of the Second International (partly, it has to be said, because the 1844 Manuscripts were not available to that generation of Marxists). But this was really just one aspect of the failure to appreciate the importance of Marx's philosophical revolution against contemplative materialism. Ignoring labour as the mediating category between subject and object, Second International Marxism reintroduced dualism into the heart of the Marxist project. Moreover ignoring the importance of the category of labour in Hegel meant that Hegel could be cast in the role of a hopeless idealist, and once inverted, Marx could be treated as an epistemological materialist (ie., a more radical version of Feuerbach!).

The Second International's determinist and evolutionist approach to history presupposed a proletariat that was subordinate to the party. If the course of history was inevitably determined, the patient and gradual marshalling of electoral forces was a sufficient strategy for arriving at a socialist commonwealth. Substitutionism lay at the heart of this conception of theory and practice: the party acted on behalf of the class, and the very conception of socialism was a re-configuration of the categories existing under capitalism. The socialist commonwealth would be planned for, not by, the producers. The negativity of labour, the autonomous struggle of workers against wage slavery, and the resolution of this in the abolition of labour as a commodity, of the abolition of the working class as a class, had no place in the Social Democratic programme. In fact socialism was relegated to the distant future through the division of the programme into minimum and maximum parts. The effect of the failure to transcend materialist epistemology was to set in place a political practice which, in privileging scientific knowledge of the world, in turn privileged the status of theory and party (as bearer of theory) above that of the experience of the class. This amounted to the return and triumph of the objective at the heart of post-Marx Marxism. Party, class, theory and practice were reified in their separation and objectivity.

This state of affairs was in some ways a reflection of the stage of development reached by the class struggle at the end of the 19th century. Workers in their newly formed mass trade unions and political parties were searching for ways to express their political independence. The contradiction at the heart of working class socialism was that the task of overthrowing still remaining feudal social and political structures (in essence republicanism) overshadowed the anti-capitalist revolution proper (abolition of wage labour). This was true of states like Germany and Britain, but even more so for the backward Czarist state in Russia.

But the bureaucratic and substitutionist political practice of the leaders of Social Democracy was quickly overtaken by new forms of the class struggle, first intimated in the Paris Commune of 1871, and further reinforced by the 1905 Russian revolution. In the Commune workers had taken power directly and proceeded to construct the rudiments of a proletarian state. In the St. Petersburg workers and soldiers soviet a similar embryonic form of state power emerged. In these two revolutionary outbreaks the soviet or workers council had made its first appearance in history. These upsurges of autonomous working class activity found their expression within the ranks of Social Democracy in the debate over the role of the mass strike tactic. Against the Kautskyite center and the Bernsteinian right were ranged a group of "lefts" — most prominently in the persons of Rosa Luxemburg, Anton Pannekoek, Otto Ruhle — all initially members of the Second International, who were attempting to give theoretical and political expression to these new forms of the class struggle.

The importance of these "lefts" was that they brilliantly anticipated the opening of a new era of the proletarian struggle, and their political evolution took them in the course of twenty years (1900 to 1920) from being left-Social Democrats to "left" or council communists. Although Luxemburg never identified as a council communist, she trenchantly criticised the gradualist reformism of the German Social Democracy for stifling the spontaneous revolutionary initiative of the masses, and went on to identify the mass strikes breaking out in Germany before the war as an expression of direct democracy and proletarian power. But Dutch Marxist Anton Pannekoek took the debate much further with his 1912 work "Marxist Theory and Revolutionary Tactics."[5] He developed the view that a new era of international capitalism was leading to forms of working class struggle that went way beyond the bounds set by Social-Democratic reforms through parliamentary institutions. These anticipated new forms received brilliant confirmation in the revolutionary events in Russia in 1917, Germany, Austria and Hungary in 1918, and Italy in 1920. In each case soviets or workers councils were thrown up by workers in struggle, assuming administrative and military functions in situations of dual power.[6]

The essence of what came to be the council communist position was that workers councils were not only entirely new forms of struggle thrown up by the workers themselves, independently of party and trade union leaderships, but were also the embryonic forms of the future proletarian state, forms which would combine, and thus overcome the division, between legislative and administrative power (as foreshadowed in the Paris Commune of 1871). And in their primary location at the point of production they overcame the division of the economic and the political that underpins bourgeois hegemony. This form of proletarian struggle that expressed the revolution against the commodity form of labour, was at the same time a revolution against the whole edifice of bourgeois political power.

The Bolsheviks, although they incorporated the experience of the soviets into their revolutionary programme, never allowed this expression of autonomous class power to fundamentally challenge, let alone displace, that of the Bolshevik party. Although Lenin's *State and Revolution* was a recognition of soviet power as the basis for a new proletarian order, by the time of the Lenin of *Left-Wing Communism — An Infantile Disorder* the Council Communists were under attack for their anti-parliamentarism, and the substituting of the party for the class at all levels of the workers state was underway.[7] Antonio Gramsci after engaging in a path-breaking theorisation of the Italian workers council movement of 1920 gradually relaxed this orientation as he moved closer to rapprochement with the Communist International (taking up the leadership of the P.C.I. in 1924), which by that time was actively suppressing the agitation of the Council communists in its ranks.

The connecting thread linking the Second International of Classical Social Democracy and the Third Communist International was their objectivist conception of history and their substitutionist political practise. The Bolsheviks differed from Kautskyism in the strategy and tactics of seizing power, but this difference has, in the hands of later Marxists, been mistakenly elevated into one of fundamental philosophical and methodological significance. It really has more to do with the peculiar set of circumstances prevailing in Russia prior to and during the revolution. Notwithstanding Lenin's brilliant strategic sense and voluntarist caste of mind, he shared, and ultimately never rejected, the philosophical interpretation of Marxism he had absorbed from the likes of Plekhanov.[8] The Bolshevik view of Marxism did not differ in fundamentals from that constructed by the major theoreticians of the Second International in the decades before the First World War.

In keeping with this theoretical and political affinity, from the earliest days of the Russian revolution the Bolsheviks demonstrated their substitutionist impulses *vis-à-vis* the factory committees and then the soviets. This is not something that can be blamed exclusively on the isolation and poverty of the young workers state, as has been the tendency of those in the Third and Fourth International traditions. By substituting the party for the class and thereby elevating the state over and above the producers, labour as the sovereign element in the revolutionary process was suppressed. Nationalised property and planning become "objective" "means" to construct socialism for the producers, not the activity of the producers themselves. What would be revolutionary activity, the practical expression of new social relations, remains the effect of "things" on the producers. This reification prevents revolutionary transformation; it denies the reality of communism in the first stages of the revolution. The view of history which emanates from this substitutionism is one in which "forces" of history act on human beings, an approach which Stalinism codified into an idealist metaphysics ("Historical Materialism" or "Histomat").

Second International socialism was distinguished not only by its reformist, parliamentary strategy for winning power, but by its conception of socialism as state ownership and direction of the means of production, a model we may call state monopoly socialism. It would rest on the mass organisations of the labour movement as the working class response to the newly monopolised stage which capitalism was entering at the turn of the century. This strategy of socialist industrialisation was also a national one — internationalism, as the response of the Second International to the First World War showed, was for rhetorical purposes only. Although the Bolshevism of Lenin and Trotsky was by contrast firmly internationalist, it continued the emphasis on state ownership and planning. The socialist industrialisation debate of the twenties conducted principally between Preobrazhensky and Bukharin, was never informed by the question of abolishing wage labour or the direct democracy of the producers at the point of production (Kollontai's 1921 pamphlet "The Workers Opposition" dealt with the latter question and her position was denounced by both Lenin and Trotsky as a danger to the revolution!). In view of the importance Trotsky was to have in the struggle against Stalinism, it is important to remember that he was the architect of the militarisation of labour in the early twenties, and an advocate of industrialisation and collectivisation that differed from the Stalinist version of the late 20s only in the insistence on more democracy and greater consistency. For Trotsky socialism was in the last analysis about the progressiveness of nationalised property relations and the superior rationality of planning. The absence of democratically functioning soviets under Stalin did not negate the proletarian class character of the workers state.[9]

Trotsky's Marxism in essence shared the objectivism and substitutionism of the Second and Third Internationals. It therefore represented the most developed expression possible of the tradition of state monopoly socialism, a tradition which included the Second, Third and Fourth Internationals. While Stalinism represented the "bad" side of this tradition, so to speak, Trotsky represented the "best" side. The "best" because while it never transcended the limitations of Bolshevism, it heroically defended what it saw as the democratic side of the October revolution against the Stalinist counterrevolution. Bolshevism, and in turn Trotskyism, inherited the Second Internationals positivist cast of Marxist theory.

Thus the revolution as the liberation of labour by-passed the bureaucratic official party organisations and programme. While the redundancy of the Second International was exposed in one fell swoop with the experience of world war, the Bolsheviks went some way towards harnessing the revolution of labour. They did, as we have said, fairly quickly truncate that revolution, and failed to appreciate the actuality of communism: communism not confined to a future goal or possibility, but in process in the form of the proletariat as negation of value, as universal negativity within capitalism. The notion of the abolition of wage labour present in the immediate class struggle, and by virtue of this, the immediate task of the revolution, was ultimately beyond the thinking of the Bolsheviks. Only Council communism strove to give full expression to this new stage of the anti-capitalist revolution.

The historic significance of council communism lay in the attempt by Marxists to express at the level of theory and programme the new forms of proletarian struggle emerging in the early years of the twentieth century.[10] The eventual decline of the council movement (following the revolutionary wave of the 1917–20 period) and the marginalisation of the council communists within the Third International, in no way negates this significance. The workers council form was to spring up again in Spain during the Civil War and in Eastern Europe in the post-Second WW period (Hungary and Poland), Chile in 1972, Portugal in 1974. It was therefore not a historically limited phenomenon. On the contrary, it represents the highest form taken by the struggle of the working class for its independence from capitalism.

By contrast the tradition and era of state monopoly socialism is at an end. The Stalinist version is now totally discredited, while Social Democracy, in its rapprochement everywhere with neo-liberal economics, has signalled its political exhaustion. Both versions, in their philosophy and programme ultimately served to prevent the independence of the proletariat from capital. The recurring tendency of the Trotskyist movement to adapt to Stalinism or Keynesianism over the last 50 years only confirms its generic affinity with the state monopoly tradition. Trotskyists wishing to engage in the reconstruction of Marxism will have to look outside their tradition. They will have to look again at the importance attached by the council communists to the workers council form, and appreciate that it represents in practical revolutionary activity precisely what Marx announced in the Theses on Feuerbach, and echoed a few years later in *The Class Struggles in France 1848–50*:

> A class in which the revolutionary interests of society are concentrated, so soon as it has risen up, finds directly in its own situation the content and the material of its revolutionary activity: foes to be laid low, measures (dictated by the needs of the struggle) to be taken; the consequences of its own deeds to drive it on. It makes no theoretical inquiries into its own task.

ENDNOTES

1 There is an important literature arguing that Marx's thought has an ontological rather than an epistemological methodological basis, without, it has to be said, concluding that what was involved was an "end" to philosophy. See for example: Carol Gould, *Marx's Social Ontology,* London 1978; Scott Meikle, *Essentialism in the Thought of Karl Marx,* Duckworth 1985; Michel Henry, Marx: *A Philosophy of Human Reality,* Indiana 1985.

2 For a brilliant exposition of this view, see David MacGregor, *The Communist Ideal in Hegel and Marx,* Allen and Unwin 1984.

3 The dominant form of modern philosophy since Descartes has been epistemology. The reason for this lies in the character of bourgeois society. The capitalist mode of production, supported by the rise of natural science, fosters, and in turn depends on a division of the world into subject and object. This dualism expresses the separation of the direct producers from those "forces" that control, order and dominate their destiny. Such separation

means powerlessness, and a conception of relating to and knowing the world which is reified, one which although created by the producers, appears alien to them, not in fact their creation at all. This is why epistemology elevates into a transhistorical and mystical problem the question of the knowability of the world. Once the producers relate directly to the world that they in fact create (which is the aim of communism), the special problem of epistemology disappears. Knowledge is then no longer a specialist and esoteric pursuit, but the practical result of the activity of the associated producers.

4 The ideas here concerning the importance of Marx's overcoming of the subject–object dualism of materialist epistemology were initially developed in my article "Commodity Fetishism and Reification," *Common Sense* no. 23, July 1998.

5 Contained in *Pannekoek and Gorter's Marxism,* Edited by D.A. Smart, Pluto Press 1978.

6 For the development of the ideas of the council communists and the experience of the workers councils, see "The Origins of the Movement for Workers Councils in Germany 1918–29," *Workers Voice* 1968 (first published in Dutch in *Radencommunismus* No.3, 1938, the journal of the Council-Communist Group of Holland; Mark Shipway, "Council Communism," in *Non-Market Socialism in the 19th and 20th Centuries,* Ed Rubel and Crump, MacMillan 1987; many documents and articles relating to the workers council movement are reproduced in *Self-Governing Socialism: A Reader,* Volume One, Ed Horvat, Markovic, Supek and Kramer, New York 1975.

7 For three accounts of this, see Maurice Brinton, *The Bolsheviks and Workers Control,* Solidarity 1970; Alexandra Kollontai, *The Workers Opposition* (1921), Solidarity 1968; *The Experience of the Factory Committees in the Russian Revolution,* Council Communist Pamphlet No. 2, 1984.

8 Anton Pannekoek in his 1938 book *Lenin as Philosopher* argues that Lenin had adopted the "middle-class materialism" of Plekhanov. By this he meant a version of materialism which represented no qualitative advance on the mechanical and contemplative materialism of the 18th century, which Marx criticised in his "Theses on Feuerbach."

9 Sean Matgamna in his introduction to *The Fate of the Russian Revolution,* Phoenix 1998, criticises Trotsky for constructing a "metaphysics of the nationalised economy," based on the idea that the statified property of the USSR was sufficient to define it as a workers state. Matgamna argues that there is in Trotsky's thinking, a logic to the forward march of the productive forces under state property which leads to socialism even if the work-

ing class does not hold power, a logic which was bequeathed to the post-Trotsky Fourth International. The significance of Matgamna's introduction is that he takes the critique of Trotsky and mainstream Trotskyism as far as it is possible to go while remaining part of that tradition.

10 See, for example, *Karl Korsch: Revolutionary Theory,* Ed., Douglas Kellner, University of Texas Press 1977.

13
Reappropriations of Public Space
Antonio Negri

1

For a good twenty years things had followed a fairly regular pattern — at least since the crisis of 1971–74, when, having digested the struggles of the 1960s and defeat in the Vietnam War, multinational capital relaunched its project of development in terms of liberal policies and post-industrial modernisation. These were the years in which neo-liberalism imposed itself: grey years, even if they were illuminated, as was the case in France, by a number of working-class offensives (that of 1986, for example) and by a succession of student explosions — the first manifestations of the revolt of immaterial labour — around which social protest attempted in vain to organise itself. December 1995 in France is significant because it marked the first mass break with the political, economic and ideological regime of the liberal epoch.

Why did the struggles of December 1995 represent such a powerful breakpoint? Why might we see them as the beginning of the end of the counter-revolution of the second half of the twentieth century?

People have begun to give answers to these questions, and the answers are often interesting. There has obviously been a growing awareness of the process of globalisation and of construction of a united Europe, which has been especially accelerated in France. There has been a feeling of betrayal of the Republican promise of the new presidency, and a whole set of contradictions brought about by the new organisation of social labour — mobility, flexibility, break-up of the labour market, exclusion, etc. There is also the crisis of the welfare state. All this has had immediate repercussions in the process of formation and radicalisation of the struggle. What seems to me important is to define the new context in which the various different demands were coming about: it is a "bio-political" context, in the sense that the struggle clashes against all the rules of discipline and control of the overall conditions of reproduction of the proletariat. Put briefly, the struggle takes its universal meaning, becomes a struggle "of general interest," in the extent to which it rejects the dictatorial choice between "liberalism or barbarism," and suggests a new threshold of possibilites for contestatory action and the expression of the desire for a new world.

However, having said that, we will only succeed in understanding the radicality and the significance of the epochal breakthrough represented by this struggle if we pose a new question: who was its protagonist? Who has been the hegemonic subject of this struggle? What is the nature of the social stratum which has succeeded, in an extremely short time, in transforming a demand-based struggle into a political struggle against globalised capitalist command? And why? What are the material factors which led to the struggle expanding and becoming politicised?

2

It is easy to give an initial answer: the protagonists of these struggles have been the "public services workers." It has been these workers, on the railways, on the underground, in tele-communications, in the postal services, in hospitals and schools, or in the energy sector etc, who have launched the struggle and guided it, and have given a general offensive meaning to demands which had begun as principally locally-based. But unless we ask ourselves what is new about what these sectors represent today, within the political and productive apparatus of advanced capitalism, this initial answer is of no particular interest. What I mean is that there have been earlier episodes in the history of working-class struggles in which the ability to block the circulation of commodities has been fundamental in initiating political confrontations (strikes by railway workers, in particular, occur throughout the history of working-class insurgency). Today, however, within the organisation of advanced capital, the ability — of workers in public service sectors such as transportation, telecommunications, education, health and energy — to attack the system of production with determining political force becomes decisive, to the exclusion of all else. Thatcher and Reagan, those muscular initiators of liberal strategy, were well aware of this when, in the early phase of restructuration, they chose to make political examples of workers in the energy sector and the air transport sector. So, how do we explain all this?

If we want to avoid banal answers, we first have to recognise that in the structure of advanced capitalism the totality of transportation, telecommunications, education and energy — in other words, the major public services — no longer represents solely a moment of the circulation of commodities or an element of reproduction of wealth, but constitutes rather the global form which structures production itself. People have told us time and again that production has become circulation, that we have to work "just-in-time," that the worker has to become a link in the social chain. Well, the strikers in the public services have shown how, by exercising an effect on one of the links of circulation, they are able to affect the entire chain of production; they have shown how, when they acted against the container, the whole content had to react. And since we are not speaking solely of the structures of production, but of the subjective forces which become apparent through them, one sees clearly why the struggles of the workers in the public services have, right from the start, "represented" the totality of workers and why, in the strategic location that they occupy, their struggle was an immediate attack on the global totality of the productive system and its new social and political dimensions.

To those who describe this struggle as "reactionary" and "conservative," and who are particularly partial to objective analysis of the process of production, we can thus reply straight away, in the terms of their own frame of reference, that these struggles, and their protagonists, have, quite the contrary, a central and decisive place within the new mode of production: they have carried the struggle through against the truly decisive point of capitalist "reform" and have, for this sole reason, momentarily blocked it.

3

But the protagonists of the struggle have not been only the working class, and more generally the workers in the public services. They have also been a million men and women who, in Paris and in towns throughout France, in order to travel to work, or simply to get around, have made efforts worthy of wartime, in conditions that were extremely difficult. The media depicted these efforts, this daily weary slog, with excessive enthusiasm — first in an attempt to organise a revolt of transport "users," and then, once this attempt had been massively rejected, to highlight the civility and conviviality of their behaviours, while moralising about the suffering being caused by the strike. However, have not industrial sociology, neo-liberal ideology and whole swathes of literature on the state been telling us for years that, in post-industrial society, users are themselves producers of the services? So how is it that these producers of ideology now start contradicting themselves by attempting to set the community of users against the service-sector workers and by attempting, by all means possible, to split them into separate communities?

In effect, the users are "co-producers" of the public services. They are "co-producers" in a whole range of senses, going from a maximum passive consumption and minimum interactivity into a minimum passive consumption and maximum interactivity. In the first bracket we could put the users of energy services, and into the second, users of telecommunications, education and health. Today, in struggle, this "co-production" has displayed a very developed level of awareness. The "users" have recognised their own interest in the struggle of the workers who produce the services together with them. If services are a co-production, then they are a co-production which is public in essence. I am not denying here that there may be opposing interests and that contradictions may emerge between supply and demand in the provision of services; I am merely pointing out that these contradictions also take place within a public dimension. Thus, when the service-sector workers turned their struggle into a defence, and an affirmation, of the public character of their production and a demand for its recognition as such, the "users" recognised themselves totally as "co-producers" of this struggle. The long distances that people walked in the snow, the hitch-hiking, the queues, the endless waiting have thus to be considered as episodes of struggle. The strike demonstrated its power not only by means of noisy trade union demonstrations, but above all by cheerful processions to work in the morning and back again in the evening. This was not a "strike by proxy," but a strike that was diffuse, embracing the whole of societal life, and one that became part of everyday reality. In the dictionary of strikes invented by the proletariat in struggle (sectoral strikes, general strikes, wildcat strikes, sit-down strikes, etc...) we now have to add a new term, the metropolitan strike.

Let us now look closer. In highlighting this metropolitan "co-production" of the struggle, we identify a concept of "public" which has a revolutionary valency. In the feelings of co-responsibility which the "users" have, as regards the functioning of — and also the strikes in — the services, one has effectively to recognise an act of "reappropriation of administration." An act which is direct and subversive. From an awareness of the nature of this act, one's thoughts therefore necessarily have to turn to what underlies it: to the identification of public service, and thus of its management and its productive functions at a very general level, as something which is in common to all. In common to all in the same way as are all products of cooperation, from language to democratic administration. A definition of "public" which no longer has anything to do with its "statist" definition.

4

The state bares its capitalist aspect when it seeks to privatise the public services. Conversely, the struggles reveal a subversive aspect going beyond the state and its function as protector of capital. Even when some of the protagnosists argue for a "French-style public service," I believe that very few people today would consider it credible to defend this left-over of the Third Republic, re-actualised by that Fordist compromise between the popular forces of the Resistance and the Gaullist technocracy which still exists despite its anachronism. For us the struggles mean that if a "French-style public service" is to continue to exist, it will pose itself in completely new terms, as a first experiment in a reconstruction of the public service within a democratic dynamic of reappropriation of administration, of democratic co-production of services. Through these struggles there now opens a new problematic, which is a constituent problematic. What we have to understand is what is meant by a new "public character of the services" which, in permitting them to remove themselves from privatisation and from the rules of the world market, permits them at the same time to extract themselves from the ideological mystifications which are born from the globalising and directly capitalist function of the action of the national state. The awareness of this problematic has been implicit in the struggles. It represents their subversive potential. Furthermore, if it is true that the services today constitute "the global form" of all forms of productivity, whether state or private — if it is true that they reveal how central and exemplary is the role of cooperation in the totality of production and circulation — then this new concept of "public" will constitute the paradigm of every new experiment in socialised production.

To sum up: the public as an ensemble of activities under the guardianship of the state with a view to permitting the reproduction of the capitalist system and of private accumulation, has here ceased to exist. We find ourselves facing a new concept of public. In other words a concept of production organised on the basis of an interactivity in which development of wealth and development of democracy become indistinguishable, just as the interactive broadening of the social relationship is indistinguishable from the reappropriation of administration by productive subjects. The elimination of exploitation here becomes visible; it appears no longer as myth but as concrete possibility.

5

But this new subjective dimension of "the public" is not something which affects only the "social" workers, in other words the workers in the social services. It is something which affects, as we have seen, the subjectivity of the co-producers of services, and thus all citizens who work. The "*Tous ensemble*" ("Everyone together") slogan of the struggles can thus be read as having revealed a new community, a productive social community which is seeking to be recognised. The recognition is two-fold. It is on the one hand the dynamic of re-composition which runs through the movement — it is the community of struggle in which all workers are co-involved by the working class who, through their position, form the essential backbone of productive cooperation (and it is the first dynamic of the process). And secondly, the recognition demanded consists in the reappropriation of the services, both by the community in struggle, and by those who, in working, use the services in order to produce wealth.

Thus the struggle functions as a prefiguration of the aim to which it is tending: the method — in other words the "being together" in order to win — is the prefiguration of the objective aim — in other words, "being together" in order to construct wealth, outside of and against capitalism.

Here I am interested in showing that within the struggle which we have lived through, and most particularly in those areas where public services were involved, the concept of "community" became enriched with essential articulations. The concept of community has often been considered, even and particularly within subversive thinking, as something which mystified the concrete articulations of exploitation, by flattening them into a figure in which the totality of the association of social subjects was given by the unity of the function, rather than by the contradictory articulation of the process of association and production. In the course of the struggle which we are analysing, we saw appearing for the first time a community which is extremely articulated, a *Gemeinschaft* which has within it all the characteristics of multiplicity — and which, as a whole productive entity, opposes itself to power.

Our reflection on the movement thus leads us to pose the problem of the transition to a higher level of productive organisation, where the "public" is considered as the ensemble of social functions which, thanks to the wealth of its articulations, does not require the separation of levels of production and levels of command. On the contrary, reappropriation of command within the productive function and the construction of the social relationship henceforth form a continuum. The problem of the transition towards an autonomous social community, towards communism, will no longer reside solely in the definition of the form of struggle against the state, but on the contrary will reside essentially within the definition of procedures and forms which will permit the reappropriation of productive functions by the community to take place.

"*Tous ensemble*" is a project of transition to communism. These struggles permit us to begin once again calling by its name the real movement of transformation of the present state of things. And while the work to be done in order to recompose in our imaginations the real movement and the development of history is immense, at the same time we can begin to give form to the utopia of the movement by means of statements which translate the desire.

6

The slogan "*Tous ensemble*" was launched and picked up by the movement, in conjunctural manner, as an invitation to workers in the private sector to join the strike movement. We have seen how the slogan gradually transformed itself. But it is true that the initial invitation, in its first signification, fell flat. Why? Why was it that the workers belonging to the "juridically" defined private sector of the economy did not join the struggle?

The explanations given for the fact that workers in the private sector did not come out on strike are grounded in realism: they range from justifications related to the structure of the waged workforce (a waged workforce which is individualised and therefore subject to immediate repression by its bosses in the event of strike action) to justifications arising from the crisis of trade unionism in the private sectors of industry and services. These explanations, for all their realism, nevertheless forget one structural element of private enterprise — the fact that in it the tendency of transformation of the productive structure into a public service structure is not evident, and that it remains hidden, on the one hand by the strong continued existence of the manufacturing industries, and on the other by the baleful predominance of the rules of private profit, often reinterpreted by means of financial models. This is perhaps the moment to say that the productive functions linked to manufacturing production are, in a thousand different ways, on the way to extinction. And that, consequently, the working-class strata within the arena of manufacturing are the most sensitive to the blackmail of unemployment, and are therefore the weakest. It is precisely for this reason that they are less capable of conducting offensive struggles. From now on they are locked into a paradox: at the moment when they enter into struggle, they will be doing it in order also to destroy the places of production in which today they receive their wages. In a sense they resemble the peasants of the French Revolution in an earlier age: they are struggling to ensure the victory not of the system of production within which they are engaged, but of another system of production in which they will be crushed.

However this interpretation applies only to the working class of the private manufacturing sector. If we look at the private sector as a whole, we find that service companies are becoming more and more of a presence. Large manufacturing concerns are massively "putting out" more and more of their directly and indirectly productive functions. They are reducing them to commercial services and inserting them into the context of social production. And it is within the private service sector that the rediscovery of the public, and thus the recomposition of the new proletariat, is possible. It is possible in the areas where the working class elements, in the private sector, have as their basic characteristics temporal flexibility and spatial mobility. In other words, in the areas where profit is formed, as it is in the public sectors, principally through the exploitation of social cooperation.

In the struggles of December 1995, the invitation extended to the private sector to join the struggle was marked by delay and confusion. This invitation was made in the traditional form of an appeal to the workers of the private manufacturing sector, whereas, in the course of the struggle, it turned out to be the working class and the operators of the service sectors, and even of private-sector services, who grasped the opportunity to recognise themselves in the new concept of public — and thus in the cooperative reappropriation of the production of wealth in the construction and democratic administration of productive society.

7

We can now return to the business of identifying the subject of the December struggle. If one stays at a superficial level, one recognises that we are dealing with workers in the "public services"; looking closer, these workers appear as "social workers" — in other words, as producers of social relations, and thereby as producers of wealth; at a third and closer look, this identification is reinforced by the fact that the clients of the services, in other words citizens in general, were active in co-producing the struggle; fourthly, it appears evident that the fact that the services are public in character makes them the strategic locus of exploitation, and thus of new contradictions through which offensive struggles will be able to develop; fifth, it is clear that service workers in the private sector (in other words those majority workers in the private sector which has been restructured into services) will be drawn into this cycle of struggles.

But the "social worker" is an immaterial worker. He is this because he is a highly educated element, because his work and his effort are essentially intellectual and because his activity is cooperative. Henceforth what we find at the heart of society and its structures of power is a production made up of linguistic acts and of cooperative activities. So the social worker is immaterial inasmuch as he participates in the new intellectual and cooperative nature of work.

But this new nature of work is still "*bios*," an entire life made of needs and desires, of singularities and of generations succeeding each other. Those involved in the struggle of December showed, through the struggle and its objectives, that the entirety of life in all its complexity is both the object of struggle and production of subjectivity — and therefore refusal of social cooperation's enslavement to the development of capital.

In any event — as the striking workers told the government — if you don't want to recognise the freedom due to this collective intellectual nature of associated labour, you will soon be forced to recognise its power and to recognise that it is inescapable — and you will find that it is impossible for you to negotiate wages, social reproduction and political-economic constitution unless you take this reality entirely into account!

Telecommunications and formation [*trans*: in the sense of education and training] are the most significant class sectors from the point of view of immateriality, of the interactive public, of the "*bios*" — here the General Intellect which Marx foresaw as being the fundamental agent of production in advanced capitalism reveals itself as *bios*. In the processes of formation, the labour force constructs itself and reconstructs itself as an ongoing process, throughout one's own life and through future generations, in full interactivity not only between active singularities, but between these and the world, the *Umwelt* which surrounds it, constructed and reconstructed ongoingly by human activity. Given that telecommunications are shortly coming to represent the totality of circulation of productive signs, of cooperative languages, they thus constitute the exterior aspect of this constant capital which human brains have reappropriated to themselves. And it is through formation and telecommunications that the processes of production of subjectivity come up against the processes of enslavement of productive subjectivities and against the construction of surplus-value-profit.

It is thus on these articulations that the struggle over the form of appropriation concentrates — because formation and telecommunications represent the highest point, and the most explicit structure, of production as public service.

8

The struggles of December 1995 are a formidable challenge for revolutionary theory. The workers in both the material and immaterial sectors have been hegemonic here — in other words, the social worker in the fullness of his productive attributes. Consequently these struggles are situated at the level of advanced capitalism or, if you prefer, post-modern and/or post-industrial capitalism. The service sector workers bring the issue of social productivity to the forefront and reveal the contradictions which are opposed to its development. The problem of emancipation from capitalist command and the problem of liberation from the capitalist mode of production are here posed in new ways, because the class struggle here presents itself in an entirely new manner. Manufacturing industry and the people who work in it are definitively losing the central role which they had had in the launching and leadership of class struggle, whereas those people who work in the services, even and particularly those in the private services sectors of the advanced economies, are powerfully attracted into entering into the field of revolutionary struggle.

Therefore theory today needs to confront this new reality. It has to work in general terms on the relationships between "general intellect" (in other words hegemonic immaterial and intellectual labour) and "*bios*" (in other words the dimension within which intellectual labour as reappropriated constant capital opposes itself to a capitalist command which has by now become completely parasitic). But above all theory needs to work on the relationships which closely link social interactivity and its political forms, production and politics, productive power and constituent power. In his time Lenin had already posed the problem of the relationship between economic appropriation by the proletariat and the political forms of this appropriation. In his time, and within the relations of production with which he was dealing, realism led him to think that the term "dictatorship" might represent a solution. However, without casting aspersions on a man who was the first to have understood the necessity of combining revolution and enterprise, our liberation utopia is radically different from what he proposed. We have the possibility of doing it — and of knowing what we are talking about, because production is today a world of interactive relations which only "democracy" can constitute and manage. Democracy, a powerful democracy of producers, that is the essential motivating core of our work and analysis today.

To build "the public" against the state, to work on the basis of a democracy of producers against the parasitism of capital, to identify the forms in which the interactivity of production (revealed by the development of services) can articulate with the (renewed) forms of political democracy, and to bring to light the material fabric of the political co-production of the social: there, in a nutshell, you have the new tasks of theory. Urgent, and extremely alive, just like the struggles which brought them into being.

When we take a closer look, we see that numerous theoreticians of social reproduction in postmodernity are already posing similar problems. A whole range of social science researchers who have not accepted liberalism as the only way of thinking — particularly in the country that is the queen of capitalism, the United States of America — are working to clarify the problem of the relationship between growing social cooperation and the production of democracy.

But the struggles of December go well beyond these thematics, because they pose the problem not simply as a possibility, but as a necessity, because they anticipate the solution by showing that democracy of the multitude is a revolutionary fact. So here we have a new theme, which is far from secondary: what does it mean to revolutionise social cooperation, by democratically reappropriating administration, in order to manage the totality of production and reproduction of society?

9

With the struggles of December 1995, we have entered a new phase of political practice.

The first problem posed is obviously that of the re-opening of the struggle after its suspension, and thus the problem of how to enlarge and strengthen the front of the social worker, in the public services, but above all in the private sector. We also have to find ways of expressing in the broadest and strongest possible terms the contribution made by social subjects in education/training (schools, universities etc), and in telecommunications, to new perspectives for the construction of revolutionary movement, and to organise the co-producing these struggles together with the citizen-as-worker.

But here emerges the second fundamental problem: how to define a form of struggle and of organisation which will be coherent with the new concept of "the public" in the terms in which it was expressed in the struggles of December. This means a form of organisation which permits, increasingly, the creation of relationships and links between category demands and general demands for a bio-political wage, for an extension of public service, for the reappropriation of administration.

Clearly, the capacity which the workers in struggle have revealed — that of reorganising themselves at the territorial level, and breaking with the traditional professional divisions of French trade unionism — could be taken up as a paradigm for a unifying recomposition of the objectives of struggle and for the general form in which the struggle is conducted. In a sense these forms of organisation prefigure new rank-and-file and mass political instances (in other words, no longer simply trade-unionist). They reveal — paradoxically by reconnecting with the organisational origins of the labour movement — a central element of the post-Fordist organisation of production: its societal diffusion. This local, territorial, intercategorial and unitary organisation really does seem to present a solid basis for the generalisation of the defence of workers' interests as regards wages and struggle over the conditions of social reproduction; and at the same time it is precisely from this starting position (and only from this) that it will be possible to launch that initiative of "public" reappropriation of administration and of services that will be capable of opening a perspective of struggle for a truly radical democracy.

TRANSLATED BY ED EMERY

Editor's Preface to Antonio Negri's "Constituent Republic"

Working in the "autonomist" tradition of Marxism, a group centering in Paris around the journal *Futur Antérior* has formulated categories which attempt a theorisation of today's revolutionary practice. This theorisation has continued in *Posse*. The central concepts of this theorisation that Negri's chapter brings to the fore, include "immaterial labour," "mass intellectuality" and "new constitution." The point of departure is a section of Marx's *Grundrisse* manuscript of 1857–58. This section reads:

> Nature builds no machines, no locomotives, railways, electric telegraphs, self-acting mules, etc. These are products of human industry; natural material transformed into organs of the human will over nature, or of participation in nature. They are *organs of the human brain, created by the human hand;* the power of knowledge, objectified. The development of fixed capital indicates to what degree general social knowledge has become a *direct force of production,* and to what degree, hence, the conditions of the process of social life itself have come under the control of the general intellect and been transformed in accordance with it. To what degree the powers of social production have been produced, not only in the form of knowledge, but also as immediate organs of social practice, of the real life process. Marx *Grundrisse* (Dietz Verlag, Berlin, 1974, p. 594; Pelican Books, 1973, p. 706)

Thus Marx: the relevance of the passage should be clear in the light of debates concerning new technology, and as a powerful counterblast against the technological determinism with which discussion of the new technology is so often linked. But Negri and his comrades delve deeper still in the passage, not merely opposing technological determinism but seeking to identify a new constitution of revolutionary subjectivity which empowers itself in, and against, present day times. The most comprehensive discussion of this argument can be found in Hardt, M. and A. Negri, *Empire,* Harvard University Press, 2000

14
Constituent Republic
Antonio Negri

1. "To Each Generation Its Own Constitution"

When Condorcet suggests that each generation might produce its own political constitution, on the one hand he is referring to the position of constitutional law in Pennsylvania (where constitutional law is on the same footing as ordinary law, providing one single method for creating both constitutional principles and new law), and on the other he is anticipating the French revolutionary constitution of 1793: "Un peuple a toujours le droit de revoir, de reformer et de changer sa Constitution. Une génération ne peut assujetter à ses lois les générations futures." (A people always has the right to revise, reform and change its constitution. One generation may not subject future generations to its own laws.) [Article XXVIII]

Standing at the threshold of present-day developments in state and society, as they were to be brought about by revolution, science and capitalism, Condorcet understood that any preconstituted blockage of the dynamic of production and any restraint of liberty that goes beyond the requirements of the present, necessarily lead to despotism. To put it another way, Condorcet understands that, once the constituent moment is past, constitutional fixity becomes a reactionary fact in a society that is founded on the development of freedoms and the development of the economy. Thus a constitution should not be granted legitimacy on the basis of custom and practice, or the ways of our ancestors, or classical ideas of order. On the contrary, only life in a constant process of renewal can form a constitution — in other words, can continually be putting it to the test, evaluating it and driving it towards the necessary modifications. From this point of view, Condorcet's recommendation that "each generation should have its own constitution" can be put alongside that of Machiavelli, who proposed that each generation (in order to escape the corruption of power and the "routine" of Administration) "should return to the principles of the State" — a "return" which is a process of building, an ensemble of principles — not an inheritance from the past but something newly rooted.

Should our own generation be constructing a new Constitution? When we look back at the reasons which the earlier creators of constitutions gave for why constitutional renewal was so urgent, we find them entirely present in our own situation today. Rarely has the corruption of political and administrative life been so deeply corrosive; rarely has there been such a crisis of representation; rarely has disillusionment with democracy been so radical. When people talk of "a crisis of politics," they are effectively saying that the democratic State no longer functions — and that in fact it has become irreversibly corrupt in all its principles and organs: the division of powers, the principles of guarantee, the single individual powers, the rules of representation, the unitarian dynamic of powers, and the functions of legality, efficiency and administrative legitimacy. There has been talk of an "end of history," and if such a thing exists we might certainly identify it in the end of the constitutional dialectic to which liberalism and the mature capitalist state had tied us. To be specific, as from the 1930s, in the countries of the capitalist West there began to develop a constitutional system which we would call the "Fordist" constitution, or the labourist welfare-state constitution; this model has now gone into crisis. The reasons for the crisis are clear when one takes a look at the changes in the subjects which had forged the original agreement around the principles of this Constitution: on the one hand the national bourgeoisie, and on the other hand the industrial working class organised within both the trade unions and the socialist and communist parties. Thus the liberal-democratic system functioned in such a way as to match the needs of industrial development and of the sharing-out of global income between these classes. Constitutions may have differed more or less in their forms, but the "material constitution" — the basic convention covering the sharing out of powers and counter-powers, of work and of income, of rights and freedoms — was substantially homogeneous. The national bourgeoisies renounced fascism and guaranteed their powers of exploitation within a system of sharing-out of national income which — reckoning on a context of continuous growth — made possible the construction of a welfare system for the national working class. For its part, the working class renounced revolution.

Now, at the point when the crisis of the 1960s concludes in the emblematic events of 1968, the state built on the Fordist constitution goes into crisis: the subjects of the original constitutional accord in effect undergo a change. On the one hand, the various bourgeoisies become internationalised, basing their power on the financial transformation of capital, and turning themselves into abstract representations of power; on the other, the industrial working class (in the wake of radical transformations in the mode of production — victory for the automation of industrial labour and the computerisation of social labour) transforms its own cultural, social and political identity. A multinational and finance-based bourgeoisie (which sees no reason why it should bear the burden of a national welfare system) is matched by a socialised, intellectual proletariat — which, on the one hand, has a wealth of new needs, and on the other is incapable of maintaining a continuity with the articulations of the Fordist compromise. With the exhaustion of "real socialism" and the etching of its disaster into world history at the end of 1989, even the symbols — already largely a dead letter — of a proletarian independence within socialism were definitively destroyed.

The juridico-constitutional system based on the Fordist compromise, strengthened by the constituent agreement between the national bourgeoisie and the industrial working class, and overdetermined by the conflict between the Soviet and American super-powers (symbolic representations of the two conflicting parties on the stage of each individual nation) has thus run out its time. There is no longer a long-term war between two power-blocs at the international level, within which the civil war between classes might be cooled down by means of immersion in the Fordist constitution and/or in the organisations of the Welfare State; there no longer exist, within individual countries, the subjects who could constitute that Constitution and who might legitimate its expressions and its symbols. The whole scenario is now radically changed.

So what is the new Constitution which our generation is going to have to to construct?

2. "Arms and Money"

Machiavelli said that in order to construct the State, the Prince needed "arms and money." So what arms, and what money, are going to be required for a new Constitution? For Machiavelli, the arms are represented by the people (*il popolo*), in other words the productive citizenry who, within the democracy of the commune, become a people in arms. The question is, what *popolo* or people could be counted on today for the creation of a new Constitution? Do we have a generation opening itself to a new institutional compromise that will go beyond the Welfare State? And in what terms would it be disposed to organise itself, to "arm" itself, to this end? And what about the "money" side of things? Is the multinational finance bourgeoisie willing to consider a new constitutional and productive compromise that will go beyond the Fordist compromise — and if so, then on what terms?

Within the social system of post-Fordism, the concept of "the people" can and must be redefined. And not only the concept of "the people," but also the concept of "the people in arms" — in other words, that fraction of the citizenry which by its work produces wealth and thus makes possible the reproduction of society as a whole. It can claim that its own hegemony over social labour be registered in constitutional terms.

The political task of arriving at a definition of the post-Fordist proletariat is by now well advanced. This proletariat embodies a substantial section of the working class that has been restructured within processes of production that are automated, and computer-controlled processes which are centrally managed by an ever-expanding intellectual proletariat, which is increasingly directly engaged in labour that is computer-related, communicative and in broad terms educative/formative. The post-Fordist proletariat, the *popolo* or "people" represented by the "social" worker (*l'operaio sociale*), is imbued with and constituted by a continuous interplay between technico-scientific activity and the hard work of producing commodities; by the entrepreneuriality of the networks within which this interaction is organised; by the increasingly close combination and recomposition of labour time and life-time. There, simply by way of introduction, we have some possible elements of the new definition of the proletariat, and what becomes clear is that, in all the sections in which this class is being composed, it is essentially *mass intellectuality*. Plus — and this is crucial — another element: within the scientific subsumption of productive labour, within the growing abstraction and socialisation of production, the post-Fordist labour form is becoming increasingly cooperative, independent and autonomous. This combination of autonomy and cooperation means that *the entrepreneurial potentiality (potenza imprenditoriale) of productive labour is henceforth completely in the hands of the post-Fordist proletariat*. The very development of productivity is what constitutes this enormous independence of the proletariat, as an intellectual and cooperative base, as economic entrepreneuriality. The question is, does it also constitute it as political entrepreneuriality, as political autonomy ?

We can only attempt an answer to this question once we have asked ourselves what exactly we mean by "money" within this historic development. In other words, in today's world, what happens to the bourgeoisie as a class, and to the productive functions of the industrial bourgeoisie? Well, if what we have said about the new definition of a post-Fordist proletariat is true, it follows that the international bourgeoisie has now lost its productive functions, that it is becoming increasingly parasitic — a kind of Roman church of capital. It now expresses itself only through financial command, in other words a command which is completely liberated from the exigencies of production — "money" in the post-classical and post-Marxian sense, "money" as an alienated and hostile universe, "money" as general panacea — the opposite of labour, of intelligence, of the immanence of life and desire. "Money" no longer functions as mediation between labour and commodity; it is no longer a numeric rationalisation of the relationship between wealth and power; it is no longer a quantified expression of the nation's wealth. In the face of the entrepreneurial autonomy of a proletariat which has materially embraced within itself also the intellectual forces of production, "money" becomes the artificial reality of a command which is despotic, external, empty, capricious and cruel.

It is here that the new fascism reveals itself — a postmodern fascism, which has little to do with Mussolinian alliances, with the illogical schemas of Nazism, or the cowardly arrogance of Petainism. *Post-modern fascism* seeks to match itself to the realities of post-Fordist labour cooperation, and seeks at the same time to express some of its essence in a form that is turned on its head. In the same way that the old fascism mimicked the mass organisational forms of socialism and attempted to transfer the proletariat's impulse towards collectivity into nationalism (national socialism or the Fordist constitution), so post-modern fascism seeks to discover the communist needs of the post-Fordist masses and to transform them, gradually, into a cult of differences, of the pursuit of individualism and the search for identity — all within a project of creating over-riding despotic hierarchies aimed at constantly, relentlessly, pitting differences, singularities, identities and individualities one against the other. Whereas communism is respect for and synthesis of singularities, and as such is desired by all those who love peace, the new fascism (as an expression of the financial command of international capital) produces a war of everyone against everyone, produces religiosity and wars of religion, nationalism and wars of nations, corporative egos and economic wars...

So, let us return to the question of "the arms of the people." We are asking: what is this Constitution that our new generation is going to have to build? This is another way of asking what are the balances of power, the compromises, which the new post-modern proletariat and the new multinational employing class are going to have to institute, in material terms, in order to organise the next productive cycle of the class struggle. But if what we have said so far is true, does this question still make sense? What possibility exists now, for constitutional compromise, in a situation where a huge degree of proletarian cooperation stands at the opposite pole to a huge degree of external and parasitical command imposed by multinational capital? A situation in which money stands in opposition to production.

Does it still make sense to ask ourselves how rights and duties might be reciprocally calibrated, given that the dialectic of production no longer has workers and capital mixing in the management of the productive relationship?

We would probably all agree that the question makes no sense. The "arms" and the "moneys" are no longer such that they can be put together in order to construct the State. Probably the Welfare State represents the final episode of this history of accords between those who command and those who obey (a history which — if we are to believe Machiavelli — was born with the "dualism of power" which the Roman tribunes installed in relation to the Republic).

Today everything is changing in the fields of political science and constitutional doctrine: if it is the case that those who once were the "subjects" are now more intelligent and more "armed" than kings and employing classes, why should they go looking for a mediation with them?

3. State Forms: That Which is Not "Constituent Power"

From Plato to Aristotle and, with some modifications, through to the present day, the theory of "state forms" has come down to us as a theory which is unavoidably dialectical. Monarchy and tyranny, aristocracy and oligarchy, democracy and anarchy, handing over from one to the other, are thus the only alternatives within which the cycle of power develops. At a certain point in the development of the theory, Polybius, with undoubted good sense, proposed that these forms should be considered not as alternatives, but rather as complementary. (Here he referred to the constitution of the Roman Empire, to show that there were instances in which different state forms not only did not counterpose each other, but could also function together: could be functions of government.) The theorists of the American Constitution, along with those of the popular-democratic Constitutions of Stalinism, thus all contentedly recognised themselves as Polybians! Classical and contemporary constitutionalism, wherein all the prostitutes of the State of Right happily wallow, is nothing other than Polybian! Monarchy, aristocracy and democracy, put together, form the best of republics!

Except that the alleged scientific value of this dialectic of state forms does not go much beyond the familiar classical apologetics of Menenius Agrippus, whose position was as reactionary as any other, given that it implied a conception of power that was organic, unmoving and animal (inasmuch as it required the various social classes to work together to construct an animal functionality). Should we write it off as being of no value, then? Perhaps. But at the same time there is a value in recognising these theories for what they are, because the way they have survived over the centuries, the effects they have had on history, and the daily effect of inertia that they exert, provide a useful reminder of the power of mystification.

The ideology of revolutionary Marxism too, albeit overturning the theory of state forms, nonetheless ends up affirming its validity. The "abolition of the state," *pace* Lenin, assumes the concept of state as it exists within bourgeois theory, and poses itself as a practice of extreme confrontation with that reality. What I am saying is that all these concepts — "transition" as much as "abolition," the "peaceful road" as much "people's democracy," the "dictatorship of the proletariat" as much as the "cultural revolution" — all these are bastard concepts, because they are impregnated with a conception of the state, of its sovereignty and its domination — because they consider themselves as necessary means and unavoidable processes to be pursued in the seizure of power and the transformation of society. The mystificatory dialectic of the theory of state forms turns into the negative dialectic of the abolition of the state: but the theoretical nucleus remains, in the absolute and reactionary way in which the power of the state is affirmed. "All the same old shit," as Marx put it.

It is time to emerge from this crystallisation of absurd positions — which are given a value of truth solely by their extremism. It is time to ask ourselves whether there does not exist, from a theoretical and practical point of view, a position which avoids absorption within the opaque and terrible essence of the State. In other words, whether there does not exist a viewpoint which, renouncing the perspective of those who would construct the constitution of the State mechanistically, is able to maintain the thread of genealogy, the force of constituent praxis, in its extensivity and intensity. This point of view exists. It is the viewpoint of daily insurrection, of continual resistance, of constituent power. It is a breaking-with, it is refusal, it is imagination, all as the basis of political science. It is the recognition of the impossibility, nowadays, of mediating between "arms" and "money," the "people in arms" and the multinational bourgeoisie, production and finance. As we begin to leave Machiavellianism behind us, we are firmly of the opinion that Machiavelli would have been on our side. We are beginning to arrive at a situation where we are no longer condemned to think of politics in terms of domination. In other words, what is under discussion here is the very form of the dialectic, mediation as a content of domination in its various different forms. For us, it is definitively in crisis. We have to find ways of thinking politically beyond the theory of "state forms." To pose the problem in Machiavellian terms, we have to ask: is it possible to imagine constructing a republic on the basis of the arms of the people, and without the money of the Prince? Is it possible to entrust the future of the state solely to popular "virtue," and not at the same time to "fortune?"

4. Constructing the Soviets of Mass Intellectuality

In the period which we have now entered, in which immaterial labour is tending to become hegemonic, and which is characterised by the antagonisms produced by the new relationship between the organisation of the forces of production and multinational capitalist command, the form in which the problem of the Constitution presents itself, from the viewpoint of mass intellectuality, is that of establishing how it might be possible to build its Soviets.

In order to define the problem, let us begin by recalling some of the conditions which we have assumed thus far.

The first of these conditions derives from the tendential hegemony of immaterial labour and thus from the increasingly profound reappropriation of technico-scientific knowledge by the proletariat. On this basis, technico-scientific knowledge can no longer be posed as a mystified function of command, separated from the body of mass intellectuality.

The second condition derives from what I referred to above as the end of all distinction between working life and social life, between social life and individual life, between production and life-form. In this situation, the political and the economic become two sides of the same coin. All the wretched old bureaucratic distinctions between trade union and party, between vanguard and mass, and so on, seem definitively to disappear. Politics, science and life function together: it is within this framework that the real (*il reale*) produces subjectivity.

The third point to consider arises from what has been said above: on this terrain the alternative to existing power is constructed positively, through the expression of potentiality (*potenza*). The destruction of the State can be envisaged only via a concept of the reappropriation of administration. In other words, a reappropriation of the social essence of production, of the instruments of comprehension of social and productive cooperation. Administration is wealth, consolidated and put at the service of command. It is fundamental for us to reappropriate this, reappropriating it by means of the exercise of individual labour posed within a perspective of solidarity, within cooperation, in order to administer social labour, in order to ensure an ever-richer reproduction of accumulated immaterial labour.

Here, therefore, is where the Soviets of mass intellectuality are born. And it is interesting to note how the objective conditions of their emergence chime perfectly with the historical conditions of the antagonistic class relationship. In this latter terrain, as I suggested above, there is no longer any possibility of constitutional compromise. The Soviets will therefore be defined by the fact that they will express immediately potentiality, cooperation and productivity. The Soviets of mass intellectuality will give rationality to the new social organisation of work, and they will make the universal commensurate to it. The expression of their potentiality will be without constitution.

The constituent Republic is thus not a new form of constitution: it is neither Platonic nor Aristotelian nor Polybian, and perhaps it is no longer even Machiavellian. It is a Republic which comes before the State, which comes outside of the State. The constitutional paradox of the constituent Republic consists in the fact that the constituent process never closes, that the revolution does not come to an end, that constitutional law and ordinary law refer back to one single source and are developed unitarily within a single democratic procedure.

Here we are, finally, at the great problem from which everything starts and towards which everything tends: the task of destroying separation and inequality, and the power which reproduces separation and inequality. Now, the Soviets of mass intellectuality can pose themselves this task by constructing, outside of the state, a mechanism within which a democracy of the everyday can organise active communication, the interactivity of citizens, and at the same time produce increasingly free and complex subjectivities.

All the above is only a beginning. Is it perhaps too general and abstract? Certainly. But it is important that we begin once again to talk about communism — in this form — in other words, as a programme which, in all its aspects, goes beyond the wretched reductions that we have seen being enacted in history. And the fact that it is only a start does not make it any the less realistic. Mass intellectuality and the new proletariat which have been constructed in the struggles against capitalist development and through the expression of constitutive potentiality are beginning to emerge as true historic subjects.

The moment of the new, the new happening, the "Angelus novus" — when they arrive — will appear suddenly. Thus our generation can construct a new constitution. Except that it will not be a constitution.

And perhaps this new happening has already occurred.

TRANSLATED BY ED EMERY

Index of Persons